Greenberg's®
Model Railroading
with
Lionel® Trains

By Roland E. LaVoie

Edited by Cindy Lee Floyd

Cover Photograph: Part of the author's 5' x 8' empire.
(See page viii and ix for the whole kingdom.)
Photographed by Maury Fei...

D1091848

Copyright © 1989

Greenberg Publishing Company, Inc.
7566 Main Street
Sykesville, MD 21784
(301) 795-7447

First Edition
Second Printing

Manufactured in the United States of America

Greenberg Publishing Company, Inc. offers the world's largest selection of Lionel, American Flyer, LGB, Ives, and other toy train publications as well as a selection of books on model and prototype railroading, dollhouse miniatures, and toys. For a copy of our current catalogue, send a stamped, self-addressed envelope to Greenberg Publishing Company, Inc. at the above address.

Greenberg Shows, Inc. sponsors the world's largest public model railroad, dollhouse, and toy shows. The shows feature extravagant operating model railroads for N, HO, O, Standard, and 1 Gauges as well as a huge marketplace for buying and selling nearly all model railroad equipment. The shows also feature a large selection of dollhouses and dollhouse furnishings. Shows are currently offered in metropolitan Baltimore, Boston, Ft. Lauderdale, Cherry Hill in New Jersey, Long Island in New York, Norfolk, Philadelphia, Pittsburgh, and Tampa. To receive our current show listing, please send a self-addressed stamped envelope marked *Train Show Schedule* to the address above.

ISBN   0-89778-054-X

Library of Congress Cataloging-in-Publication Data

Greenberg, Bruce C.
    Greenberg's model railroading with Lionel trains.

        1. Railroads—Models.   2. Lionel Corporation.
I. LaVoie, Roland, 1943-   . II. Floyd, Cindy Lee.
III. Title.   IV. Title: Model railroading with Lionel trains.
TF197.G6678 1989   625.1'9   89-11711
ISBN 0-89778-054-X

TABLE OF CONTENTS

ACKNOWLEDGMENTS

When I first conceived of this book several years ago, I wanted to make it different from the many guides to Lionel already available. Of course, many of these books are excellent, as I wanted this one to be. I decided that my best bet would be to make this book a personal approach rather than a strictly technical one. As I explain in the Prologue, shared experiences are at the heart of this great hobby. In sharing all my experiences, I am only carrying on a long tradition among model railroaders — "keeping the faith," as it were. That has turned out to be a wise decision. Just as I hope to show you some aspects of running Lionel trains, I, too, have learned from more experienced hobbyists.

I first learned about operating and maintaining these trains from **Mr. Frank D'Olonzo**, now retired, who generously shared the wealth of his knowledge with me when he had his little train shop. I am forever in his debt for this unselfish generosity. I also learned that I must listen to the many voices of Lionel train enthusiasts if I expected to learn anything. Two examples of that listening show how critical it really is. Once I was running my trains at a Greenberg show with a battered but still serviceable ZW Transformer. A child near the layout made a comment about "all the smoke." Of course, I thought he meant the locomotive smoke, but when I looked back at my ZW, I saw wisps of acrid smoke curling from beneath the cover! Shutting down the layout, I called for help! **George Koff**, an old "pro" at this sort of thing, took the transformer apart, showed me the short circuit, and taught me on the spot how to repair it. On another occasion, I was doing a track-cleaning demonstration, sanding down some rusty tracks with emery cloth. One of the Philadelphia Greenberg staffers, **Joe Brancato**, tossed a roll of grits paper at me and told me to try it out. That was my introduction to a very valuable track-cleaning tool! There have been dozens more incidents of this sort, and I have tried to do the same for others as was done for me. Above all, be a good listener — and you will learn!

I've tried to listen to others for this book, too, and now is the time to pay them some homage. If I've forgotten anybody, please chalk my neglect up to premature senility rather than ill intentions! Since no one book on Lionel Trains is the product of any one mind, please take note of the article writers whose expertise has created Chapter X and has enriched the book beyond measure. The are **Albert Bailey, Arthur L. Broshears, John Kouba, William Mayer, Jack Robinson, Tom Rollo, Richard Sigurdson, Ed Stencler, Carl Weaver,** and **Richard Ziegler.** These people really know their stuff!

In the editing process, it is always wise to share what one has written with others for their critical commentary and suggestions. In more earthy terms, good readers can keep me from making a total fool of myself! The readers for this book have caught many utterly egregious errors, added suggestions of their own, and in many ways improved upon my original manuscript. In no particular order, these great railroaders are **Dr. Peter Riddle,** who wrote all the way from Nova Scotia; **William Berresford; Joseph Breinter,** a fellow LaSalle University grad; **Charles Briggs** and his handy *Heath Handbook of Composition;* **Tom Budniak** (The Accessory Man); **Pat Iurilli; Lauren Mudge** (who really loves those old railroad timetables); **Clark O'Dell** (Yes, Clark, I still have that black 2314 Searchlight Tower for you); **Bob** (Mr. Lionel Paper) **Osterhoff; Tom Rollo,** the Squire of Milwaukee; **Chris** (Fellow Teacher) **Rohlfing; Richard** (Mr. Catalogued Sets) **Shanfeld; I. D. Smith,** the best darn repair expert I'll ever know; **Carl Weaver,** a fantastic and generous Märklin Man; **Dr. Charles Weber,** whose irreverence I really treasure and enjoy; **Jim Sattler,** the Lionel Pride of Hawaii; and **Glenn Halverson,** my young Fundimensions partner in crime and collaborator. Seventeen people — all of whom made some really thoughtful suggestions and additions! Of course, I had to make some judgments about which suggestions to include, not only because they may have contradicted me, but also in many cases because they contradicted each other! This proves that there is no one way to repair and operate these trains, and if I omitted anybody's suggestions, it's because I had an amateur audience in mind or I had to resolve conflicting advice in some manner. Don't shoot the piano player, boys; he is playin' the best he can!

William Hakkarinen graciously opened his home to the Greenberg photography staff and spent the entire day assisting with photography. **Robert Long** gave us permission to use several photographs taken by the Reading Railroad (Atlantic City Railroad).

If you think the mere production of a manuscript ends the writer's job with a book, think again! At the Greenberg offices, there is a really dedicated group of people who orchestrate all the revisions, make corrections, proofread incessantly, plan photo layouts, tar paper the roofs, tote barges, and lift bales. I cannot begin to thank **Cindy Lee Floyd** for the unbelievable patience she has had with me over the course of this and other books. Her cyclonic energy and unflagging good humor have encouraged me over some really difficult obstacles. Cindy organized the text and coordinated communications with all of the many readers and assistants. **Maureen Crum** (staff artist), and **Sam Baum** were responsible for the layout and design of the book. Maureen was also responsible for preparing the book for the printer. **Donna Price** proofread the book for style and consistency and also showed her artistic talent by creating the layout drawings for Chapter XI. **Donna Dove** applied her expertise, with the help of the computer, to produce many of the drawings. **Maury Feinstein,** (staff photographer) provided most of the photographs for this book. He spent many hours rearranging houses, cars, trees, bushes, people, etc., to prepare for the 'perfect' shot. **Bill Wantz** assisted in printing photographs and making the necessary photostats. A sincere thank you to everyone in the Greenberg Organization for making me look so darn good! Of course, **Bruce and Linda Greenberg** deserve a great thank you from me. After all, they have put up with my eccentricities for a long time and listened to every demented idea which has crossed my nerve synapses. They have done so with complete faith in me, great common sense, and tremendous encouragement.

A very special thank you should go to the long-suffering members of my family, who must wonder sometimes about the mental balance of a middle-aged teacher who plays with toy trains. My wife Jimmie has been a model of patience with me; there's a seat at the direct right hand of the Almighty waiting for her because she has understood why I need this creative outlet. My son Tom has opted for tennis instead of toy trains, but he's his own young man, and he's helped me at several shows and appreciated what I have tried to do over the years. I am indeed a man twice blessed!

Finally, I have saved the dedication of this book for some truly special people. They are my colleagues and students at Cherry Hill High School East. As an English teacher, I have always wanted to be a published author, of course. Not in my wildest dreams did I think that such publication would be with a book about Lionel trains! My colleagues in the English Department have always been good friends who have encouraged me at every turn. They too have some pleasant memories attached to Lionel trains; I hope I have awakened some of them. As for my students, past and present, I cannot say enough good! My English and Creative Writing students and especially the students on the staffs of *Demogorgon* and *Vignettes*, our two student literary outlets for which I am the advisor, have transferred their boundless enthusiasm and energy right to me. It is really touching to see how much they have cared for this particular teacher's welfare and success! With considerable affection, I dedicate this book to those colleagues and students. I owe them more than I can ever mention!

Despite the hard work and occasional aggravation, I have truly enjoyed writing this book. As you begin or continue your involvement with Lionel trains, I hope you will find it helpful. Above all, remember and perpetuate the cooperative spirit these trains seem to engender. Enjoy yourselves!

Roland E. LaVoie, Cherry Hill, New Jersey, May 1989

PROLOGUE

A WELCOME: THE PURPOSE OF THIS BOOK

"The Child Is Father To The Man."
— William Wordsworth

"I Started Out As A Child . . ."
— Bill Cosby

As I write these opening lines, I am looking at the cover of the 1988 Lionel Trains catalogue. These catalogues have been produced every year by Lionel since 1902, except for 1967, when the firm was in deep financial trouble, and 1943 and 1944, when the war precluded toy train production. Then, as now, the catalogues fascinate the reader with a whole world of trains and accessories which have been designed as toys for children — and for those who steadfastly refuse to abandon youthful pursuits. This catalogue has a beautiful Lackawanna 4-8-4 Northern steam engine, a Great Northern electric, and a Santa Fe Alco RS-3 diesel splashed in rich colors across its cover. They look ready to sprint and roar along their tracks at the reader's command.

Part of the fascination people have always felt for Lionel trains is that they come alive when they are operated. Joshua Lionel Cowen, the founder of the firm which bears his middle name, once said that children would become bored with trains just running around in a circle; they had to be "in on the action."

Lionel 1988 Catalogue cover.

And action is just what Lionel has always supplied to its customers. If you have attended a train show recently, you may have seen Lionel layouts with all kinds of operating cars and accessories, some of them with the most clever engineering imaginable. A railroad cop chases a hobo around and around the packing crates of a gondola car, with no hope of ever catching him. Logs, barrels, and coal are dumped from their special cars into waiting accessories which convey them to new locations on the layout. A big gantry crane swivels its magnet into place to dump scrap steel into gondolas at the wrecking yard. A milkman delivers little cans of milk onto a platform, and cows and horses move in and out of their corrals and cars. Crossing gates descend, lights flash, and a little gateman swinging his lantern greets the oncoming train.

All that action brings delight and amusement to railroaders of all ages. The little railroad you design is all yours. It doesn't rely on anyone's imagination except your own. The real significance of these trains is that they represent a little world of your own creation — a microcosm of your own values, preferences, and priorities. Your layout is your empire; it responds to your commands, and if you are its benevolent dictator, you are also totally responsible for its continued operation. The real accomplishment of a fine Lionel layout is that you are the absolute master of a small part of the world; that's not a bad feeling in an age when so many events seem out of our control!

Your Lionel railroad will bring enjoyment to you, as it did to those who grew up with these trains (as I did) when the toy train was king of the world of toys. However, bear in mind that you may also be introducing a whole new generation of young people to the constructive imagination and educational value these trains can teach them. I'll never forget one incident a few years ago when I was operating my layout during one of the Greenberg train shows in Philadelphia. As my Chessie Steam Special passenger train chugged around my outside "express" track, a little girl with Shirley Temple curls in her hair stood at one corner of the layout. She was perhaps three years old, and she could barely see above the table top. As it happened, my No. 1045 Operating Flagman was right in her line of sight. This accessory features a rather over-sized human figure dressed in a conductor's uniform and mounted on a bright red base. When the train passes, he raises his right arm and waves a white flag. The little girl saw him wave his flag, and from her point of view he was waving it right at her! She squealed in delight and ran off to find her parents so that she could show them her new-found wonder. That is the essence of Lionel's magic. These trains touch us personally.

The author's 5′ x 8′ Lionel layout as exhibited and operated at the Greenberg Train Shows. The "crowded" atmosphere of this layout gives the impression that it is much larger than it really is. Note the profusion of lights and operating accessories. Photographed by M. Feinstein.
(See pages 134 and 135 for a detailed diagram of this layout; also see page 133 for drawing showing track pieces used.)

Since there are so many personal associations with these trains, it follows that a book about them with a touch of personal experiences — my own — may strike a responsive chord among you, the readers of this book. I have many stories to tell you, and these stories may seem familiar to many of you because there are so many common experiences with Lionel trains. I will tell you of the catastrophic time I "fried" six uncoupler tracks on one of my layouts because I miswired them. I will relate great collisions I have known and repaired. I can tell you numerous tales of the people I have met in my twelve years of involvement in this hobby.

I will not neglect the practical advice I can give you, either. This book is designed for the newcomer to Lionel trains or for the railroader who is re-introducing himself (and, increasingly, herself) to an old friend with pleasant memories. You will learn, first of all, how to acquire a good collection of trains to operate without taking out a second mortgage on your home. Then I will tell you what I know about sound platform construction, and in the process I hope to destroy once and for all the myth that Lionel trains need too much room in the home for a great layout. I will talk about wiring, scenic tricks, track work, accessories, lighting, and, of course, basic repair and maintenance. Later in the book, you will find some advanced techniques contributed by some of my train friends, who were gracious enough to share their experiences with me for this book. Finally, since there is no substitute for reading and study of these trains, I'll supply you with an annotated bibliography of the best literature available and a glossary of model railroading terms.

I have never been too far from trains myself, both the real thing and its toy equivalents. At my particular age, 45, I am just old enough to remember the last years of steam locomotive operation on the old Pennsylvania-Reading lines. I grew up in the small town of Collingswood, New Jersey, not far from the old Pennsylvania and Reading Seashore Lines main tracks. I hope you will allow me a bit of nostalgia as I tell you how I got into this hobby, hoping that you will recognize some parallels in your own experiences.

As a boy growing up in the 1950s, I experienced quite a few stimulating incidents which kept trains of all kinds in the foreground of my imagination. I had two sets of American Flyer trains as a child, and I distinctly remember the heated arguments I had with my best friend, as to which was the better make, these

The author at age 11 with his four-year-old brother and American Flyer layout. These trains have long since been lost from the family's possession.

or Lionels. After all these years I will concede that he was right, although I must stress that American Flyer made some fine trains which were in some respects superior to Lionel's.

Real trains were fascinating, too. My grade school was right next to the PRSL tracks, and many a dull lesson was brightened for me by switching operations at the coal tipple right across from the school's playground. Years later, I remember the number of the little Pennsylvania 0-6-0 switcher involved, 1644, and I have even managed to secure some pictures of it. I can still hear its little teakettle whistle. It pulled battered black Reading coal hoppers and a little red square-cupola caboose which was faithfully reproduced by Lionel as its No. 2457.

One incident I recall rather vividly summarizes the absolute fascination the trains of that era had for youngsters like me. I turned 14 in the summer of 1957, and on one hot, oppressive day I was riding my bike with some friends on the platform of the old Haddonfield, New Jersey passenger station, which looked so much like Lionel's 132 and 133 models produced at that time. I was standing next to my bike on the brick-paved platform about three feet from the edge of the tracks when the crossing gates on nearby Kings Highway descended to the accompaniment of ringing bells and flashing red lights.

I expected the usual train of Budd railcars to approach from the west around a curve, but not this time. A deep, throaty steamboat whistle sounded an urgent "Get Out Of My Way!" from around the curve, and I knew that whistle could only be found on one engine, the mighty Pennsylvania K-4s Pacific steamer. The big Pacific, its drive rods thrashing madly, came flying around the curve, and before I knew it the train towered above me, only a few feet from where I stood.

I was absolutely transfixed as the smoke-belching iron horse passed me with an unbelievable mechanical roar and rush. The wind and dust of the train's passage nearly blew me over as I watched a long train of maroon and black P-70 passenger coaches rush by me in a monstrous blur. Then I turned to watch the end of the last car disappear around a curve to the accompaniment of huge swirls of dust and the engine's strident whistle notes. In a minute, the serenity of the day had reasserted itself over the sudden, violent disturbance of what I now know was an Atlantic City Race Track special express. Over thirty years have passed, but I have never forgotten the overwhelming sights and sensations of that brief minute.

As the usual concerns of education, a career in teaching, and a marriage and family occupied me into my adulthood, my interest in trains subsided but never really disappeared. I had a bachelor apartment in Audubon, New Jersey during my first few years as a teacher in the late 1960s, and it was next to the Conrail tracks over which long, long trains of coal hoppers pulled by straining black SD-40 diesels lumbered on their way to the Atlantic City Power and Light Company. My furniture would shake and sway in tune with the rumble of those trains. Once there was a derailment, and I walked to an overhead footbridge to watch a burro crane attempt to pull a battered hopper back onto the rails.

Some years later, when my son turned four, my late father-in-law suggested that I get him a set of trains for his birthday. I got a ready-to-run HO set which did not run right, and my father-in-law told me to "exchange it for a real boy's train — get him a Lionel!" I did just that, getting him a 1973 set called the Blue Streak. It was pulled by a little blue Jersey Central 8303 plastic-bodied steamer, which we have to this day. Later on, I ran into some sales at the local K-Mart and added some more freight cars from the 9700 Series. I remembered how much fun I'd had with these trains, and as my son and I watched the little blue engine chug around a hastily constructed oval of track on a dining room table, I decided to seek out more of these trains.

In the process, I found a little hobby shop in Collingswood operated by a fine and knowledgeable gentleman, Frank D'Olonzo, who has since retired. As is typical of toy train hobbyists, Mr. D'Olonzo answered my every question with great patience, and I learned from him the basics of what I am now telling you in this book. By 1978 I had sold my soul to the ghosts of Cowen, Gilbert, and Marx. I was hooked!

In 1980 I acquired an all-silver 9134 Virginian covered hopper. This was an unusual variation; the usual version has a blue roof. Mr. D'Olonzo suggested that I write a letter of inquiry to Mr. Bruce Greenberg, who had just published his 1979 Price Guide to Lionel Trains. I did so, expecting a typical form letter in return. Imagine my surprise when I received a well-detailed, friendly personal response from Mr. Greenberg! This was the beginning of a lively personal correspondence between us. He was to hold one of his train shows at the Philadelphia Civic Center, and he suggested that I come to the show and introduce myself. I did so, and I was enthralled by the tremendous variety of trains and exhibits I found. Here was a whole new social world as well as an entree to a hobby!

Mr. Greenberg found that I was an unusual combination of trained proofreader, English teacher, and Lionel Trains enthusiast, so eventually he asked me if I would be interested in doing a little editing for him. I was, and am, interested in doing so! Before too many years had passed, I had become an exhibitor at his shows and the editor and author of several editions of the Lionel Guides. That first letter was the beginning of a highly pleasurable personal and professional association for me.

Now, in the summer of 1988, I find myself writing these words so that I can share my own experiences with you. I exhibit my "insanely crowded" 5' x 8' Lionel layout in six or seven Greenberg shows a year, and I have been involved in many writing and editing pursuits — an important creative outlet for me. My train collection has grown to about 550 pieces of rolling stock as well as 125 accessories. My show layout is my only one, and perhaps that is just as well, since I appreciate it more by seeing it less. I feel privileged to do clinics and demonstrations with showgoers, and in the process I have met some fine and interesting fellow hobbyists. The generosity of toy train people is simply superb; that is why I am now trying to share with you what I have learned. The ideas I will relate are the sum total of many shared experiences, and that sharing can and does carry over into the real world.

I believe that shared experiences are the heart and soul of this hobby. I cannot write the definitive book about every facet of Lionel trains and their operation, but I can tell you what I have learned, what I have felt, and what I have seen since I discovered this wonderful diversion which has enriched my life in so many ways. I hope to communicate some of the joy of discovery and the enthusiasm I have felt, in the hope that you can experience the same feelings. Before I do that, however, a little background into the history of this hobby and some explanation as to why Lionel trains are the best ones for your enjoyment are in order. Then we shall get to work!

A night view of the old P R S L station in Haddonfield, New Jersey. The author was standing under the shed roof on the left during the incident described above. Photo courtesy of Mr. Robert Long of the West Jersey Chapter, National Railway Historical Society.

Chapter I

A BRIEF HISTORY OF TOY TRAINS AND THE LIONEL CORPORATION

"Sir, a whole history!"
— Shakespeare, *Hamlet*

"And so we beat on, boats against the current, borne back ceaselessly into the past."
— F. Scott Fitzgerald, *The Great Gatsby*

Toy and model trains have been around for a long time. In fact, the first model trains appeared soon after the real trains did. Not long after the first real railway in Germany was completed from Nürnberg to Fürth in 1835, German toy makers had produced the first model locomotives seen in that country. It's not too surprising that toy trains appeared so soon, for railroads were on the cutting edge of technology in the Nineteenth Century, and toys have always reflected what was new and enterprising in the real world.

One of Ives' first locomotives produced in the first or second year. From the collection of the late J. Wiley.

The earliest toy trains were designed mostly as pull toys, although in the latter half of the Nineteenth Century clockwork trains had appeared. These toy trains operated by a spring-wound motor which was wound with a key. In addition, many live steam toy trains were produced in Europe, especially in England. These trains had locomotives which burned alcohol to produce steam in miniature boilers to provide power to the cylinders — in other words, they worked just like the real steam

engines. Needless to say, these live steamers were not paragons of safety for young children!

By the late Nineteenth Century there were many manufacturers of toy trains in Europe, but a few giants predominated. The German toy manufacturers had taken the lead in toy train manufacturing, and they were to dominate the marketplace until the First World War. The two largest toy train makers in Germany were the Bing Company, famous for its fine models of American steam locomotives, and the Märklin Company, which is the oldest toy train manufacturer still in existence today. Both firms exported toy trains to the United States, to where we now shift our attention.

One of the earliest trains with sectional track was advertised in the Marshall Field 1892-1893 Catalogue.

In the 1890s some American toy train makers had emerged as domestic leaders within the marketplace. The Ives' Company of Bridgeport, Connecticut had made pull-toy trains since the 1860s, and these toys had achieved great popularity. A little later, spring-powered clockwork trains appeared. However, the real surge in popularity came with the first electrically-operated trains in the last decade of the Nineteenth Century. Märklin had introduced a real breakthrough, the first sectional tracks, in the late 1800s. The earliest manufacturer of American electric trains was the Carlisle and Finch Company of Cincinnati. This firm put out

Carlisle and Finch mining locomotive and three hopper cars. R. Sullens Collection, M. Feinstein photograph.

an electric trolley car in 1896 and followed it with steam engines and a little mining train, all highly prized by collectors today. Lionel introduced its first operating unit, an electrically-powered gondola, in 1901. It was quickly followed during the next few years by Voltamp, Elektoy, Knapp, and Howard. None of these firms lasted beyond the 1920s. Although Ives was the largest American manufacturer of toy trains, it did not introduce its first electrically-powered locomotive until 1910.

Lionel, therefore, was not the first to introduce toy electric trains. Every major innovation came from other firms active during the time of Lionel's founding. The chief reasons for Lionel's domination of the marketplace for toy trains can be found in the personality and skills of its founder, Joshua Lionel Cowen, who began his enterprise in late 1900 or early 1901. Cowen was not the innovator he claimed to be, but nobody could summon up better engineering expertise or more skilled marketing ability.

Joshua Lionel Cowen was born to Jewish immigrant parents in New York City's Lower East Side, that great simmering stew for the tidal waves of immigrants between 1860 and 1920. A restless, imaginative young man, Cowen was always tinkering with motors and gadgets. He later claimed that one of his experiments blew up his parents' kitchen, although no real proof exists for this. He was fascinated with transportation vehicles of all sorts and, like most boys his age, trains held a special magic for him. It must be remembered that Cowen grew up at a time when every young boy dreamed of becoming a locomotive engineer. The tabloids of the time, such as *Frank Leslie's Illustrated Weekly*, featured lithographs and stories of young boys saving the Lightning Express from sure catastrophe on a washed-out bridge. Kate Shelley, largely forgotten today, was a young girl who saved a train from a bridge washout and was made a national heroine for her exploit. The legend of Casey Jones dates from 1902, during the earliest years of Cowen's train manufacturing career. In late 1900, as the legend has it, Cowen had just finished a contract with the United States Navy for shell fuses. At 22 he typified the entrepreneur of the time, waiting to develop and market an idea which could make him successful and wealthy. These were great years for such men. Cowen had perfected a small electric motor, but he had nothing for its practical use. Supposedly, he was standing outside a store display window when he came up with the idea of a powered gondola to carry sale goods inside the window, thereby attracting customers. He rented a small shop on White Street and began manufacturing his gondolas in early 1901. He soon discovered that people were more interested in the gondolas than the goods they carried.

all, a trolley car which sold very well. The fledgling train company also offered stations and accessories during those first years.

A big step in the prosperity of Lionel was the introduction in 1906 to three-rail track with 2-1/8 inches between the rails. This was the real start of the Lionel firm which was to dominate the toy train world; Cowen called this new track "Standard Gauge," and other manufacturers soon offered similar track under their own names.

By the end of the First World War the German firms had ceased to dominate the American marketplace, and Lionel's chief competition came from the venerable Ives firm and the newer American Flyer Company, which made its trains in Chicago. All three firms manufactured O Gauge trains as well as Standard Gauge, but now Lionel's marketing superiority began to make itself felt.

THE TRACK
Catalogue No. 310.

Lionel's sectional track pieces from 1904.

Cowen capitalized on some brilliant marketing techniques. He stressed fascination with electricity, the wonder of its age. He devoted many pages of his catalogues to a description of the manufacturing process. It is to Joshua Lionel Cowen that we owe the linkage of the toy train to the Christmas season. In the early years of this century, it was the custom for people to build a Christmas creche, or display scene, around the base of the Christmas tree. Often these creches had religious themes, but they also displayed miniature streets, houses, and the like. It was Cowen's idea to promote a toy train as part of these creche displays, and when the idea caught on, the toy train became associated forevermore with the Christmas season.

Sometimes, especially in his comparisons with other train makers, Cowen stretched the truth, but the Lionel Corporation did in fact turn out a high-quality product, thanks to a bright manufacturing supervisor named Mario Caruso. Cowen insisted on the best quality materials for his trains, even though their price would be higher. Caruso encouraged many talented Italian craftsmen to come to America to produce the trains, and these people were very

One of Lionel's earliest gondolas.

Lionel's first products ran on two-rail track with 2-7/8 inches between the rails. These very early items included a derrick car, a small electric engine, powered passenger cars, and above

LOOK OUT FOR THE THIRD RAIL

Manufactured by
Lionel Mfg. Co.
(Incorporated)
4 and 6 White Street
NEW YORK CITY
Western Sales Office
Monadnock Block   CHICAGO, ILL.

1906 Catalogue cover ("Look Out for the Third Rail").

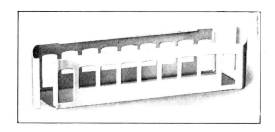

Sometimes Lionel's quality comparisons were highly exaggerated, as was the fashion in 1923. However, the firm really did make a high-quality product.

devoted to their art. It wasn't long before Lionel developed a fine reputation for quality goods. The firm also managed to produce its trains far more efficiently than the Ives Corporation did — a decided advantage in marketing the trains. Ives, too, cared about quality, but that company's manufacturing process was far more dependent upon manual workmanship than was Lionel's. Ultimately, the toy train future belonged to the efficient.

Cowen also exploited the father-son bond of toy trains better than any other manufacturer. His ads would show a picture of a disinterested father reading his newspaper in his easy chair while his young son played with the trains; the ads would carry the stern wording, "This father never knew his own son!" In Cowen's eyes, if you were a real dad, you made your son into a real boy by getting Lionel trains for him!

By the 1920s Lionel had become the acknowledged king of the toy train world. During these years Lionel produced some of the most beautiful toy trains of its history, including the 200- and 500-series freight cars and the magnificent Transcontinental Limited, nicknamed by collectors as the "State Set." The passenger cars in this set even had detailed interiors, right down to miniature porcelain fixtures in the rest rooms. Lionel's competitors, Ives and Flyer, also came out with some beautiful electric trains. These years are known as the "Golden Age of Toy Trains." Although Ives produced some of the most magnificent toy trains ever seen in the 1920s, it was in financial difficulty from the mid-1920s due to inept management. In 1928 Ives' creditors forced it into bankruptcy. The Ives company was sold for only $73,000 to the joint venture of Lionel and American Flyer. This

partnership lasted one year and in 1930 Lionel became the sole owner of Ives, which it continued as a separate corporation but under Lionel management. The result of this corporate juggling was some very strange trains put out under the Ives name. These trains, now called "transition pieces" by collectors, are among the most avidly sought toy trains of all. Some of the freight cars had Ives couplers, Lionel bodies, and American Flyer frames and trucks!

The Great Depression affected Lionel just as much as it had other firms, and by the mid-1930s Lionel found itself awash in red ink. Ives trains were marketed with a combination of new designs created for it under its new management and re-stamped Lionel equipment. In 1933 Lionel discontinued the Ives line and, with that abrupt ending, the Ives Corporation passed into toy train history. Or did it? Supposedly, one provision in the terms of sale of the Ives Corporation was that Lionel had to keep the name alive on at least one piece of equipment. Lionel accomplished that by keeping the Ives name on the lowly O27 Gauge track clip! It is more likely that Lionel was merely protecting the Ives name for copyright and patent purposes. American Flyer remained as a competitor, and that firm was joined by Marx at the low-price end; but Lionel had no equal.

Lionel had to find a new way to attract people to toy trains, since the expensive sets of the 1920s were clearly out of the reach of most families. In the early 1930s, Lionel began to market inexpensive trains under the Winner nameplate. This was the beginning of the now dominant O27 Gauge. Later on, Lionel began to abandon its reliance upon the brightly-colored Standard Gauge trains in favor of greater realism. By the mid-1930s, Lionel was marketing O Gauge models of the latest streamliners, the City of Denver and the Flying Yankee. Lionel also came out with a great seller, the Mickey Mouse Handcar, in 1934. By the end of the 1930s, Lionel had mastered new manufacturing processes in die-casting and compression-molded plastics, paving the way for a whole new generation of realistic trains. New electrically-operated accessories and couplers gave Lionel operators a toy train which would respond to the simple touch of a button. In 1935 Lionel perfected an extremely realistic steam engine whistle which soon won great favor. Lionel's tour de force came in 1937 with a brilliantly executed, full-scale model of the New York Central's J1-a Hudson steam locomotive.

By 1941 the changeover was complete for Lionel. The last Standard Gauge trains were made in 1940; they would not return until the recent Lionel Classics revivals in 1986. The onset of the Second World War brought a halt to toy train production as Lionel converted its factories to the war effort. Lionel made navigational instruments and communications equipment for the United States Navy during the war, winning many commendations in the process.

Throughout the war, Lionel's managers made their plans for toy trains after the war years. Cowen himself, still active and vital in his sixties, had definite ideas about what would sell because he possessed the services of Arthur Raphael, Lionel's marketing wizard, who was years ahead of his time in the art of market surveys. Raphael's story has yet to be told, but marketing experts have been amazed by his advanced marketing methods. The firm also had a brilliant design engineer named Frank Pettit, who became the inventor of many of the great action accessories which were to give Lionel its postwar predominance. It was clear that if Lionel produced the right trains and accessories after the war was over, some great years would be ahead for the company.

Cowen, Raphael, Pettit, and company saw to it that the right trains were in fact produced. The public was clamoring for toy trains, since none had been available since 1942. Lionel's chief competitors by this time were the rejuvenated American Flyer company, which had been taken over by the creative A. C. Gilbert, and the Marx Corporation, which had given Lionel some stiff competition at the lower end of the market since the early 1930s. Each company raced to be the first to reintroduce toy trains to the American public. Corporate spies tried to find out what each company was planning. By strenuous efforts, Lionel was able to catalogue one train set by Christmas of 1945, and all through the next year Lionel introduced some of its greatest innovations, including smoke and knuckle couplers. At Flyer, A. C. Gilbert had gone one step further. He introduced smoke and a "choo-

1945 Catalogue cover.

choo" sound to Flyer, and he made his new trains in two-rail S Gauge, smaller — and less expensive — than Lionel's trains, which kept their three-rail track.

Despite Flyer's best efforts, Lionel retained its market dominance. Flyer's two-rail track was electrically limited; Lionel's retention of three-rail track meant that its trains could do more electrical "tricks," and Lionel took full advantage of its electrical edge by producing an astonishing variety of operating accessories, more than American Flyer could manage. By 1950, the firm's "Golden Anniversary," Lionel had become the largest privately-held toy company in the world. Sales went up and up, every year. Then, in the early 1950s, the first signs of real trouble appeared for the company.

In 1952 Arthur Raphael, Lionel's creative marketing genius, died suddenly, and no one of comparable ability was there to replace him. Had he lived, Raphael might have prevented Lionel from some of the disastrous marketing decisions it would make in the next five years. In addition, the spectre of television was threatening to replace toy trains as an activity. Lionel failed to recognize the increasing popularity of HO trains and slot cars, and when the firm finally did market these items, they were poorly planned and manufactured. Lionel was a one-product firm, and by the mid-1950s Lionel had to diversify or fall by the wayside. Despite the production of some of its most magnificent trains in

Folklore has it that this Mickey Mouse handcar set saved the Lionel corporation from the clutches of the great depression. However, the truth is, Lionel's more realistic trains — such as the streamline Flying Yankee — put Lionel back on its financial feet. The legend is a great story anyway. M. Feinstein photograph.

1954, Lionel's sales and profits began to plummet. The toy market was changing, and Lionel failed to change with it.

Joshua Lionel Cowen was still active with the firm in the early 1950s, but by 1959 he was 82 years old, and he had seen enough. He and his family sold their shares in the company to a group of investors led by Roy Cohn, the McCarthy-era lawyer.

By this time, trains were simply one of four competing lines of Lionel Toys.

Cowen then retired to Florida, where he died in 1965 at the age of 88.

During the 1960s, the trains continued to be produced, even though they had been cheapened considerably. Corporate mergers and battles raged within the firm, each one battering Lionel's tarnished reputation even more. Lionel's worst years began in late 1966, when Lionel's Hillside, New Jersey tooling was auctioned off and the firm moved its remaining production to a small facility in Hagerstown, Maryland. The trains nearly passed into oblivion by 1969, but Lionel wasn't a dead issue yet. The name still had magic, even though the trains no longer did.

Recognizing a good name when they saw it, the officers of General Mills made inquiries about the prospective purchase of

Lionel Auction Catalogue.

the manufacturing rights to the trains. At the time, General Mills was acquiring toy firms as part of that new business phenomenon, the conglomerate. A deal was struck, and by early 1970 General Mills had moved Lionel's equipment and parts warehouse to a facility in Mount Clemens, Michigan where the trains are still made today. Under the division name of Model Products Company, later to become Fundimensions, General Mills began to market Lionel trains to a whole new generation of people. Beginning modestly, the new Lionel line experienced success, and by 1973 a new toy train market had begun to emerge, thanks in part to a newly-found nostalgia for the past on the part of the American public.

In 1973 the General Mills management discovered a market for toy trains which had not been tapped before, even by Cowen — the collector's market. In that year Fundimensions put out a special General Motors 50th Anniversary diesel locomotive. This engine sold so well that Fundimensions cultivated the collector market, eventually producing special limited-edition trains while it also marketed Lionel to its usual childhood audience. By 1979 there were two distinct lines of Lionel trains — traditional and collector. These separate lines have continued to the present.

Lionel was not quite through with its corporate adventures. In 1983 Lionel moved its production facilities to Mexico, claiming better economy and citing better labor costs. The General Mills management forgot that these trains demanded a very high proficiency of assembly, and the move to Mexico was destined to end in failure because skilled workers could not be trained. Lionel fell two years behind in its production, and by 1985 the Mexican production had ceased and the trains were back in Mount Clemens. General Mills then turned Lionel over to the Kenner-Parker Toy Division in late 1985, but one further change in management was forthcoming. Just as Lionel's customers had gotten used to the Kenner-Parker changeover, Richard Kughn, a wealthy real estate developer in Detroit, purchased the entire company, renaming it Lionel Trains, Inc. Once again, Lionel had become a privately-held company.

The first two years of Lionel Trains, Inc. management have seen tremendous expansion into new and highly competitive markets. To meet the challenge of the German firm of LGB (Lehmann Gross Bahn), Lionel has begun to market its own Large Scale trains in the huge G Gauge. Lionel is also marketing resurrections of the great old prewar trains under the name of Lionel

8960 Southern Pacific U36C, available with dummy unit only in Southern Pacific Limited Set of 1979, a set which sold out even before it was distributed. A. Rudman Collection, M. Feinstein photograph.

Classics. Several engineering breakthroughs promise a whole new era for the toy train devotee; one of these is RailScope, a video transmission system inside a locomotive which sends an "engineer's eye" television picture to a receiver. The traditional line has been expanded, and the collector line features some excellent designs of new products as well as resurrections of old favorites. With the toy train marketplace enjoying a rejuvenation, Lionel is meeting its competition and thriving once again — just as it did in Cowen's glory days.

You can see, then, that Lionel indeed has an illustrious history. I respond to that because I believe these trains to be reflections of the culture and value systems of the society which produces them. Lionel's promotional literature and the trains themselves tell us a great deal about the firm's view of management, promotion, and manufacture. In fact, many toy train "archeologists" have been busy for the last fifteen years in reconstructing the entire manufacturing history of a century-old toy company, just by examining the "artifacts" themselves. This pursuit makes for some interesting scholarship and fun, over and above the enjoyment of the trains themselves!

Now, however, it is time to discuss the real advantages of collecting and operating Lionel trains above any others available to you. Needless to say, I am reflecting my own prejudices here, but if you are just beginning your sojourn into this hobby, you will see how there are philosophical as well as practical reasons for joining the Lionel passenger consist. If your experience is anything like mine has been, you're in for a pleasant journey — and so is your family. Climb aboard! Some comfortable chairs in the parlor cars of your imagination are waiting for you!

The 1973 8359 gold Chessie which commemorated the 50th Anniversary of GM diesels was not marked with its catalogue number, 8359. Author's Collection, B. Greenberg photograph.

CHAPTER II

THE ADVANTAGES OF COLLECTING AND OPERATING LIONEL TRAINS

"You know what the most exciting sound in the world is, Uncle Billy? That's it — a train whistle!"
— James Stewart as George Bailey in Frank Capra's
It's A Wonderful Life

I have already pointed out that Lionel trains have a rich history. The significance of this is that they reflect the concerns of their times and thus offer insights into the changing history of the United States in the Twentieth Century. What I have not stressed yet is the scholarship involved in the research into these trains. By examining the trains themselves and noting variations in the manufacturing process, we can reconstruct the history of an entire company right through the present day. We can look at the literature — the catalogues, service manuals, and instruction sheets — and find out what advertising "pitches" worked in a given time. We can even note changes in language over the years. If you are intellectually inclined, Lionel trains have much to offer you. Many toy train collectors and operators have relished playing Sherlock Holmes over Lionel trains!

Another intangible reason to develop an interest in Lionel trains involves social concerns. All of us want social outlets of all kinds to meet new friends and share experiences. Most hobbies offer this, but the pursuit of Lionel trains can introduce you to some interesting people from all walks of life. I have come to meet lawyers, fellow teachers, ministers, business executives of all kinds, farmers, oil rig workers, construction and maintenance employees, salesmen, and even sports and entertainment figures through my association with Lionel trains. (Yes, I've even met real railroad workers and executives!) The common bond everyone shares can lead to a real education about people for you and your family. Meeting the many people associated with this hobby can help you avoid becoming locked into just one little world, because inevitably you will share the political and social concerns of many segments of our society. That's a real education!

Increasingly, you will be joining a sorority as well as a fraternity. The world of Joshua Lionel Cowen was exclusively male, and young girls were supposed to be onlookers but not participants within the world of toy trains. Lionel's one attempt to lure girls to trains in the 1950s, the notorious Girls' Set, was a sales disaster, for good reason! That notion has changed along with our society. Although the toy train world is still male-dominated, women have taken up the collection and operation of Lionel trains in increasing numbers in the past ten years or so. I believe this to be a welcome addition because these trains can be enjoyed by everyone. In the future, there may be just as many women train scholars and operators as men.

One important philosophical reason for developing an interest in Lionel trains is their educational value. Remember that setting up Lionel trains involves a great deal of decision-making, and in the end you will be exercising your own creativity instead of playing with someone else's designs. The operator of Lionel trains will learn a great deal about electricity and its functions, just as Joshua Lionel Cowen had the sense to foresee. The operation, repair, and maintenance of small electric motors can lead to a career interest. The problem-solving and visualization skills involved in designing, building, and operating a Lionel layout can enrich the developing intelligence of young children better than almost any other toy. Young children can also profit greatly from the exercise of gross and fine motor skills needed to operate a set of Lionel trains. The reading and research involved in the building of a collection and the operation of a layout can stir a great interest in reading. In an age when literacy is so important to our newly-emerging technical society, an interest in reading can pay great dividends. As an educator, I recognize the many instructional advantages Lionel trains can offer to the whole family, not to mention the great creative outlet these trains can provide.

If you want more formal association with people in the hobby, I'd suggest that you join one or more of the collecting and operating clubs which have arisen in the years of the hobby's development. The addresses of these clubs can be found in the appendix at the back of this book. I can only list the national organizations here, but many divisions, chapters, and local train collecting organizations are probably in your area. It is estimated that there are about fifty thousand serious collectors of toy trains in the United States alone, and at least that many more people are scale modelers and operators. These totals would triple if you included the more "casual" collectors and operators of toy and model trains. (I will be telling you about the differences between scale railroaders and "tinplaters" in the next chapter.)

Some of the "Friday Night Irregulars" pose for a group photo. From left to right: Hans, Gary, Frank, Jack (front), Mitch (center), Bob (rear), George, Denis, and Tom (partially obscured). Presiding over this assembly are the store's two proprietors, Joe Gordon (left) and Joe Bratspis. Note the extensive stock! Author's photo.

The Train Collectors Association (TCA) is the largest tinplate organization in the country, with nearly 20,000 members. The TCA sponsors several regional divisions and chapters throughout the country; this organization, founded in 1954, operates the superb Toy Train Museum in Strasburg, Pennsylvania and publishes a fine magazine of toy train information and scholarship, the *TCA Quarterly*. The TCA is noteworthy for its twice-a-year train meets at the York, Pennsylvania fairgrounds. These shows, for members only, are the largest train markets in the country; they usually feature seven buildings full of trains!

The **Lionel Collectors' Club of America** (LCCA) is another large organization which specializes in the collection and operation of Lionel trains. Like the TCA, the LCCA has a national convention, often featuring special rolling stock made for the organization by Lionel Trains, Inc. These cars are usually highly prized special issues. The LCCA publishes a terrifically interesting, lively magazine called *The Lion Roars*. This journal features up-to-the-minute information on the latest doings of Lionel Trains, Inc., as well as fine articles and operating tips.

The **Lionel Operating Train Society** (LOTS) is a relative newcomer on the toy train scene, but it has built a good membership in the last few years and it features national conventions and yet another fine journal, *The Switcher*, which features layout contests, maintenance tips, and many other articles of concern to the Lionel layout operator. Like the LCCA, LOTS has special cars made for the club by Lionel Trains, Inc.

The **Toy Train Operating Society** (TTOS) does not limit itself to Lionel operations, but many great articles appear in its journal which can add to the dimension and strategy of the Lionel layout operator. The TTOS also publishes many articles of great historical significance, in addition to featuring national conven-

tions where all kinds of exotic trains from the past can be seen operating in all kinds of gauges. Highly specialized collectors of scarce antique toy trains favor the TTOS and are frequent contributors to its activities.

The **National Model Railroaders' Association** (NMRA) is mostly concerned with scale model operation in O, S, HO, N and Z Gauges, but that does not mean Lionel does not get a share of attention. There is one special interest group (SIG) within NMRA, the tinplate SIG devoted to Lionel trains. In any case, the Lionel operator can profit a great deal from the electronic and scenic skills of the fine railroad craftsmen who belong to this organization. Since scale modelers insist upon absolute realism, they can offer many decorating tricks which can readily be adapted to Lionels. This organization is also on the cutting edge of the latest electronics, including the use of computer technology.

Actually, based upon my own experiences with Lionels, I have been half tempted to form my own organization which sometimes reflects the real toy train world of errors, mistakes, and confusion. I think I'll give it the acronym FLORIDA, which stands for Frustrated Lionel Operators' Railroads In Drastic Alteration! Actually, the train associations mentioned above can become important sources of information for you as well as sources for the trains themselves through the many club "meets," as they are called. I recommend that you join any or all of these organizations; the dues are not prohibitive, and the journals alone are worth the cost.

By now, you're probably wondering about the practical advantages of collecting and operating Lionel trains, now that some of the philosophical underpinnings have been established. Are there reasons for choosing Lionel over any other make of trains available? Yes, as surely as trains run on rails! You'd better believe there are practical advantages to these trains, especially if you're considering trains as a family hobby!

First of all, consider the gauge, or size, of Lionel trains. Lionels are made for O Gauge and O27 Gauge, which means there is a space of 1-1/4 inches between the outside rails of Lionel's three-rail track. Larger gauges, such as LGB's G Gauge, may be easier to play with, but they are also much more expensive and for some, limited in play value. A new line in G Gauge, Playmobil, might change that eventually for very young children, but for now the size of Lionels is appropriate for children from about eight years and older. The American Flyer trains are made in two-rail S Gauge (by Lionel Trains, Inc., ironically), and they are very impressive. However, the two-rail configuration leads to wiring complexity and limited operational value. The smaller gauges favored by scale modelers, HO, S, N, and Z, are not very durable if they are inexpensive and, if they are of high quality, much more difficult to maintain and repair. For a family hobby, therefore, Lionel seems the best choice. To be sure, not all "tinplaters" agree with this assessment, especially the "Flyer Guys." However, my experience with toy trains still points to Lionel as the best choice for a family hobby.

Another significant practical advantage of Lionel trains is that they are available in absolutely staggering varieties and quantities. Remember that these trains have been produced for nearly a century. A quick glance at the Greenberg publications about Lionel trains tells an interesting story. There is a two-volume guide to the prewar Lionels produced from 1901 to 1942. It is matched by a two-volume guide to the postwar Lionels of 1945-1969, and there is a hefty one-volume guide for the Lionels of the modern era produced from 1970 to the present day. The Greenberg Company is planning a large volume just for the many accessories Lionel has produced over the years. No toy company documented itself better than Lionel, so there are two books of Lionel catalogue reproductions (with two more in the planning stages), a four-volume service manual for the postwar trains, a one-volume book for prewar parts and instruction sheets, and a large volume of Lionel paper and catalogue listings. A new service manual has just been issued for the trains of the modern era. And these are only some of the books available! Clearly, you

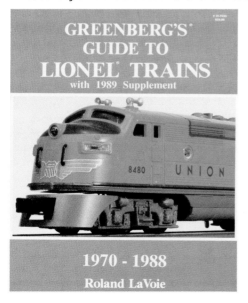

1989 cover of *Greenberg's Guide to Lionel Trains* **1970-1988.**

will not lack for choices when you look for Lionel trains! (Just which choices to make will be the subject of the next chapter.)

More important than the sheer quantity of Lionel trains available to you is the unbelievable variety of these trains. You have three distinct eras to choose — prewar, postwar, and modern era. The couplers of the prewar rolling stock are not compatible with the other two eras, but postwar, and modern era Lionels are completely interchangeable. Steam, diesel, and electric engines, boxcars, hoppers, gondolas, crane cars, bunk and tool cars, refrigerator cars — you name it, Lionel has produced it! Operating accessories? Lionel's production will do everything but jump up and sing grand opera! Buildings and structures? Signals? Tracks? Believe me when I tell you that they are all available! Naturally, a Lionel collector and operator accumulates trains based upon personal preferences. My point is that with Lionels, you have ample room to pick and choose. No other American manufacturer has produced these trains in so many varieties. To paraphrase the popular song of the 1960s (with apologies to Arlo Guthrie and Alice), "You can get anything you want at the Lionel Train restaurant!"

In terms of money, the Lionel operator and collector can build an excellent collection on a very limited budget (as I think I have) or an even better collection on a lavish budget, as some more monetarily blessed friends of mine have managed to do. Used Lionels for operation are a great value; for example, a 2034 Steam Engine produced in 1953 can be found used in great operating condition for about $35 at the time of this writing. This little engine does not have smoke or a whistle, but it has an excellent spur-gear motor which runs very well. If you want smoke and a whistle in your steamer, an old 2025 in excellent condition will cost you about $150 at this time. This locomotive represents Lionel's finest craftsmanship. I have mentioned that I have about 600 locomotives and cars in my own collection. That must seem like a tremendous quantity, but I know a few people who possess that many locomotives, not to mention thousands of pieces of rolling stock! By combining used and new equipment, you can build a terrific starter set for yourself, including all the tracks, transformer, and even an operating car or two, for about $200 to $250 today — not bad, considering the quality you can find. If that seems too much, Lionel Trains, Inc. sells good starter sets, ready to run, for less money. There's something for every budget in Lionel trains! I'll have more specific purchasing advice in the next chapter.

Another significant practical advantage to Lionel trains is their quality of construction and operation. Like any toy manufacturer, Lionel has made its share of shoddy equipment. However, these trains are, extremely reliable and durable. Many a Lionel locomotive has dived off a layout onto a floor and come back for more punishment. On the whole, the electric motors in the locomotives are simple and rugged; they are also relatively easy to repair, thanks to all the repair literature produced by Lionel over the years. Lionel issued service manuals in the same way that auto companies still issue parts and service manuals — they're that comprehensive. No other toy company has ever provided so much service and operating guidance, and you should take full advantage of this literature so you can maintain and operate your trains yourself. There's no guesswork with Lionels!

Electrically, Lionel's use of three-rail track has always paid great dividends. As you'll see later on, you can take advantage of the extra ground rail to operate accessories automatically, using the train itself to turn the accessories on. Wiring procedures are relatively simple, and the electrical devices themselves are highly reliable. Lionel's transformers are protected by circuit breakers for the most part, and since they are basically very simple devices, there's not much that can go wrong with them. They also can handle considerable abuse without burning out. It should tell you something that I run my own layout with a 34 year-old ZW Transformer and a 41 year-old R Transformer! These two transformers have been flawless performers for the past seven years. Most of the accessories work by either solenoids or vibrator motors, both of which are simple and reliable mechanisms. I have an operating gateman on my layout made in 1939. After nearly half a century, the little gateman flings open the door of his shack and meets the train with his lantern every time without fail! Finally, you must consider that no other toy makes a better long-term investment than Lionel trains. Collectors of dolls and other antique toys may dispute this with some justification. However, I have seen the toy train marketplace grow tremendously over the years, and some astute purchases now are likely to accumulate value later on. I hasten to add that Lionel trains are not meant for the speculator who wants to make a quick fortune (although some recent limited production has offered even that opportunity). These trains are excellent long-term investments which, in the meantime, can be enjoyed by the whole family in a thoroughly constructive activity. I doubt that these trains will lose their value; I sometimes think of my own collection as a form of savings. The whole issue of play versus investment is a complex one, but speaking for myself I do not view Lionel trains as bank-vault articles. I believe in running these trains as they were meant to be run, for only then do they truly come alive, as I hope you will soon discover.

All of these advantages — the history, the social contacts, the quality, and the quantity — add up to an unbeatable combination of stimulation and enjoyment. If you're just beginning your involvement with Lionels, you have some great fun ahead of you! Let us assume, therefore, that you have made your decision to collect Lionel trains as a hobby and build the best operating layout you can. Once this decision is made, you need to address several other questions before that layout-building project gets started. Which Lionel trains should you look for? Where can you get them at the best prices? How can you find out which Lionels are "out there?" Should you buy new Lionels, used Lionels, or a combination of both? In the next chapter, I will try to help you answer these and some other questions. Please read on for just a little bit more before you accompany me to the garage or basement, get out your tools, and start building that train layout!

CHAPTER III

WHICH LIONEL TRAINS SHOULD YOU GET —AND WHERE YOU CAN GET THEM

"In a minute there is time
For decisions and revisions
Which a minute will reverse."

— T. S. Eliot

"Devilish MacBeth hath by many
of these trains sought to win
me into his favor..."

— Malcolm, in Shakespeare's *MacBeth*

Every once in a while, just for the sake of nostalgia, I flip through the old Lionel catalogues. One particular 1946 catalogue page seems quite appropriate for our discussion of the choices available to you. This ad was one of Lionel's best. It shows a father, nattily dressed in a checked tweed sport coat, looking through a store display window at a complex and well-equipped Lionel layout. In view are the 38 Water Tower with real water, the 671 Pennsylvania Steam Turbine belching clouds of white smoke, and several other colorful trains and accessories. His son, about eight years old, looks at this layout with eyes the size of fruit jar lids. The father asks in bold script the magic words inscribed at the top of the page: "Which LIONEL do you want, Son?"

As you begin your foray into the world of Lionel, that's a very appropriate question to ask of you. I've already pointed out that there are seemingly endless varieties of Lionels from which you can make a choice, but that very quantity can cause great confusion. Lionel trains are relatively expensive; they were that way many years ago, too, when the $89 one could pay for the Transcontinental Limited in 1927 was a very handsome week's salary. By the standards of inflation, the $11.95 you paid for an operating milk car outfit in 1951 was more, in proportion to your salary, than the $45 or so the same outfit would cost today within the used toy train market. The question then becomes (since most of us are not Sultans of Oman): Which Lionels represent the best values and will bring us the most for our money?

To help you answer that question, it is necessary to do a little classification and division. First, let me explain the differences between scale modelers and "tinplaters," as Lionel enthusiasts are sometimes called. These differences have important monetary considerations as well as operating ones. Then, we should talk

Inside cover of the 1946 Lionel Catalogue.

about the three major eras of Lionel trains, prewar, postwar, and modern era, showing how used trains can be an excellent value and can mix effectively with new ones. Finally, we must consider the question of where these trains can be secured at the best prices. Each source has its advantages and its disadvantages. I have some very specific advice about the question of quantity vs. quality as well, based upon my own experiences — sometimes costly! You must have a good working knowledge about the toy train marketplace to make your dollar stretch as far as it can.

SCALE VS. TINPLATE

Within the world of trains there is a distinct division between scale modelers and operators of toy trains. This division is a matter of philosophy and talent as well as equipment. The two sides often poke good-natured fun at one another; scale modelers are called "rivet counters" and toy train collectors are "junkmen."

There's no real right and wrong to the issue, but it is certain that many scale modelers face much more demanding standards when it comes to operating layouts if they wish to achieve something more than trains simply running around a track. The more demanding scale modeler insists everything on his/her layout be proportioned exactly to scale, as if the real world were shrunk down to the size of the particular layout. Of course, that's not completely possible; couplers would have to be almost microscopic in size, and mountains would have to protrude through holes cut into ceilings!

Most often, scale modelers work with HO Gauge, although there is a good number of people who work with the larger O Scale and the smaller N and Z Scales. To complicate matters, some work with narrow gauge scales with complex-sounding names such as HOn3 (HO scale, 3-foot narrow gauge). Narrow gauge and regular gauge scale model trains are sometimes found side by side on the same layouts, too.

Many scale modelers are very exacting people. The really dedicated scale modelers often hand-lay their track, tie by tie. The scale modeler tries to "super-detail" the layout's rolling stock so that the smallest pipe or rivet is right there on the piece of rolling stock. The overriding philosophy of the scale modeler is to be absolutely true to the prototype, both in appearance and in operations. Many scale modelers have computer-controlled their

layouts so several members can operate the trains exactly as they are operated in the real world, order cards and all. (If you like this idea, I'd suggest you consult Eugene Villaret's *Realistic Revenue Operations*, a Greenberg publication, for a fine introduction to this demanding skill.)

In fairness, it must be said that many fine scale modelers got their start in tinplate, especially with Lionels, so among many scale modelers there is great respect for Lionel trains. Unfortunately, there are also a few scale modelers who feel they have "outgrown" toy trains, and these few create unnecessary conflict by looking down their noses at tinplate operators. That's a shame, because they do not recognize that all model railroaders are indulging in one form or another of fantasy. I believe your particular fantasy with trains is worthy of basic respect, whatever form it takes. For scale modelers, the imitation of reality is itself the fantasy they pursue. Tinplate layouts can also be just as realistic as the finest scale layouts, too. Go ahead and do your own thing as long as it pleases you! Garry Moore, the great radio and television comedian and host of years past, liked to run his Lionels blindfolded, cause spectacular wrecks, and unpile them with his wrecking train. The wrecker crane was a favorite toy of Burt Lancaster, too. Did they deserve derision from the purists? I think not! As I have said before, you are the benevolent dictator of your own empire. Show off your trains to others, but remember the

Alan Schappell's Module for N-TRAK 1987 REGIONAL EVENT at Greenberg's Great Train, Dollhouse & Toy Show, Philadelphia Civic Center, August, 1987. From the cover of Greenberg 1987 Summer Catalogue.

layout is mostly for you and your family, and do what pleases you regardless of commentary, whether it is well or ill meant! Perhaps the English poet and essayist Samuel Taylor Coleridge gave all of us good advice when he said that literature, to be enjoyed, involved a "willing suspension of disbelief." He could just as easily have been talking about model trains of all kinds!

Needless to say, the work of scale modelers can be really spectacular. In their work with scenics and electronics, scale modelers are far ahead of most tinplaters. They do not skimp on expenses, either, since their equipment is not the inexpensive toy HO trains one sees in toy stores (at least, among the more serious scale modelers). Some of the superdetailed freight and passenger car kits are very costly, and the best scale engines are made of finely machined brass; these are more costly than most Lionels.

Tinplaters get their name from the fact that tin is used to coat the track work used with toy trains. These are people who are concerned with collecting and operating trains which were, and are, designed as toys to be played with, not as exact scale models. The tinplater looks for action and play value in his layout, not necessarily exact realism. The tinplater's trains are, on the whole, much easier to work with than the scale modeler's, though they are not necessarily less expensive. Additionally, many collectors of tinplate are much more concerned with the history of their product than are scale modelers, simply because the tinplater has different priorities.

The tinplater "gets away" with things on his layout which would horrify some of the more serious (or pompous) scale modelers. For example, I have a 1045 Operating Flagman on my layout who is taller than the trains he flags down! The Marx Operating Banjo Signal is better suited to the G Scale trains such as Lionel Large Scale or LGB. Yet both accessories are on my layout because they work so well and they have undeniable charm. Of course, the three-rail track used by Lionel is not exactly true to prototype! (Believe it or not, the New Haven Railroad used three-rail track with a powered center rail for its electric locomotives for quite some time! Scale modelers say that there is a prototype for just about everything!) In addition, the Lionel

1045 Operating Flagman.

Giraffe Car, Life-Savers Tank Car, and Operating Aquarium Car, among others, wouldn't exactly thrill a die-hard scale modeler!

Despite some differences in operating philosophies, scale modeling and tinplate operation have many details which are useful, one to the other. Lionel has marketed its "Standard O" line for some time; many of the locomotives and freight cars are exactly proportioned to O Scale. So good are some of these models that scale modelers have often used the Lionel bodies on more realistic trucks in their O Scale layouts. Additionally, the whimsy and humor of tinplate often works its way onto scale layouts. I remember one great scale building portrayed in *Model Railroader* some time ago; it was a "firecracker factory" with chimneys decorated like large firecrackers. The scale modeler who constructed this building, E. L. Moore, put a ragged hole in the roof and a human figure half inside and half outside the hole, explaining that "Johnny Simpson couldn't resist the urge to sneak a smoke now and then." Scale modelers often add such humorous details, especially demented signs on buildings — "Willie Finderr Detective Agency" or "Either Ore Company." The late John Allen, one of the greatest scale modelers of the last twenty years, used mirrors to expand the apparent size of his layout, sometimes producing some really strange and delightful effects with them. (The Kalmbach Company has published *Model Railroading With John Allen*; a reading of this book will convince you of Allen's superb abilities.)

From the other side of the ledger, the great scenic tricks used by scale modelers have much to offer the tinplate operator and collector. Examples of this are plentiful; one of the clearest might be the manufacture of pine trees out of furnace filter material and plastic straws. The furnace filter material is wound around the brown-painted straws and then dipped in a mixture of green-dyed ground foam to give it a rich tree-like texture. The uses of ground cover such as ballast material, coal, grass, and earth come from the work of scale modelers. The fine arts of "kitbashing" and "scratch building," to be explained in the scenery chapter, have been perfected by scale modelers. Of course, nearly all of these excellent scenic techniques are adaptable to Lionel trains.

Why choose tinplating over scale modeling? There is no law that says one is superior to the other; the disciplines are merely different. I, for one, value the historical and research values inherent to Lionel trains, as well as the great play value, ease of construction and maintenance, and — quite frankly — the nostalgia value. Lionel trains can be made to approximate the real world quite closely. On the other hand, they can also give the railroader a much wider range of equipment representing the best of the make-believe world.

Lionel trains lend themselves much better to family activity, in my opinion, and that's the most important consideration for many people. Their larger size makes them the only reasonable choice for a family activity, even though the larger G and Lionel Large Gauge trains have much to recommend them. The HO and N Scales are not too appropriate for family activity because of their fragility and relatively high frustration level. The historical and investment perspectives associated with Lionel trains are not to be found in the HO or N Gauge worlds. There is, as you will soon discover, some remarkable literature about the history of Lionel trains, both the products and the company itself, which is not to be found anywhere else in the toy world or even in the larger world of collectibles. In their investment performance, Lionel trains have been unique in the world of toys. No other mass-produced moderately-priced toys have enjoyed such impressive value appreciation while simultaneously providing their owners with such creative recreational experiences. Lionel trains are special indeed, and they provide unique advantages which make them the preferred choice for family train activity. They can be repaired and serviced by most operators, too — no small advantage in an age of high labor costs! Expert service can be obtained at numerous approved Lionel Service Stations, just like many home appliances.

WHICH LIONELS SHOULD YOU CHOOSE?

As I've said, the choices in Lionel trains are bewildering. Since it makes a great deal of sense to buy used Lionel equipment as well as new, there are three time periods to choose from and literally thousands of choices which could be made. I believe there are three general rules for your selection of Lionel trains, as follows:

RULE 1: **Purchase the trains which appeal the most to you.** This isn't as evident as it may sound. You'll be barraged by advice to buy a certain piece because it will have great collector value as an investment. That may be all well and good, but what if you simply can't work up an appreciation for the piece? Two examples should suffice. In 1977 Lionel began its production of the Mickey Mouse Disney set, which included a U36B locomotive, caboose, and 13 Hi-Cube style boxcars. This set is highly prized and very valuable today. I never cared much for it because I think the set has a cheap look, but some of my friends go crazy over it when they find it. I really like and own the Blue Comet passenger set and locomotive produced in the late 1970s, but some of my friends think the two-tone blue color scheme is too gaudy. Since you have to live with your trains, purchase the ones which really appeal to you. I think it's a mistake to acquire a particular piece just for its collector value. Its aesthetics are important, too.

RULE 2: **At the outset, put as much money as you can into the locomotive and the transformer, even at the expense of other components.** This is more than just a matter of finances; it's also a matter of common sense. The transformer you choose at the outset should be capable of more than just running the train. It should also be capable of running accessories and have enough power for expansion of your layout. Otherwise, you'll just have to trade in your little transformer for a bigger one later. You may even want to get a transformer which can run at least two trains right from the outset, even if you don't use the full capacity of the transformer until later. This is also a powerful argument against buying a ready-made train set such as you see at toy stores. Although there are many fine sets available, I believe that it makes more sense to build your own set out of both older and newer components. Later on in this chapter, I'll have some specific recommendations about transformers. As for the locomotives, it stands to reason that you'll want an engine with the best features you can get. Most people want their steam engines to have smoke and a whistle, and the diesels should have the best motors you can secure.

There's a practical reason to get a better locomotive right from the start, too. Most of Lionel's older, less expensive locomotives have two-position reversing units. This means that there is no neutral position; the locomotive will only go in forward or reverse. That places some severe limitations on operations, since you'll want to have power in your track and your locomotives

standing still so that you can operate some special cars such as the operating milk and cattle cars. If at all possible, make sure that your locomotive has a three-position reversing unit which includes a neutral position. The latest Lionel production features a newly-designed can-type motor with an all-electronic three-position reversing unit. These locomotives are excellent choices for the Lionel beginner.

RULE 3: **At the outset, concentrate upon acquiring quantity rather than scarcity until you are familiar with the toy train marketplace.** Every collector and operator — this author included — has been "stung" by poor choices in the marketplace. Sometimes that's due to just plain carelessness. Recently, I came across a big 2555 Single-dome Tank Car produced from 1946-1950. The car was in its original box with its protective liner, and all the decals were perfectly intact — unusual for this car. I bought it at a decent, but not spectacularly bargain price. When I took a second look, I saw that the plastic top dome piece was broken and one of the ladders was missing! Since I knew this particular dealer, I felt fairly sure he didn't know about the damage, either. I decided to use a "junker" tank car to replace the dome and ladder instead of returning the piece. Once again, I had to learn to examine every piece carefully before purchase!

The best way to avoid problems with purchases of rolling stock and accessories at the outset is to concentrate at the lower end of the market first, to build up familiarity with what is scarce and what is common. Once you have acquired a supply of the common but attractive pieces, you can then use your knowledge to acquire higher-quality and scarcer pieces intelligently. At the beginning, buy locomotives and rolling stock which you believe look and run well. Get familiar with their operating characteristics and gradually shift your focus to other parts of the marketplace, as your budget dictates. I have never had a huge budget to work with, but I believe I have done very well with my own collection by following just this procedure. You will find that your focus will narrow from the entire production of Lionel trains to a more specific area — boxcars, for instance.

As a beginning collector and operator, one of the best strategies is to read extensively about Lionel trains and their operation. In the marketplace, there are many excellent books written by experienced collectors and operators of these trains. Secure them and consult them frequently. Your collection of toy train literature should include some Lionel catalogues, a price or collector's guide, and a repair and operating manual. I have given you an annotated bibliography in the back of this book for that reason.

Incidentally, you should have absolutely no hesitation in buying used Lionel equipment. Lionel, then and now, made its trains to last. Used equipment is fully compatible with new stock and can be a great operating bargain. You might see a locomotive which is a great operating piece but is not cosmetically good enough for collectors. Such engines are often great bargains for the layout operator, as long as they are operationally acceptable — and most of them are. If you've also learned the fine art of repairing and restoring used tinplate pieces, you can come up with some real bargains. (See the Repair and Maintenance chapter in this book.) Time and labor are effective substitutes for money in this hobby.

As an example of this phenomenon, consider another purchase of mine — ironically, from the same dealer who sold me the broken tank car! One of my finer locomotives, a big 2046 Hudson-type Steam Locomotive which can usually pull a train

Very attractive 8801 Jersey Central Blue Comet of 1978 — Lionel at its best. R. LaVoie Collection, M. Feinstein photograph.

2555 Sunoco. Note the decals and detailing of this fine all-metal tank car. P. Bennett photograph.

through a brick wall, broke down during a Greenberg train show demonstration; it has since been overhauled. I continued running my trains with a reserve locomotive, but I thought it prudent to see if I could pick up another Hudson-type steam locomotive at the show. These engines usually sell for $150-$200 at the present writing — not exactly a small sum of money! I found a 2065 Hudson which was in decent cosmetic shape but hadn't been run in a long, long time — perhaps as much as 20 years. After buying the engine and its tender for $100, reflecting the fact that it needed work, I gave it a complete overhaul when I got it back home, repairing some motor parts and replacing some others. I spent about three hours restoring it. I now have a fine-running Hudson engine, complete with a good whistle tender, at a great price. With some experience and the accumulation of some "junk" spare parts, you can do this, too — but not right away! Learn how Lionels work and get a good repair manual first!

Now that we have considered some general rules, let's take a look at some specific categories of Lionel locomotives, rolling stock, accessories, and transformers which seem to be good bets for the beginner.

LOCOMOTIVES

Lionel's steam locomotives offer some fine opportunities for the beginner. There were many fine steamers made during the prewar years, but since these have couplers which are not compatible with postwar and modern era rolling stock, they are best left to the specialists. Still, given their great quality, you might want to get a prewar steamer and equip it with its own prewar rolling stock. I possess a great 224E Steamer made in 1938; it may be fifty years old, but it still runs well and I can use it with some of the old prewar freight cars or even put a postwar tender behind it and pull my regular rolling stock with it. Of the postwar steamers, your best bet would be to acquire one which features smoke, a whistle, and one of Lionel's best features, Magnetraction. This feature magnetized the wheels of the locomotive so it would grip the track and pull more cars, using a little more voltage from the transformer in the process. The 2037 Steamer, made in the late 1950s and early 1960s, is a good choice at a reasonable price which includes all those features. You could also look for a used 2026 Steamer, which lacks Magnetraction, at a slightly lesser price. The 675 and 2025 Steamers made from 1947 to 1953 represent Lionel's steam engine art at its finest. All of these engines are fine "runners." In the modern era, the latest steamers such as the 8402 Reading offer a smooth-running motor, smoke, and a headlight at a very reasonable price. I personally prefer the postwar steamers because of their rugged AC spur-drive motors, but price may well dictate your choice.

The modern era diesels are better choices, on the whole, than the postwar diesels at the beginner's end of the market. The GP-7, GP-9, GP-20, and U36B models produced from 1970-1980 are plentiful, even new, and reasonably priced for the most part. They operate well with basic maintenance. These diesels feature a motor which is mounted integrally with the truck casting — a weakness, since if they are overloaded the main drive gear can strip. This gear cannot be replaced, so you must replace the entire motor and truck assembly — a nasty proposition. Some of the

2037 Lionel Locomotive. This common engine has all of Lionel's best features — smoke, whistle, and Magnetraction.

Top Shelf: 9717 Union Pacific (compare with later 9755), 9718 Canadian National. Middle Shelf: 9719 New Haven "Coupon" Car which retains the 1956 built date of its 6464 predecessor, 9723 Western Pacific. Bottom shelf: 9724 Missouri Pacific (compare with later 9219 operating version), 9725 MKT Stock Car (compare with earlier 9707). A. Rudman, L. Caponi, F. Stem, and R. LaVoie Collections.

bigger diesels and electrics have a motor which is separate from the power truck; this is a more expensive but better arrangement. Actually, you should not have too much trouble if you do not over-burden your diesel with too heavy a train. The latest diesels have two can-type motors mounted into the trucks. These are very strong pullers which can handle a medium-length train at a very low voltage. I would start with something like the 8352 Santa Fe GP-20 or the 8369 Erie-Lackawanna GP-20, with the older and newer drive assemblies, respectively. If these engines lack a diesel horn, or if the steamer lacks a whistle, don't worry — you can supply the same effect with the fine new diesel horn or steam whistle sheds just introduced by Lionel Trains, Inc. They sound great!

ROLLING STOCK

For layout operators, the rolling stock produced since 1970 has a distinct advantage over the cars produced from 1945-1969, the postwar years. The older Lionel freight and passenger cars had mostly rugged metal trucks, but the wheel sets on these cars had flat-surfaced flanges and the wheels turned on the axles. This produced considerable friction; it meant that the layout operator had to use a powerful locomotive and relatively high voltage to pull a longer train. (As an operating rule, I recommend that any train you run on your layout should not exceed 14 volts of indicated power from the transformer; this will prevent any chance of excess heat from the transformer and/or burnout of any of the motors or other components.)

When Lionel trains were reintroduced in 1970, General Mills made its rolling stock with a real innovation — the fast-angle wheel sets. Most of the trucks were made of a special, low-friction plastic called Delrin. The wheels were fixed to the axles, which turned inside special "pockets" in the trucks by means of a needle-point bearing. In addition, the wheel surfaces were cast on a slight angle instead of flat. This meant that the piece of rolling stock was capable of "differential" action when it went around a curve. The newer metal trucks feature this differential action and low friction as well. For the operator, this means that a given locomotive can

8352 Santa Fe, one of the first GP-20s, and 8369 Erie-Lackawanna of 1983 with twin can motor drive system. A. Rudman Collection, M. Feinstein photograph.

2025 Steam Locomotive. Look closely at the complex and attractive drive rod linkage.

pull many more modern cars than the older cars — a significant operating advantage. I would not reject out of hand the running of the older cars, but the newer cars really roll well and spare your locomotives considerable stress. I possess a Santa Fe Fairbanks-Morse diesel made in 1981. This powerful locomotive has two big, rugged AC motors and is a legendary hauler. A few years ago, I put this engine at the head end of a huge train of 48 newer freight cars on one of the Greenberg show layouts, and the engine absolutely ran away with the train! It could have pulled at least 15 more cars. Not many of you will be pulling 60-car trains on your layouts, but it's a comfort to know your locomotives have plenty of reserve power when they pull the newer cars.

BOXCARS

There are literally hundreds of choices you can make in this area, and these cars come with virtually every road name and color scheme you can want. The older 6454 Boxcars made from 1946-1953 aren't too glamorous, but they add a realistic look to a train and are still reasonably priced. The newer boxcars offer much better and more colorful choices. I would look for the less expensive boxcars out of the 9200, 9400, and 9700 Series, most of which are still available brand-new. These cars have a stamped-steel frame and opening doors, and they look great; they are direct remakes of the postwar 6464 Series which has acquired extensive collector interest.

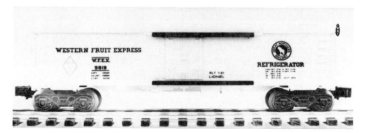

9819 FGEX Refrigerator Car. R. LaVoie Collection, M. Feinstein photograph.

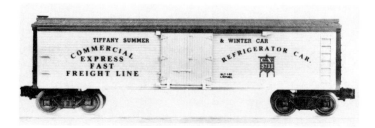

5711 Refrigerator Car. R. LaVoie Collection, M. Feinstein photograph.

REFRIGERATOR CARS

Clearly, the newer cars have the advantage in this category. They also represent the best single value in Lionel rolling stock today. The 9800 Series features beer cars, candy cars, food cars — you name it! These cars are made of heavy plastic with opening doors, wood-scribed sides, and incredibly colorful electrocals. Do you like beer? Examples come in Coor's, Budweiser, Schlitz, Old Milwaukee, and Carling's livery, and if you like something a little stronger, there are the Favorite Spirits cars featuring Wolfschmidt's vodka, Bailey's Irish Cream liqueur, Johnnie Walker Scotch, and many others. Candy, you say? There are Good & Plenty, Brach's Candies, and Bazooka Bubble Gum examples. Sodas? There are bright Pepsi cars in this series. You get the idea! Additionally, if you like an old-time look you would do well to seek out the 5700 Woodsided Reefer Series, which are very realistic, though not as colorful as the 9800s. (Railroads used the term "reefer" in a much more innocent time as a nickname for their refrigerator cars, before the word acquired a slightly more sinister meaning!)

9260 Reynolds Hopper. R. LaVoie Collection, M. Feinstein

HOPPER CARS

In the postwar years, the big "quad" hoppers (four compartments) gained great popularity, and many of these are still available. In the modern era (since 1970), that tradition has continued with the "billboard" type advertising various products and those using real railroad names. The quad hoppers are plentiful and reasonably priced. The smaller hoppers, both postwar and modern, are available in huge quantities at low prices. Try for examples where both couplers are operating versions — in some small hoppers, one or both couplers are non-operating, or "dummy" couplers. Lately, Lionel Trains, Inc. has introduced some charming little iron ore cars which are well worth the acquisition.

6462 NYC Gondolas. R. LaVoie Collection, M. Feinstein photograph.

6208 B&O Gondola. R. LaVoie Collection, M. Feinstein photograph.

GONDOLAS

The postwar 6462 model of the long gondola was made by the zillions, and you can't go to a train source without seeing some of these at inexpensive prices. For hauling goods on a layout, the 6462s are very versatile; they can come in black, red, or green colors. Other numbers can come in blue or yellow, and most have New York Central markings. The modern gondolas are a bit more varied, and many of these can be acquired inexpensively, too. Short gondolas are also plentiful and reasonably priced; some of these come with loads such as cable reels and canisters.

6560 Crane. R. LaVoie Collection, M. Feinstein photograph.

CRANES AND SEARCHLIGHTS

Crane cars, those "big hooks" needed to clear wrecks, have always been prized and sought after by collectors. As a result, they have been mostly limited production items in the modern era and are not always available at decent prices. However, in the postwar years the red and black 6560 Crane was produced in great numbers. Before you buy a used example, make sure there are no cracks in the cab and that both wheel pulleys work properly. The 6560 Crane is probably your best bet. For searchlight cars in the older era, you might be able to get a die-cast 6520 fairly cheaply, but this car is heavy to pull around on a layout. The modern derivatives of the old 6822 are readily available at decent prices in

such markings as Conrail, Reading, Louisville & Nashville, and Canadian Pacific. You should have no trouble securing one of these at a reasonable price. If you are a little more ambitious, you could try to get a postwar Searchlight Extension Car or perhaps a Rotating Searchlight Car, both of which are die-cast.

OPERATING CARS

Lionel has always been famous for its action cars, with reason, and there are a few which you should try to get right away. One car which is legendary and almost indispensable is the "Automatic Refrigerated Milk Car" produced from 1947-1955. So popular was this little white wonder that two and a half million of these cars were made! Bigger versions have been made since, but they lack the charm of this car, where a man dressed in white flings little metal milk cans onto a platform at the touch of a button. It's certainly not rare and expensive! The Cattle Car and Platform was popular, too, but I would recommend a modern horse or cattle car because the older unit is difficult to keep in proper adjustment. I also prefer the older Log and Coal Dump Cars to the new ones because they are much more durable. Another great operating car which is readily available in both older and modern versions is the whimsical Giraffe Car, where a giraffe sticks his head out of a hole in the car top and ducks when he comes to a "telltale" pole. Also worth consideration is the Operating Barrel gondola, which is a very charming piece available at reasonable prices, especially in the case of the older 3562-25 gray versions. In General, try at first to acquire operating cars which are simple to set up and operate; leave the more complex ones until later on, when you have acquired an operating and repair manual and are more experienced as an operator.

3472 Milk Car. R. LaVoie Collection, M. Feinstein photograph.

7904 San Diego Giraffe Car. M. Feinstein photograph.

TANK AND VAT CARS

Lionel has made tank cars in one-dome, two-dome, and three-dome varieties. Of the older tankers, the 6465 Sunoco Two-dome Car is very plentiful at a low price. You could build a whole

Top shelf: 9278 Lifesavers and 9313 Gulf. Bottom shelf: 9321 A T S F and 9324 Tootsie Roll.

fleet of these little silver tankers for very little money! In the modern era, there are tank cars of all three varieties which are plentiful and colorful. You can get the old, traditional look of the black or silver tank car, or you can indulge your fancy by getting a single-dome tanker made to resemble a roll of Life-Savers (somewhat scarce now) or a Tootsie Roll (still plentiful). I personally prefer the modern single-dome tank car because of its metal platform and ladders around the dome. The vat cars are real charmers; they come in Heinz Pickles, Libby Pineapples, Mogen-David Wine, Budweiser, and Dr. Pepper versions. Four round vats are contained inside the car's metal and plastic framework.

flatcars look terrific, but the trailers have a hard time staying on the cars when they go around a curve at anything but a low speed. There's a good flatcar with a bulldozer and road scraper kit available, but the dozer and scraper are a little fragile. Perhaps your best bet is to fasten the trailers more securely to the flatcar (an easy process) or to get plain flatcars inexpensively and supply your own loads. There are plenty of good choices out in the market, but I like the TOFC cars despite their operational instability, which can be fixed easily with twist-ties. You might also check into the older 6414 Auto Carrier car, a nice piece which can be fitted easily with small Matchbox cars.

9285 Illinois Central Gulf TOFC Flatcar.

9177 Northern Pacific Railway Bay Window Caboose. M. Feinstein photograph.

9121 L & N Flatcar with dozer.

9271 M & St. L. Bay Window Caboose. M. Feinstein photograph.

FLATCARS

The older flatcars carried pipes, logs, military equipment, trailers, and even Christmas trees. Some are still common, but depending on the load they carried, many have become scarce and expensive. In the modern era, the TOFC (Trailer-On-Flat-Car)

CABOOSES

There is no more persistent concept about the railroads than the notion of the little red caboose at the end of the train. The older Lionel years produced some excellent candidates for your acquisition. For example, the Southern Pacific-style square-cupola

Above: All the tracks and platforms are busy at Dallas Penn Station about midday when the Overland Limited arrives. The Alton Limited and the Blue Comet prepare for their departures while the two-car "400" of the Chicago & Northwestern occupies the South (right) track. Expansion of passenger service has taxed the capacity of the station on almost a daily basis. The station was designed and built by the Floyd Howes firm of Cheyenne, Wyoming. W. D. Hakkarinen, M.D. layout, M. Feinstein photograph.

Below: Derailment on the main line! Workmen try to shore up the big Chessie Caboose with timbers as a "Big Hook" strains mightily to re-rail it and clear the line for traffic. A supervisor stands atop a tool car's roof and a little boy, not realizing the danger, gets too close to the action. One of the workmen will tell him to back off, we hope! Author's layout, M. Feinstein photograph.

caboose was made in tremendous quantities in both lighted and unlighted versions. Although the unlighted versions can be purchased for very low prices, I prefer lighted cabooses, so I would look for the 6357 or 6457 models, which are quite plentiful and well-detailed, especially the 6457. Another good bet is the 2457 all-metal Pennsylvania model from 1946-47, which looks terrific behind a steam engine. The modern cabooses come in more varieties, most of which are quite affordable. I particularly like the N5C "Porthole" cabooses, which are brightly lighted and very colorful. Also noteworthy are the big bay window models which are very well-made and reasonably priced for the most part. Thanks to the variety of cabooses in more recent years, I have been able to secure a caboose in road markings to match every one of my locomotives. The more expensive extended vision and wood-sided scale cabooses are really spectacular pieces!

PASSENGER CARS

Because of rising prices and collector influence, it's not easy to acquire a nice set of passenger cars. The older cars are best left to collectors because of their prices, but there are some possibilities in the modern cars. The 9500 Series has a fine, realistic look, and these cars are affordable in Pennsylvania, Milwaukee, and Baltimore and Ohio versions. Operationally, however, they have a glaring weakness — a non-operating coupler which mounts to the car body instead of the trucks. These are easily broken, and if your track work is irregular these cars can uncouple unexpectedly. After some tinkering, I was able to get my Pennsylvania set to run pretty well, but not without some annoyance. In a real pinch, you can fasten the couplers together with twist-ties! (Wide radius track will prevent this problem, but not all layouts are suited for such track.) The 9500 cars with six-wheel die-cast trucks and operating couplers can get a little "pricey" for the beginner. Recently, Lionel Trains, Inc. issued a new series of Pennsylvania cars based upon the old 2400 Series made in the postwar years. These have operating couplers and lighted interiors and are priced very well; along with some new cars in Amtrak markings, these new offerings are probably your best bet if you want to make up a passenger train. If you want bigger passenger cars, check out the Madison-style cars made by Williams, not Lionel. These cars are really magnificent behind a large steamer or diesel engine. The large aluminum O Gauge passenger cars will only run on O Gauge track; they won't clear the switch boxes of the O27 switches. They happen to be rather beautiful pieces and good investments, despite their expense.

ACCESSORIES

Lionel is justly famed for its fine action accessories, whether they are old or new, and these little wonders add real life to anyone's layout. Most of them operate by either vibrator mechanisms or solenoids, both of which are rugged and reliable. At the outset, it is wise to acquire the simpler accessories until you get some experience in operations. Then, the more expensive and complex accessories would make sense.

The best group of accessories for beginners is the variety of track side signals. Look for the older 151 Semaphores, 152 or 252 Crossing Gates, 154 Highway Flashers, and 153 Block Signals. Most of these are made to operate with a weight-activated contactor, but the use of special insulated track sections is much better. That is a topic which I will discuss in the chapters on track work

and wiring. Look for one of the old 45 Gatemen — the little tin shack made from 1935 to 1949. Newer versions are available, but I think the old tin shack has real charm. I possess 15 of these, all different, and the one I have on my demonstration layout was made in 1939. It has operated flawlessly for six years. Other good bets at reasonable prices include the 356 Operating Freight Station, the 445 Signal Tower, the 125 Whistle Shack, the 2127 Diesel Horn Shed, and the 494 Rotating Beacon. I like plenty of lights on my layout, so I have invested in many of the old Lionel and even Marx searchlight and floodlight towers, which are very inexpensive. Let your imagination be your guide for Lionel's accessories!

TRANSFORMERS

I have some very specific advice about Lionel transformers because this is a special case for the Lionel operator. In recent years, the Consumer Products Safety Commission has prevented Lionel from making transformers with more than 100 watts of output, although I have never heard of any cases of injury resulting from the high-output transformers of the postwar years. This means that the prices of the big postwar transformers have risen dramatically in recent years — more operators chasing fewer available transformers. However, there are some solutions for this dilemma.

If you want to begin with a single-throttle transformer, your best choice is to seek out a 1033 model made in the 1950s. This 90-watt transformer was Lionel's finest smaller transformer; it has whistle and direction controls and accessory terminals. It will run a single train and several accessories with no trouble. Several of these transformers wired in phase (refer to the chapter on wiring) can run several trains and many accessories. There are other good models, such as the 110-watt RW, but the 1033 and its later derivatives, the 1044 and the 4090, are the best bets for the beginner.

If you want a double-throttle transformer, your choices are varied but somewhat expensive. Lionel Trains, Inc. has issued a solid-state MW Transformer which is a fine performer; it is similar to models produced earlier by Troller, among others. Of the older transformers, the SW is somewhat scarce, but it has two throttles and 130 watts and is not too highly priced. The best of the older transformers are the KW, a 190-watt powerhouse, and the best of them all, the ZW, a 275-watt giant. Unfortunately, both of these units are comparatively expensive, especially the ZW. Another answer to the double-throttle problem is to acquire an old Z model made from 1938 to 1947. Then, get yourself two 167C Whistle and Direction Controls and wire them into your main train circuits. For less than half the price of a ZW, you will then get almost the same capability, because the Z has 250 watts and four separate throttles. That's enough for two trains, a lighting circuit, and an accessory circuit.

A frequent practice of operators who have complex layouts is to use one transformer as a main power supply for the trains and a secondary transformer for the accessories and lights. On my demonstration layout, I have a 275-watt ZW (acquired several years ago before its price went through the roof — thank goodness!) which supplies four circuits, two to run the trains and two for some of the operating accessories. I added two more circuits with an old 100-watt Type R transformer, which is ideal for this use. This transformer powers all the lights from one circuit and the majority of the accessories from the other. The power drain on my layout is so ferocious (when I run a passenger train, there are at least 60 light bulbs in operation) that I could easily cook your dinner on the heat produced by the ZW if it were not for the R working as an auxiliary! When you purchase your transformer, allow for future expansion of your layout, because power needs multiply rapidly. Get the best one for your money for openers.

WHERE ARE THE BEST PLACES TO GET LIONEL TRAINS?

Now that we've discussed the best types of equipment to pursue, it follows that we should talk about the best sources for your trains. Each source has specific advantages and disadvantages, so a thorough discussion of each should allow you to make some well-informed decisions about your sources of supply. Regionally, if you live along the Eastern Seaboard you are more fortunate than people in the Midwest and the West, because toy trains are more plentiful along the East Coast. However, wherever you live you will still have options.

Remember one thing: Regardless of your source, it really pays to shop around! Not too long ago, I noticed a 9700 Southern Boxcar advertised by a big mail-order house as "new in the box" for $70. The same car, even brand new, can be purchased for as little as $20 at most shows and train shops! If you become a collector of these little trinkets, patience is a real virtue. I searched for a particular version of the 6560 Crane Car for nearly five years before I found one recently. Investigate all of the possibilities before you invest your money! Here are your possible sources, with their advantages and disadvantages as I see them:

TOY STORES: Many big discount toy stores such as Kay-Bee, Kiddie City, Toys 'R Us, and others carry Lionel trains, especially around Christmas time. Beginners in the hobby often seek out these stores first because Lionels are, after all, toys. The big toy stores feature the lower-priced end of Lionel's production, especially ready-made sets. Selections of rolling stock and accessories are quite limited and prices tend to be somewhat high. In fairness, many toy stores cut their Lionel prices drastically after the holiday season, sometimes by half. However, selection is quite limited. Unfortunately, the store employees are not very knowledgeable about these trains as a rule. Lionel trains demand a certain interplay between customer and dealer for maximum enjoyment, and the toy stores cannot ordinarily provide this expert advice. Some department stores may emphasize toy trains enough to be exceptions, but I think you have much better potential sources for the trains.

MAIL ORDER FIRMS: There are at least a dozen mail order sources for Lionel trains which are big enough to offer good prices; most place big display ads in *Model Railroader* or *Railroad Model Craftsman,* among other train magazines. These firms are ferociously competitive with the newest Lionel production, so there are good bargains available through mail order. Most of the firms offer good service, but before you order you should read the firm's return policies and shipping requirements. Some firms do not give refunds; instead, they offer credit vouchers towards future purchases. There's usually no trouble if you understand the firm's policies and stick to new production, but I think purchasing used Lionels from mail order firms is somewhat risky. The firm might advertise its pieces as "like new," but when you get the piece, you might disagree with that assessment. For used trains, the Train Collectors Association (TCA) and other clubs have developed standard definitions of conditions, which you should study and insist upon. For example, the condition "excellent" means that the item shows evidence of being run, but has no easily detectable cosmetic flaws such as rust on locomotive frames. If you buy used Lionel from mail order firms, you're buying sight unseen, and that's always risky. Check the return policies for used Lionel very carefully before you buy.

TRAIN SHOWS AND "MEETS": All over the country, there are large and small train shows and swap meets which can offer real values in Lionel trains. For example, the Greenberg train shows along the Eastern Seaboard are the biggest public train shows in the country. In the Midwest and Far West, the Great American Train Shows are other noteworthy public shows. Some of the Great American Train Shows can be quite large; my friend Tom Rollo of Milwaukee has done very well at the DuPage County monthly train meets near Chicago. Many, many other smaller independent train shows and meets are sponsored by several organizations; some are open to the public, and some are limited to club membership. The "granddaddy" of all the train meets is the members-only TCA train meet and show at the York County Fairgrounds in York, Pennsylvania, which is held twice a year in the spring and fall. So large is this gathering that train collectors from all over the country poke around in seven buildings full of trains! Divisions and chapters of the TCA hold their own train meets regularly, and the other train clubs sponsor shows as well.

These shows and meets can help the beginning Lionel operator a great deal. There are, of course, many professional dealers at these shows, but there are also people who rent tables just to unload their surplus trains, meet people, and make a few dollars more as recreation than business. Many of the shows offer operating clinics, where you'll get a chance to watch demonstrations and talk with experienced operators and collectors of Lionel trains. There's a wide variety of Lionel available, often at excellent prices. Since there are so many dealers of new and used Lionel trains at these shows, you can shop around. I've done very well at these shows for myself.

The only trouble with buying trains at these shows is that often, you really don't know with whom you are dealing. Unless you buy from a reputable firm or individual, you can't really return a piece if it doesn't work out — you're stuck with it. You will find that the overwhelming majority of these dealers are good, honest people, but as in any business, there are always a few unscrupulous people who will sell defective merchandise knowingly or try to pass off a reproduction piece as an original. I would suggest that you always ask for a receipt with the seller's name, address, and phone number. And if the piece is a major purchase for you, then you should ask for a simple declarative sentence: "I certify that this _____ is completely original with original paint." If you have any doubts, you should consult a veteran collector who will be happy to assist you. As a participant in the Philadelphia-area Greenberg shows, I have gotten to know the most reliable of the dealers, and I tend to limit my purchases to them rather than risk purchases from people I do not know. It won't take long for you to develop that kind of knowledge, either. At these shows, there are plenty of experienced train experts who will be glad to give you their opinions as to whether a given piece is a good value or not. The shows also have test tracks so you can check the operational worthiness of a given piece. I am fortunate in one respect; at least two-thirds of my train dollars go to the next source, which I consider to be the best source of all.

Left: The CN freight train with its empty ore cars is slowly working its way up the grade. The mixed freight, pulled by the 773, is also straining up the grade. Multiple levels add great interest to Neville Long's layout. Note the heavy earth moving equipment. N. Long layout and photograph.

Below: Traffic on the B & A is heavy as a Hudson-powered passenger express begins to run around the freight on the siding. Conrail still allows steam on the former B & A line, even though Union Pacific and other foreign powers may also pull run-through freights from the West. The B & A Hudson, with its white "circus clown" face boiler front, will be replaced at Albany with a New York Central gray Hudson on the through Boston to Chicago New England States Express. W. D. Hakkarinen, M.D. layout, M. Feinstein photograph.

TOY TRAIN HOBBY SHOPS: If you are fortunate enough to live near a hobby shop which has a good supply of new and used Lionel trains, this is the best source of all. To be sure, many of these shops charge a bit more for the trains, but that's understandable, considering their overhead. Additionally, many of these shops have price structures which are just as reasonable as those in train shows and meets. The real advantage of purchase at a good hobby shop is that the owners and dealers tend to know these trains and give excellent advice to the beginner. They usually service the trains they sell, often with expert repairmen, and their trains frequently carry guarantees even when used. You should test a locomotive before you buy it, and perhaps reserve a new piece of equipment with a small down payment and lay away trains at some shops.

These hobby shops can often become an important social outlet for the operator and collector as well. I frequent (maybe "hang out" is a better expression!) a place known as the Toy Train Station in Feasterville, Pennsylvania, about 20 miles from my home. Along with about a dozen other operators and collectors, I spend my Friday nights there after a hectic work week to get rid of job tensions and relax with my hobby. As a result, I've made many good friends; the proprietors of the shop are wise enough to recognize that this social phenomenon leads to word-of-mouth recommendation and increased sales, so they encourage us "Friday Night Irregulars." There's a lot of laughter and good-natured kidding, and all of us bring in our latest "finds" to show the others. We hover like vultures about to pounce when the proprietors purchase a collection and put it out for sale!

If you find a shop like this, you're extremely fortunate, because the nature of the hobby is such that the "regulars" spend a great deal of time advising beginners from their own experiences. You will learn very quickly about the best operating pieces and the best monetary values from both the proprietors and the experienced collectors in these shops. Since you have a coterie of experts on hand, a guarantee of performance, reliable repair services, good train selection, and excellent prospects for answers to all your questions, it's hard to beat the tinplate hobby shops as sources for your purchase of Lionel trains. The magazine *Model Railroader* has a directory of train shops arranged by state and city. Look up one which sounds promising and drop in. You might try the good old Yellow Pages, too. You may be in for a pleasurable experience! People who collect and operate Lionel trains come from all walks of life and are, as a rule, extraordinarily pleasant people, as I have found.

Class, it is now time for a bit of review before we move on.

We have talked about the train hobby philosophically and practically, and we have studied a little history in the process.

We have detailed which Lionel trains are best to seek out, and where you can get these trains.

Got your tool kits ready? It's time for us to go out into that garage or up into that attic and build that Lionel layout! I would request that you read the next three chapters in their entirety before you start putting saw to wood and hammer to nail, though, because these chapters are interrelated so much. Let's examine platform construction, track work, and wiring. Then your trains will be ready to go.

Above: A Lionel 675 Steam Locomotive pounding down the main line with a long line of freight cars. Note the close proximity of the freight house to the line and the handsome rock croppings. W. Hakkarinen, M.D. layout and photograph.

Below: A view of the yards on LaVoie's layout. The fourth track from the rear has a 397 Coal Loader, 3462 Milk Car Platform, and a 3356-150 Horse Car Corral. It is early Sunday morning and the yard is quiet. M. Feinstein photograph.

CHAPTER IV
PLATFORM CONSTRUCTION AND LAYOUT DESIGN

"Some people see things as they are and ask why. I dream of things that never were and say, why not?"
— George Bernard Shaw

"The Platform Committee will now come to order!"
— Any political convention

As we begin to plan and build our Lionel layout, I once again turn to the Lionel catalogues for inspiration. This time I'm looking at one of the most remarkable catalogue covers of modern times, the one for 1973. Very few catalogue covers capture the spirit of Lionel trains as well as this one does. A young boy in pajamas and bathrobe is seated cross-legged in the middle of a simple oval of track, gleefully watching a freight set made that year, the Blue Streak, its little blue 8303 Jersey Central Columbia Steamer thrashing its drive rods as it hauls its freight cars around the track oval, which is simply placed on the rug without any other decoration. Behind the boy, a man, obviously his father, smilingly sits on the floor as he holds the little blue 50-watt transformer controlling the train. Behind the father is an equally gleeful grandfather — three generations of males enthralled by the trains, as they always have been. To one side of the chair, the family dog looks on balefully, not quite sure of this strange sight. Finally, on the extreme right of the photo, the barest wisps of evergreen tree branches appear, unmistakably suggesting a holiday scene.

I think this catalogue cover captures a great truth about these trains, and it is this: the most basic of layouts, even a simple unadorned oval, is a captivating sight all by itself. How much more fun, then, can await you with a well-planned operating layout with "the works?" I also respond to this cover because that Blue Streak train set was my very first Lionel set, the one I got for my own son but which instead launched me into this hobby. I still treasure that little blue locomotive and run it once in a while.

Any worthwhile project in life demands a certain amount of planning. If you're going to build an addition onto your house, you'd better draw up some preliminary plans. Financial planning for the future is extremely important to provide for emergencies, the expenses for education of your children, and many other

1973 Catalogue cover.

elements of a worthwhile life. It is no different with a Lionel train layout. Never underestimate the importance of planning!

Perhaps a little anecdote might illustrate this idea. (Besides, it's a great excuse to tell a crazy story at my own expense!) One stormy night last summer, I was spending time with the "Friday Night Irregulars" at the Toy Train Station, as I often do. A rather violent thunderstorm came up, and all at once a blinding lightning flash and a deafening peal of thunder shook the building. All the lights in the area went out — street lights, shop marquees, and everything else in the immediate area. It was Stygian black inside the shop. I happened to be standing next to the test track oval, and one of the cars placed on it was a flatcar with a white "cruise missile" on it. For the first time, I was able to notice that the little missile glowed in the dark. As I called this fact to the attention of my friends Tom and Mitch, the following conversation ensued:

ME: "Hey, Tom! Mitch! Look at this! I didn't know the cruise missile on this car glowed in the dark!"

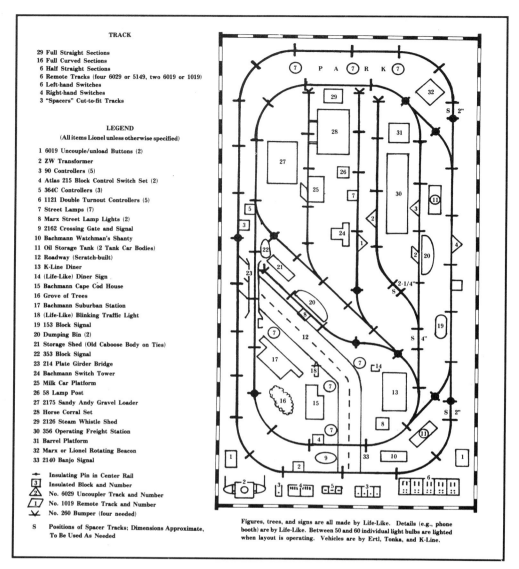

TRACK

29 Full Straight Sections
16 Full Curved Sections
6 Half Straight Sections
6 Remote Tracks (four 6029 or 5149, two 6019 or 1019)
6 Left-hand Switches
4 Right-hand Switches
3 "Spacers" Cut-to-fit Tracks

LEGEND
(All items Lionel unless otherwise specified)

1 6019 Uncouple/unload Buttons (2)
2 ZW Transformer
3 90 Controllers (5)
4 Atlas 215 Block Control Switch Set (2)
5 364C Controllers (3)
6 1121 Double Turnout Controllers (5)
7 Street Lamps (7)
8 Marx Street Lamp Lights (2)
9 2162 Crossing Gate and Signal
10 Bachmann Watchman's Shanty
11 Oil Storage Tank (2 Tank Car Bodies)
12 Roadway (Scratch-built)
13 K-Line Diner
14 (Life-Like) Diner Sign
15 Bachmann Cape Cod House
16 Grove of Trees
17 Bachmann Suburban Station
18 (Life-Like) Blinking Traffic Light
19 153 Block Signal
20 Dumping Bin (2)
21 Storage Shed (Old Caboose Body on Ties)
22 353 Block Signal
23 214 Plate Girder Bridge
24 Bachmann Switch Tower
25 Milk Car Platform
26 58 Lamp Post
27 2175 Sandy Andy Gravel Loader
28 Horse Corral Set
29 2126 Steam Whistle Shed
30 356 Operating Freight Station
31 Barrel Platform
32 Marx or Lionel Rotating Beacon
33 2140 Banjo Signal

↧ Insulating Pin in Center Rail
▣ Insulated Block and Number
△ No. 6029 Uncoupler Track and Number
▱ No. 1019 Remote Track and Number
✕ No. 260 Bumper (four needed)

S Positions of Spacer Tracks; Dimensions Approximate, To Be Used As Needed

Figures, trees, and signs are all made by Life-Like. Details (e.g., phone booth) are by Life-Like. Between 50 and 60 individual light bulbs are lighted when layout is operating. Vehicles are by Ertl, Tonka, and K-Line.

This is a complete plan for a 4' x 8' Lionel layout I once exhibited at the Greenberg Train Shows. Note that all the accessories are "blocked in" so the actual construction of the layout can follow a specific plan. Try this one yourself!

TOM: "Where, Roland?"

ME: "Right over here, Tom!"

MITCH: "ROLAND, ARE YOU POINTING IN THE PITCH DARK???"

ME: [Expletive deleted]!

If there's a moral to this story, I suppose it would be never to plan something in the dark. Always think your layout through before you do something you'll regret later!

Actually, the building of a Lionel layout in your home involves a complex set of interrelated decisions, all of which have to be solved before the actual construction of the layout. That's why I want you to read through this chapter and the next two, on track work and wiring, before you begin your actual construction. For now, let us consider the basic decisions you have to make. The first one, quite appropriately, is the size of your layout.

Unfortunately, many people have come to believe that Lionel trains require a great deal of space. Therefore, the conventional wisdom goes, a tinplater can't put very much onto a stand-ard 4' x 8' train platform and had better consider smaller trains if a complex layout is desired. To this conventional wisdom, I say, "Hogwash!" If you do your planning properly, you'd be amazed what you can actually put onto such a small platform. In fact, we're going to use the 4' x 8' platform as a kind of building block. I built a 5' x 8' layout for demonstration purposes at the Greenberg Train Shows; that's one foot shorter than a regulation ping-pong table. On that layout, I've managed to shoehorn two complete loops to run two trains, four freight sidings, a trolley track down a somewhat narrow "Main Street," and at least a dozen operating accessories. I need two transformers to handle the power requirements of this layout. I've never possessed a house with a basement or adequate garage for a train platform, so I've always had to build small. This is my fifth layout, and it has run nearly flawlessly for five years despite being banged around in the back of a truck in its journeys from Maryland, where it is stored, to the Greenberg shows. It is capable of many more operations than I actually demonstrate, and it is loaded with play value with all its accessories, push buttons, and switches. It would be surprisingly easy to build this layout for yourself. Too many times, people look at a complex Lionel layout and tell themselves they could never create such an enterprise. That's simply not true! With some practice and — above all — careful planning, you can indeed build a terrific operating layout, one that goes far beyond just running trains around a loop!

Obviously, your first decision concerns where in your home your layout is to be placed. This is just as obviously a family decision, since the trend in housing has been to build smaller homes without basements or attics, where Lionel layouts found such great homes thirty or forty years ago. If you plan your layout for an attic, remember that often attics are roaring hot in summer and very cold in winter. Garages can work out very well if the space is there and if they are protected from the elements, but most are not. Spare rooms inside a house tend to be somewhat small. Here, some careful thought and planning can turn apparently small spaces into an unexpected bonus. In garages, I've known people who suspend their Lionel layouts from pulleys attached to the ceiling when the layout is not in use. Some people have insulated and finished off their attics into great train rooms. Even when space is at a real premium, you can build a small layout on casters so it can be rolled under a bed for storage. Other layouts can be made so that they fold up against a wall when they are not in use. Use your ingenuity, and there are ways to build good Lionel layouts in nearly every home, even the smallest apartments and condominiums!

Once you have conferred with your family (which is only fair) and selected the proper space for your layout, it will then be time to examine some track plans which will fit into your particular space.

There are two ways to do this. One way is to consult a good book of track plans. Several publishers of books about toy trains have diagrams of track plans suitable for Lionel; perhaps one of these can serve as a good model. I applaud these track plans because of their guidance, but I wonder sometimes if exact repetition of these plans is really the best answer. For one thing, Lionel's track plans over many years have placed a great stress upon the construction of reversing loops in the layout. These loops use a non-derailing switch to reverse the direction of the train around your main track loop. I believe these loops waste a great deal of precious space, except on large layouts. My priority is the construction of busy freight yards because dead-end freight spurs and

switches allow for complex switching operations, which I prefer, and for the placement of many Lionel operating accessories. Reversing loops do not allow for freight spurs as a rule. Despite what I see as a planning flaw, many Lionel Trains, Inc.-designed layouts show great ingenuity.

The second method of planning a train layout for yourself is to visit some operating examples, either at train shows or at friends' homes. By observing the construction techniques and operating methods of these real-life layouts, you can decide your own preferences more clearly. Even if the layouts you observe are too large for your own home, you can adapt many of the construction and operating techniques on these layouts for your own layout. Pay close attention to the use of operational techniques; do they seem simple enough to control or too complicated for your situation? Before I built my own series of layouts, I observed quite a number of operating layouts, and I picked and chose the best of these layouts for my own example. This is a wise procedure, because you will be building upon successful experience.

Of course, when I did all this, I examined some operating layouts and some track plans before I built my first layout. Then, not really knowing a great deal about carpentry, I did what I thought was best. My first two layouts were very simple; they featured a 4' x 8' sheet of plywood cut down to 4' x 6' to fit a room in my former house. I did not frame the plywood; instead, I simply bolted four table legs onto the corners. Large error! I found that the plywood eventually warped without reinforcement, even though my second layout used thicker wood. My third layout was the first one I used for demonstrations at the Greenberg shows, and it was the first one which used two-train operation. I reinforced the plywood from below with thick sheets of particle board, but to my dismay that one warped, too. My fourth layout featured a much better track plan, and finally I had the sense to mount the train board on a framework of 1" x 4" lumber. This one, a 4' x 8' layout, lasted much better, but I still wasn't satisfied with its performance. I wanted to use larger equipment on an O Gauge outside track, and I wanted more sidings and operating accessories while still maintaining a small layout. Thus I built my fifth and current layout, which is built in two 4' x 5' sections to form a 5' x 8' layout.

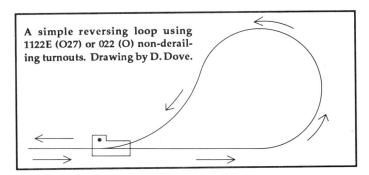

A simple reversing loop using 1122E (O27) or 022 (O) non-derailing turnouts. Drawing by D. Dove.

I've been very happy with the performance of this layout. I can do complex switching maneuvers because of a wiring system called Cab Control (more about that in the wiring chapter). The track work has held up extremely well; the only repairs in five years have been a couple of "jumper" wires to correct corroded center rail pins causing voltage drops and a replacement of one of the eight remote-control switches. The operating accessories are sensibly placed and work very well. Because of the mixed gauge of the rails — O Gauge on the outside loop and O27 Gauge on the

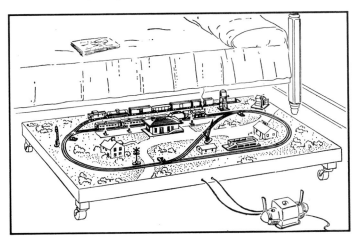

A small "rollaway" under-bed layout from 1949 Lionel Instructions book.

Above: The Union Pacific's old engine yard is a frequent spot for railroad photography as the rust-colored rocks of southern Wyoming provide an overlook. Mom and the kids look for arrowheads and other Indian artifacts while Dad watches the fueling and switching operations. W. D. Hakkarinen, M.D. layout, M. Feinstein photograph.

Below: Plasticville buildings are inexpensive and easily reworked by cutting and regluing. A four-story apartment house was built from a number of the common stations and repainted light gray. The red brick four-story office building was built from Plasticville schoolhouses. A foot patrolman writes a ticket on the illegally parked red coupe. Greenberg 48-foot layout, M. Feinstein photograph.

Above: It is a busy day at the old horse corral as we load up the horses for their journey to the Kentucky Derby. Note the Marx floodlight towers and Lionel 2318 Control Tower in the background. A separate Marx spotlight illuminates the corral. Maybe there's been a terrorist threat against the horses, judging by that mean-looking soldier sitting on the bench. Author's layout, M. Feinstein photograph.

Below: The center sections of the Greenberg 48-foot show layout are four feet wide and the dual tracks on each side carry heavy passenger and freight service. As the consequence of its enormous mileage, 2343 Santa Fe F3 has been remotored twice. The Lionel trolley is actually a mid-1950s No. 60 with a new body. Ongoing equipment maintenance is provided by I. D. Smith. B. Greenberg photograph.

inside — I can run the larger Madison-style passenger cars on the outside as well as the six-wheel truck diesels and other larger pieces of Lionel equipment. It is, however, the characteristic of all Lionel operators never to be totally satisfied. Some day, I'll probably dismantle this layout and build an entirely new one!

Bear in mind that the continuous loop layout is not your only choice, even though it is by far the most common layout built by tinplate operators. You should also consider the point-to-point layout, which duplicates real railroading much more precisely. This layout works best if you have a long and relatively narrow space for the operation of your trains. Instead of a continuous loop, the point-to-point layout features one strip of main line track with (usually) reversing loops at either end. Some point-to-point layouts have several such lines. With such a layout, you can start switching operations at one end of the layout and gradually work your switch train to the other end after many movements of cars in spur sidings. In addition, you can have a fast express operate continuously by using the reverse loops at either end of the layout. Such layouts allow high-speed running because of the long stretches of straight track. Continuous loop layouts like mine are generally "slow-order territory," especially if they are small.

Another choice you could make would be the **perimeter** layout, a great layout to install around the walls of a room. In this format, the layout board is built around three sides (sometimes all four) of a room, with wider sections at the ends to allow for the turning of trains in the opposite direction. It is similar to the point-to-point layout because reversing loops are built into the ends of the layout, but it differs from the point-to-point layout because it uses more than just one straight section of platform. The operation of the perimeter layout is great exercise for the muscles of the neck!

Once you get some experience building layouts, you will be able to increase their complexity and thus the fun of operating them. Some tinplaters have built fine cabinetry under their train platforms so they can store their train equipment. Others have created magnificent central control panels with transformers, levers, and buttons for all the accessories. Some of these control panels look as if they belong inside the control center of a nuclear power plant! What you do with your layout depends upon your existing level of construction skill and the level of layout building skills you acquire over the years — actually, that learning experience is part of the fun, as I've learned for myself. However, it is wise to remember that complex layouts are not an absolute requirement for the enjoyment of Lionel trains. Keep it simple at the beginning, allow for expansion and change, and make your layouts more complex as your skills develop.

For the actual laying out of the track, you can choose from several plans or simply experiment with loose sections of track on the bare platform once it is built. I've found this "mock-up" system to be very effective for me. Once my potential trackage is in place on the bare platform, I can operate a locomotive on it to check clearances, operations, and speed, among other things. There are several commercially available templates for Lionel trains which can help you prepare a blueprint in miniature for the space you have built. However, I have found that the mock-up system of planning trackage allows for the greatest creativity. Remember that one of the great advantages of the toy train layout is that you're exercising your own creativity, not taking advantage of someone else's — including my own! Visualize the accessories you're going to use on your layout. Do they fit in specific spaces you have allowed on the platform? You can even put them in place without wiring them in the mock-up system to see if you've allowed for proper clearances. You can check trestle and bridge clearances first without having to make complex changes later on. Once you have a suitable track plan in its mock-up stages on the platform, commit it to paper before you begin installing the track work for good. You might want to pencil-outline the perimeters of all the transformers, accessories, controls, etc. right on the layout board, as I did with this last layout which has served me so well. Here again, careful planning is the answer to a layout packed with operating fun!

Another decision you'll have to face is whether to make your layout permanent or portable. Sometimes you may have to face moving your entire layout for one reason or another. If you

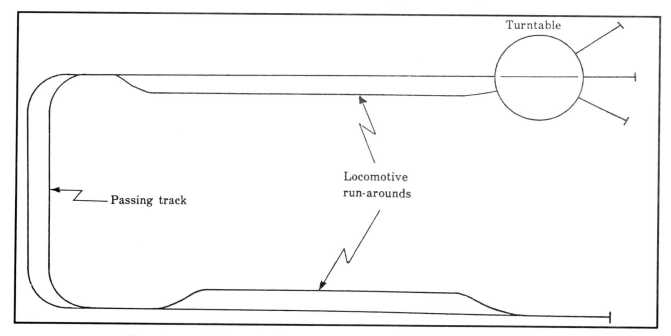

This point-to-point layout is suitable for a perimeter layout. Drawing by Carl Weaver.

change residences relatively frequently, as so often happens in the working lives of Americans, you may very well have to build your layout so that it can be moved without being torn down completely. I faced a rather unusual decision in this regard because if I were to exhibit my layout at the Greenberg shows, as I wanted to do, I had to construct a layout which looked permanent but was easily transportable. By observing the show people and their construction methods, I was able to devise this type of layout. It has cafeteria-style folding legs on two 4' x 5' sections. When I set up the layout at the shows, I use nine junction tracks to join the two sections of the layout. Since I planned my track work in mock-up with the two sections joined, I never have any trouble fitting these sections together. I camouflaged these junction tracks by attaching them to asphalt shingle roadbed sections with twists of wire; the shingles are a close match for the permanent roadbed on the layout, and it takes an observant eye to pick up the difference. The electrical connections underneath the layout are joined at the two sections by a computer-type clip with 24 connections grouped in six color-coded sections of four wires each. When the portable elements are taken off the layout at the end of the show, I separate the two sections and gather the junction tracks and clamps. Then (with some help!) I place two large lids made of furring-strip framework and old paneling atop the two sections. These "coffin lids" are then attached to the layout sections with T-shaped brackets and screws. Then the legs are folded up and the sections are ready for shipment. Your layout probably will not have to meet those rigid specifications for portability, but if you face a move and don't want to sacrifice your layout by tearing it down completely, certain elements of it can be made portable enough for transplanting into a new location.

Now it's time to get specific about building techniques. Let us assume you are going to build a standard 4' x 8' platform table, just so we can all start at the same point. What is the best way to build your platform and its framework? Which type of table leg will support the layout the best? What type of lumber is best, and what type of board should be placed on top of the framework? These are questions which we now address. I must stress here that I am not a skilled carpenter. The following discussion is certainly not the only way to build a fine layout! The late Linn Wescott pioneered the simple and sturdy L-girder method of construction; the Kalmbach Company still sells his many excellent books. Carl Weaver has a thorough discussion of the L-girder method in his Märklin book (see Appendix). As an alternate to my methods, it may suit your needs better.

Let us begin, then, with a discussion of the materials you will need for a basic 4' x 8' platform. Most people who construct their first layouts make the mistake of overbuilding; that is, they use materials which are too heavy for the purpose. As an example of this, some people use table tops made of heavy particle board or even 3/4" thick plywood. This produces a sturdy table top, to say the least, but layout builders soon realize their mistake when they start drilling holes through the table top for all the wiring. Aching wrists teach a lesson very well! So do the hernias associated with lifting an entire layout even a few inches from time to time. It simply isn't necessary to build your layout like a fortress. Particle board has to be the most devilishly stubborn substance for wiring openings or wood screw holes!

The frame members will be extremely important, since they will prevent the table top from warping, hold the platform legs, and bear the load stability of the entire layout. I like to use 1" x 4" pine or fir for these members, since it is quite strong without being

too heavy. For a 4' x 8' layout, you will need six pieces of 1" x 4" x 8' lumber, allowing for a little spoilage and for three reinforcing cross members within the frame. Put two of these lumber pieces aside for the long part of your frame. Cut two pieces of lumber into 3' 10-3/4" (46-3/4") lengths, not exactly four feet. If you cut the short parts of the frame to four feet, you'll have a frame too large for the sheet of wood used for the table top. Join the long piece and the short piece so the short piece is inside the long piece. For a preliminary joint, I like to use L-shaped metal brackets which attach to the boards with four wood screws each. Repeat this procedure with the other pieces of lumber until you have constructed a rectangular frame with metal brackets at each corner. Alternatively you can use 8D resin-coated nails and carpenter's glue. Please remember that lumber measurements are nominal. You may have to adjust your lengths to suit the lumber you are using. Rely on that good old tape measure to be sure!

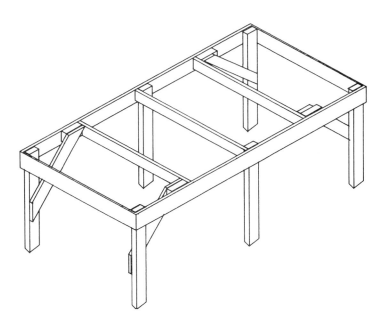

The 4' x 8' frame is best assembled on the floor. Cut your crosspieces to 46-3/4" approximately. **If you are using three-eights or half-inch plywood, only four crosspieces are needed, two at the end, two in the center. If you are using 1/4" plywood or 1/4" lauan, five crosspieces are needed.** Note the leg placement in the five-crosspiece version. Drawing by D. Dove.

Next, it is appropriate to solidify the joints with wood screws. In each end of the long pieces of the frame, drill two holes which will accept 1-1/2" slotted wood screws. If you want a more finished look to your frame, countersink the screw holes with a countersinking drill bit. Do not attempt to sink the screws without drilling first, because you could split the wood. When this is done, you should have a solidly built rectangular frame.

To keep the frame from any threat of stress, you should attach three crosspieces to the frame, one in the center and the others two feet from each end of the rectangle. Once again, cut your crosspieces 3' 10" long (46-3/4") to compensate for the 5/8" thickness of each long frame members. Attach these by once again drilling two screw holes through the long frame members. Use a T-square to make sure that these reinforcing pieces form a right angle with the rectangular frame. Finally, cut out three U-shaped openings in the reinforcing boards to serve as wire pass-through

The left end of the Greenberg 48-foot O Gauge show layout as shown from the rear. The suburban town has Plasticville and other houses. One Plasticville ranch house has been repainted dark red. The many Life-Like brand trees give a pleasant visual appearance. White correction tape provides the street lines. Note that the streets curve and the cul-de-sac provides a safe place for children to play. M. Feinstein photograph, scenery by T. Zissimos.

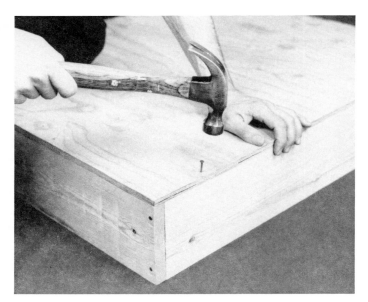

Nailing the top to one of the short side pieces of the skirt. To make a stronger table, thinly coat the contacting surfaces of skirt and table with wood glue before nailing. M. Feinstein photograph.

Nailing the long piece of the table skirt into the shorter piece substantially strengthens the table. However, wood splitting is a potential problem at this point. Hence, drilling a starter hole through the long skirt piece is recommended. Gluing before nailing is also recommended. M. Feinstein photograph.

openings once the platform is secured to the table top. You can do this easily with a saber saw or fine-bladed hand saw.

With the reinforcing pieces on this frame, you do not have to worry too much about the thickness of the sheet of wood you will use for the table top. I prefer nothing more thick than 1/4" Lauan wood, for two reasons. First of all, Lauan wood is easy to work with but quite inexpensive. You don't have to worry about securing finished lumber because you will be decorating your platform anyway. Secondly, Lauan holds screws very well — better, in any case, than particle board — but it is so lightweight you don't even have to use a drill to make many of your wiring holes. I have found that I can punch a wire hole right through the thin Lauan board with a scratch awl. Wood splinters from these holes can be removed from below, and you'll save a great deal of time in wiring your layout if you punch rather than drill holes. The board's thinness does not matter, since it has been reinforced from below by the three crosspieces in the framework. As an alternative, consider 3/8" or 1/2" plywood.

To attach the table top, coat the top surface of the framework with carpenter's glue and place the 4' x 8' Lauan board atop the framework. Secure the board to the frame by using half-inch wood screws around the perimeter (one screw every foot and a half should do) and across the reinforcing crosspieces. I prefer screws to nails in this case because screws are far less likely to work themselves loose over time. However, this is not necessary for a layout that is not moving. You might also want to use pieces of 1" x 2" furring strips to attach to the perimeter of the layout at table top level. These strips will serve as "bumpers" to prevent damage to the joints of the table top and the framework. I use these strips for another purpose — to support the weight of the "lids" I use for transportation of the layout.

Now we must discuss the attachment of legs for the layout, and here things can get a little tricky. First of all, you must make a decision whether you want folding legs or non-folding, permanent platform legs. If you want permanent legs, I suggest the use of square pieces of 2" x 2" wood for the purpose. They should be cut so the height of your table top is between 30 and 36 inches,

depending upon your preferences. Some builders prefer 40" heights. I have always found it easy to work with 36" legs. Cut six of these pieces to the desired length, four for the corners and two at the mid-points of the layout. The center legs will keep the layout from the distressing phenomenon of "hogging," or sagging in the middle. I learned this the hard way; one of the long frame members of my 4' x 8' demonstration layout cracked and had to be reinforced because I put legs only on the corners. Another method of solving this problem is to place the legs inward about 1-1/2 feet from each end. If you choose this method, you may need only four legs instead of six.

To attach the legs, begin at the corners with the layout inverted on the floor of your garage, attic, or construction surface. Position a leg in each corner, holding it in place with two "C" clamps. The end of the leg should be as flush with the frame corners and table top as possible. Drill a 1/4" hole through the framework and the leg about midway through the framework board. Into this hole, place a 1/4" x 3-1/2" carriage bolt and secure it with its nut and a lock washer. These bolts are much more sturdy than mere wood screws. Alternatively you can use 1/4" x 2-1/2" or 2-3/4" law screws to fasten the frame to the leg. Drill out the hole using a 3/16 bit, then using an appropriate wrench or a ratchet with a socket that matches the lag screw heads. (The law screw heads may be either square or six-sided.) Repeat the process through the other framework member, this time staggering the hole so it is drilled one inch from the top of the frame member. Follow the same procedure with the center legs except that you'll be drilling one of your holes through the middle cross brace.

Permanent legs should be reinforced further. To do this, cut pieces of your remaining 1" x 4" lumber at a 45-degree angle so they can be attached to the legs and to the framework. Attach two of these pieces per leg to the legs themselves and to the layout frame pieces, this time using 1-1/4" wood screws. As a final (though optional) step, attach 1-1/2" wood screws through the

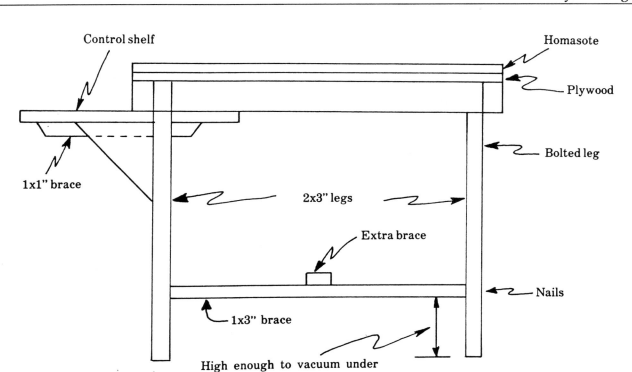

Control shelf

Homasote

Plywood

1x1" brace

Bolted leg

2x3" legs

Extra brace

Nails

1x3" brace

High enough to vacuum under

The end view of the table. Note the 1" x 3" or 1" x 4" brace. If a leg is accidentally kicked, the brace will help hold it in position. Drawing by Carl Weaver.

table top itself down into the ends of the legs. This structure is a lot of trouble, but you will be rewarded with a long-lasting layout. Many layout builders also like to add a reinforcing brace between the legs to reduce the chance of flex when a leg or the layout is bumped or pushed.

If you want folding legs, you have several choices you can make, although your construction necessarily gets a bit tricky. First of all, you can make your 2" x 2" wooden legs folding instead of permanent by hinging them to the frame member and attaching a metal locking strip. If you're going to do that, you should remember to cut square sections out of your cross braces in the framework so the legs can fold completely up into the layout. Based upon some negative experiences, I strongly recommend against the use of metal card table legs which attach in the corners of the framework. These put the entire layout load upon the corners unless you add two more folding legs at the center — a tricky proposition with these legs. By far, the best choice for metal folding legs is the cafeteria table-style leg set. These legs attach to the layout platform itself and to the centers of the frame members rather than in the corners, and they bear the layout load much

closer to the center of the layout. Their locking mechanisms are much more secure than those found on card table legs.

To attach cafeteria-style legs to your platform, you'll have to modify the frame construction details I gave you earlier. First of all, you should use sturdier 2" x 4" frame pieces at the ends of your frame rather than the 1" x 4" pieces, since this will be where the legs attach to the frame. In addition to that, attach two 1" x 4" pieces of lumber, flat side up, between the ends of the frame and the cross members two feet inside the frame at each end. These will be the attachment places for the folding mechanism of these

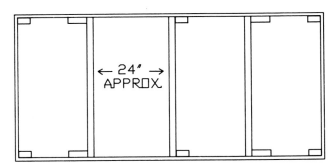

← 24' → APPROX.

Top view of 4' x 8' layout with five crosspieces. If you use 1/8" or 1/4" plywood or Lauan, five braces are recommended. Drawing by D. Dove.

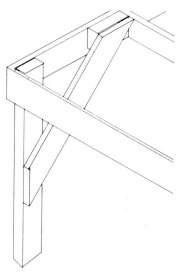

Bracing the 2" x 4" leg with 1" x 4" brace. To hold brace in position, while drilling holes and inserting screws, use a large "C" clamp. Drawing by D. Dove.

You can assemble the frame with nails or screws. Screws provide very secure fastening but resin-coated nails with glue applied to the crosspiece end makes a solid joint. If you are nailing the pieces, you can assemble the pieces on the floor. Put a crosspiece against a convenient wall. Put a little glue on the crosspiece end. Nail from the long piece. Then do a second crosspiece. Measure its location from the end. If there are a total of four crosspieces, then the center of the second piece is 32" from the end. After you have two crosspieces nailed, add the second long piece to the other side and nail it. Have a helper put his or her foot against the first side, so that it will not move when you nail.

legs. Now, after your attachment of the table top, fasten the U-shaped brackets which hold the legs themselves to the end of the frame. Measuring carefully, attach the folding mechanism pieces to the internal lengthwise frame pieces you have installed for that purpose. These folding legs should be very sturdy if they are attached in this manner. Make sure you follow the manufacturer's instructions.

Once all this is done, you can wipe the sweat off your brow, secure in the knowledge that you have constructed a sturdy platform for your trains which does not carry unnecessary weight. Of course, you will have to modify these basic instructions, depending upon the type and size of your layout and your knowledge of carpentry, which may very well be a lot better than mine!

Many railroaders like to use a sheet of Homasote atop their layouts to deaden the noise of the operating layout. This practice has advantages and disadvantages, in my view. Homasote is indeed a good sound insulator. It can add rigidity to your platform, and it can even be hollowed out during the making of your scenery so you can simulate a body of water. It will also eliminate the need for any cork or rubber roadbed. However, when Homasote gets moist in high humidity it has a nasty tendency to warp. In addition, it increases the length of the wiring holes you'll need to drill in great profusion, and sometimes it does not hold screws too well. Since there are other ways to deaden the sounds of your trains, I don't recommend the use of Homasote. However, many layout builders disagree with this assessment. Here, your best bet is to consult with someone who has used Homasote on a layout before you make your decision.

Before I close this chapter, I should mention a more advanced type of construction which has found favor among many model railroaders. This is called the open-top platform; what I have outlined above is called a closed-top platform. In the open-top platform, no wooden sheet is used on the basic framework of the layout. Instead, strips of wood cut to the curvature of the track plan are fastened in place one by one. During the scenery-making process, the open spaces are filled in with all manner of effects such as mountains, lakes, and so forth. The big advantage of the open-top platform is that it allows railroading on several height levels on the same platform and far more complex scenery. Of course, it is quite complex to build and somewhat daunting for beginners. The Sievers Benchwork Company offers several track plans for Lionel trains using pre-cut benchwork which is assembled by the layout builder into an open-top configuration. Such commercially available benchwork eliminates planning mistakes, although it can be somewhat costly. Most Lionel layout builders begin with a closed-top platform and graduate to open-top construction later on, and since this book is intended mostly for the beginner, it is not the place for an extended discussion of the open-top platform.

Now that we have surveyed the basics of platform building, it is time to turn to another topic — track work. We have already discussed some of the planning factors essential to a good operating layout. However, what kinds of three-rail track are available? What turnouts, crossovers, and operating track pieces are appropriate? What is the best way to fasten track to the table top? How can the rather dull-looking Lionel track be made to look more realistic? These questions are part of the next chapter — Tricks With Track.

CHAPTER V

TRICKS WITH TRACK

"The rails go westward in the dark. Brother, have you seen starlight
on the rails? Have you heard the thunder of the fast express?"
— Thomas Wolfe

"To do things railroad-fashion is now the by-word, and it is worth the
while to be warned so often and so sincerely by any power to get off its
track ... We have constructed a fate that never turns aside."
— Henry David Thoreau

The Strasburg Rail Road, just outside Lancaster, Pennsylvania, has been a terrific tourist railroad for almost thirty years now. It is the oldest operating short-line railroad in the country, having a history which goes all the way back to 1832. In the late 1950s, when it was almost abandoned, a dedicated group of railfans raised enough money to take over the railroad, which was in a sad state of disrepair.

In the course of time, the Strasburg railfans acquired some freight and passenger cars and, most importantly, a steam locomotive from the Canadian National Railroad. In preparation for passenger excursions which would raise money for the line, the railroad's board commissioned the rebuilding of the track all along the line, a distance of about four and a half miles. The board ordered new ties, rails, splice plates, and all the necessary items for the rebuilding of the track. Finally, the track was ready, and the steamer began its operations. Now the line would really catch on — or so the railfans thought.

To the dismay of the Strasburg's operators, it soon became apparent that the track work that had been done so conscientiously by volunteer workers was no match for the load stresses placed upon it by the steam locomotive. Rails warped and kinked; splice plates worked loose; whole ties were driven into the ground. Smooth curves rapidly became erratic tangents. Learning its lesson quickly, the Strasburg's board rebuilt the entire line, this time to sturdier and heavier specifications. Once the track work had been done correctly, it was much easier to maintain.

Lionel railroads are, in principle, no different from the Strasburg Rail Road. If you're going to have a smooth-running layout, the trains, the scenery, the wiring, and the platform will not make very much difference if the track work is not properly done from the start. The purpose of this chapter is to acquaint you with the types of track available as well as to show you how to lay and fasten it to your platform properly. I will also discuss some

A gasoline-powered combination railcar of about 1910 vintage makes a stop at the Groff's Grove picnic area of the Strasburg Rail Road in Strasburg, Pennsylvania. Note the track work and the rivet detail. R. LaVoie photograph.

methods of deadening the train sound by cushioning the track, some unusual mixtures of different sizes of track which can be of great benefit, and some ways to "dress up" the rather plain Lionel track so it looks more realistic. One method of decorating your track will be a little outrageous, so stay tuned to this chapter!

At the outset, it is important for you to realize that new track is not your only option. The three-rail track used in tinplate operations has been made for many years by many different manufacturers, and a surprising amount of this track has survived. Very little can go wrong with track. In used examples, all you have to do is check to see if the insulating pieces are in place on the center rail and examine the rails for denting and warping. Don't worry about rust, grime, and dirt; used track can be restored very easily if you are willing to spend the time and the labor, which are often substitutes for money in this hobby. That, in fact, is the biggest advantage of restoring used track for your layout. Used track is often available for a fraction of the cost of new track, and if the restoration is done correctly, you will achieve a highly realistic look for your layout as well. Later in this chapter, I'll detail the best methods for restoring used track.

TYPES OF TRACK AVAILABLE

Before we talk about the restoration of used track, it is best that we survey the types of three-rail tinplate track available at the present time. Several manufacturers besides Lionel make this track, and since the toy train hobby has grown so much in the last few years, there is trackage available for almost any use on any size layout. At the present time, Lionel Trains, Inc. is offering the following types of track:

O27 GAUGE

— Regular straight track sections
— Regular curved track sections
— Half straight and half curved sections
— 35" long straight track sections
— Wide radius O54 curved sections
— Wide radius O42 curved sections
— 45˚ and 90˚ crossover sections
— Remote-uncoupling track sections
— Manual turnouts (commonly called "switches")
— Remote-control turnouts (27" and 42" radius)
— Steel and fiber track pins
— Straight and curved track ballast pieces
— Steel and nylon track pins

O GAUGE

— Regular straight track sections
— Regular curved track sections
— 40" extra long straight sections
— Half straight and half curved sections
— Wide radius O72 curved sections
— 45˚ and 90˚ crossovers
— Regular remote-control turnouts
— Wide radius remote-control turnouts
— Remote-uncoupling and operating car track
— Straight and curved track ballast pieces
— Steel and nylon track pins

Besides all that track, another manufacturer, the K-Line Company, offers the following track pieces which Lionel is not making at the present time:

O27 GAUGE

— Wide radius O72 curved sections
— Insulated straight track sections
— Double straight sections
— 36" extra long straight sections (Lionel's are 35")
— Wide radius O42 remote-control turnouts

O GAUGE

— Wide radius O42 curved sections
— Insulated straight track sections
— O72 straight track sections (14-3/8" long)
— 36" extra long straight sections (Lionel's are 40")

— Wide radius O42 remote-control turnouts (Note: These should not be confused with Lionel's No. O42 manually-operated O Gauge switches, which have a regular 31" radius.)

K-Line also offers its "Super-K" track sections, which are somewhat similar to the old Lionel Super O sections and have molded plastic ties over the entire track length. Similar track with molded plastic ties is made by the Williams Company.

The Gargraves Company has been offering track for Lionel which is considerably different from Lionel's tinplate track. Gargraves track has flat T-shaped surfaces on its rails, not the rounded surfaces so common to ordinary tinplate track. It comes in two lines, a regular three-rail section and the "Phantom Line," which has a blackened center rail to give the track a more realistic two-rail look. Both versions come in tinplated and stainless steel forms. Gargraves also sells wide-radius turnouts which operate like those used by scale modelers; these turnouts use separately-installed switch motors such as those manufactured by Tenshodo. The switch machines can be installed underneath the layout, so the Gargraves remote-control switches eliminate clearance problems with larger O Gauge Lionel equipment caused by the integral switch motor casings on other types of turnouts. The Gargraves track sections also feature wooden basswood ties over their length. These track sections look very realistic and are favored by many layout operators.

For the beginner, however, Gargraves track has some disadvantages worth noting. For one thing, it is not possible to make electrical connections on Gargraves track with Lionel's lockons without taking some ties out of the track. If you aren't willing to take ties out of the track, the electrical connections to the track must be soldered — a tedious process. Small holes can be drilled in the sides of the rails and sheet metal screws can secure the wire, but that's precision work for the beginner. Cargraves now sells its own special wire connectors. In addition, the track sections are sold as straight pieces only, and curves must be made by bending the track sections. That's not an easy job. If you are the slightest bit careless, you can kink the track section and ruin it. The excess lengths of rails on curved sections must be snipped off. Believe it or not, one of the favorite tricks of layout operators who use this track is to bend it around their home water heaters! This produces curves which are the proper radius for layout operation. Another method is to bend the track around a circle of Lionel O Gauge track. The Gargraves rails are bent right inside the Lionel rails with the Gargraves track upside down. For layout operators who have better than average skills, Gargraves track is worth the use because of its highly realistic appearance and the extra traction afforded the locomotives because of the flat rail surfaces. At a beginning stage of model railroading, Gargraves track may prove to be too daunting an experience.

There are even more special track sections available to the Lionel operator. Right-Of-Way Industries makes some really special track sections for Lionel trains. These sections include a complex yard set, a "wye" turnout, a three-way turnout, a double crossover, a double slip switch, crossovers in no less than five different angles, and switch machines and control panels of every description. The really advanced Lionel operator can take advantage of these sections to make up incredibly complex yard configurations.

Now, to throw some further gasoline onto the fire, let me mention some track sections which are no longer made but are frequently available as used track sections. The Marx Company, one of Lionel's biggest competitors, made long O27 straight track sections and 34" wide radius curved sections. Before the Second World War, American Flyer still used three-rail track, and its O Gauge sections came in 34" wide radius sections. These can still be found readily, believe it or not. Finally, Marklin and Bing, two German manufacturers, made O Gauge curved sections which are actually banked to allow for higher-speed operation on curves. Even these ancient track pieces show up from time to time, even though they haven't been made for over sixty years!

Are you confused by all this track talk? I wouldn't blame you! Perhaps it is best to try to sort out the variety by explaining what is meant by curved track radius and by making some specific recommendations about track and switches.

The radius of a curved section of track refers to the width of its curvature, and different radii have different uses on a layout. Lionel's O27 and O Gauge track pieces are the same gauge, which refers to the distance between the rails. However, the O27 track forms a circle 27" in diameter, while the O Gauge track forms a 30" circle. That's not the only difference between these two basic types of track. The O Gauge track is not truly compatible with O27 Gauge track because its rail surfaces are higher than those of the O27 sections. Additionally, O Gauge track is much more sturdily built than is O27 Gauge track, which had its Lionel origins in the early 1930s with inexpensive clockwork and electric train sets. Since O27 Gauge track is less expensive, it is more commonly used than O Gauge. The track pins used in O Gauge track are much thicker than those of O27 Gauge track, too.

As you've probably surmised, there are other curvatures available besides the 27" and 30" curvatures of regular Lionel track. The O42, O54, and O72 curved track sections form circles with 42", 54", and 72" diameters. The type of radius you choose has to do with the type of equipment you'll be running on the tracks and the amount of space you have on your layout. If you're limited to a layout of 4' x 8', as many people are, you are better off with standard sections of O or O27 Gauge track. The curved sections with wider radii allow for higher speed running on larger layouts. It is also worth noting that some of the larger Lionel rolling stock pieces, such as the Fairbanks-Morse diesels and the aluminum passenger cars, will not run on O27 Gauge track because of the tight radius and because these pieces will not clear the O27 Gauge switch boxes when they go through turnouts. All of Lionel's locomotives and rolling stock will clear the O Gauge track and turnouts. However, you can put more O27 Gauge track in a limited space because of its tight radius, so this smaller track does have a significant advantage for many operators.

On my own 5' x 8' layout, I used O Gauge track on my outside loop and O27 Gauge track on my inside loop and yards. The O27 Gauge track had to be "jacked up" to match the height of the O Gauge track, but that's not a difficult process. The real difficulty was in adapting O27 Gauge turnouts to the O Gauge track on the outside loop. Supposedly, it is not possible to do this, and indeed it is impossible to mate O27 Gauge turnouts with O Gauge track if they are the currently-produced variety. The reason for this is that the center rails of these turnouts cannot be widened to accept the larger O Gauge track pins; there is a plastic nib just inside the rail which holds the O27 Gauge pins in place. However, one older type of O27 Gauge turnout can indeed be adapted to O Gauge track. The 1121 Turnout was made from 1937 to 1951, and I have found this type of O27 Gauge turnout to be extremely reliable. It does not have the non-derailing feature of the newer turnouts (though it can be made to work that way), but it is a simple, reliable turnout which has illuminated signal hoods and controllers. Often, these 1121 Turnouts are available for less money than their more modern equivalents, and their reliable operation seems to be one of Lionel's best-kept secrets.

To adapt an 1121 Turnout to O Gauge track, you must widen the rails to accept O Gauge pins and elevate the turnout itself so it is at the same height as the O Gauge track. Widen the rail openings carefully with a scratch awl or other such tool. Don't use too much force, or you'll pull the rail loose from the turnout frame. Then, using one of the switches as a template, cut out two sections of asphalt shingles and place them underneath the turnout. These shingles will boost the turnout to the height of O Gauge track. This adaptation is a godsend to a small layout because it allows for closer placement of an inside loop to an outside loop. Since O27 Gauge track has a tighter radius than O Gauge track, I was able to place my inside loop very close to the outer loop, allowing for more trackage inside the layout for switching operations.

If you're going to use O Gauge track with O27 Gauge track, your best bet is to raise the height of the O27 Gauge track over the entire layout. This isn't as hard as it sounds. Since I knew I would be ballasting my track, I didn't worry about the O27 ties being raised off the platform surface — they would be hidden by the ballast work. I was fortunate enough to find a large supply of Mainliner rubber O Gauge ties for this purpose. These hard rubber ties were made commercially in the 1950s, and supplies of them can be found from time to time. If you can't find these ties, there is another solution. Simply purchase strips of balsa or basswood from your local hobby shop and, using a razor saw, cut them to the proper length. If you use wooden strips 3/8" thick, the O27 Gauge track will be boosted to O Gauge height. (For standard O27 Gauge applications, use 1/4" balsa ties.)

BUILDING YOUR ROADBED

Once you have decided on the proper track plan and track to use, it is time to actually fasten the track to the layout platform. Of course, there are other considerations such as wiring and special track sections, so make sure you have made allowances as needed. (Read the next chapter on wiring before you actually fasten the track work.) In your mock-up of the layout plan, make sure that none of the track work is stretched or kinked. If the track work doesn't quite match for any reason, as it may not on some plans, you will have to cut special sections of track for the odd areas. This is an easy process. Small holes can be drilled in the sides of the rails and sheet metal screws can secure the wire, but

Closeup of 1121 Turnout as seen on R. LaVoie's layout. M. Feinstein photograph.

that's precision work for the beginner. Gargraves now sells its own special wire connectors. Measure carefully the exact length of track you'll need and mark it off with pencil on a section of track. Wrap the track in a rag and fasten it to a vise. Using a fine-bladed hacksaw, cut the rails to their proper length. Before reinserting the track pins, you might want to buff off the track ends with fine sandpaper. Many railroaders keep sections of these "fitter" tracks handy for special applications. If necessary, loosen one of the ties with a screwdriver blade and move it as needed; then, re-crimp the tie.

In fastening the track to the platform, avoid using nails if you can, since the vibration of the trains can work them loose and you'll wreck some track sections if your hammer slips. Screws are preferable, even though it will take you a bit longer to fasten the track. Usually, appropriate lengths of No. 4 or No. 6 screws are available in hobby shops for this purpose. When you screw the track sections down, don't overdo the operation by using too many screws or by over-tightening them. Remember that the purpose of these screws is simply to keep the track in place. If you use too many screws, you'll introduce too many rises and falls in your train's operation, and you certainly want your trains operating smoothly without too many "bumps" to complicate matters. The best strategy is to use one screw per track section at the track junctions; alternate the screws between the inner and outer tie holes as you go along. There may be some places where an extra screw is needed to level the track on a curve. To check this, use a small level as you fasten the track to keep your track work as even as possible. As you assemble your track, make sure your track pins are clean and tight. A special pair of pliers is available for this purpose; it has a small hole to crimp the rail around the pin securely.

If you desire, you can use any of several methods to deaden the sound of the trains as they go around the track. In my case, the rubber Mainliner ties accomplish this purpose to a certain degree, but I was fortunate enough to find them, for they are no longer made. (One wonders why this item hasn't been re-manufactured.) One option you have is to lay your track onto cork roadbed. Some specialty train supply houses sell this roadbed in O Gauge sizes for O Scale modelers, but it will work just as well for Lionel's O and O27 Gauges. If you've used a sheet of Homasote board atop your wooden platform, you will not have to worry too much about sound deadening. Just make sure your track screws do not penetrate into the wooden sub-base, because they will transfer the train's vibration into the wood and increase the noise. Using templates, you can also cut strips out of an old rubber rug pad, as long as these will be camouflaged by ballasting the track work later on.

TYPES OF TURNOUTS

The various types of Lionel turnouts have specific applications to your layout; you'll find that each has advantages and disadvantages for your particular situation. (I use the term "turnout" to avoid any confusion with the word "switch," although many tinplate operators use that term to refer to the device which shunts a train onto another track.) I've already discussed my favorite among the older O27 Gauge turnouts, the 1121 model made between 1937 and 1951. As a rule, these old turnouts have very few liabilities and several advantages, especially on small layouts. They're lighted both at the turnout itself and at the controller box, so they provide a fine indicator of the turnout's position. Their inner works are all metal, so there's little danger

of damage to the mechanisms. They work by direct drive without any rack and pinion gearing, eliminating any chance that they bind up, as many of the newer O27 Gauge turnouts do. You'll find the controllers of these turnouts often have decayed wiring, but the control boxes are very reliable, so it is worth it for you to get out a soldering iron and rewire the controller boxes, a fairly easy operation. Three-wire cabling is sold by the foot at many parts dealers for this purpose. If you rewire the control boxes, it is necessary to solder the new wiring in exactly the same sequence as the old wiring. Some of these 1121-100 Controllers have a ground wire attachment at the center wire of the three; on the 1121 turnout, this wire connects to the center terminal. However, many of the later control boxes have their ground wires working off one of the end wires in the three-wire cable. These were controllers meant for the newer 1122 Lionel O27 Turnout, which had its ground wire attachment on the terminal pin closest to the switch box. To avoid confusion as to which of the three wires is the ground wire, you might want to mark off the ground wire in some way, or — better yet — use color-coded wire so that one color always represents the ground wire. In my rewired 1121 control boxes, I know that the red wire is always the ground wire for the switch. When you hook up the wiring, check to see if the turnout position matches the position of the control box. If the turnout is in its straight, or green, position and the controller box shows a red light, simply reverse the positions of the two operating wires at the turnout itself. The controller and the turnout position will then agree. Each 1121-100 Controller services a pair of turnouts.

The old 1121 Turnouts lack a non-derailing feature. This feature is not too important on smaller layouts, where presumably the operator can see readily if the turnouts are in the correct positions. However, on larger layouts and on layouts with reverse loops, a non-derailing turnout is desirable. (In fact, a reversing loop is rather difficult without non-derailing turnouts.) You'll need two insulated pieces of track to make the 1121 Turnouts non-derailing. (I'll tell you how to make your own such tracks later in this chapter.) Install the tracks next to the curved and straight branches of the turnout; make sure that you have installed nylon pins where these tracks meet the turnout as well as at the other rail end of the track section. Attach lockons to the center rails and the insulated outside rails of the two tracks. Then, run a wire from the No. 2 clips of the lockons to the proper outside posts of the turnout wire connections. If you've installed the tracks correctly, when the train hits the special piece of track it will complete a connection which will throw the turnout frog if it has been set against the train. Without this, you could be facing a nasty derailment! My own layout is small enough so I can do without a non-derailing feature, but at least I have the option of converting the 1121 turnouts to non-derailing status if I should so choose. I suppose that if enough of my locomotives dive off the layout onto the floor, I'll know it's time to make my turnouts non-derailing!

The later 1122 and 1122E Turnouts, made from 1952 to 1969, have a non-derailing feature built into them so all you will need are the nylon pins attached to the inside rails of the switches. In 1952 Lionel completely redesigned its turnouts, mainly to provide the non-derailing feature. The first design of these turnouts was not entirely successful. The outside rails were split into segments; contact was a little erratic. In addition, the light sockets in the first 1122 Turnouts were too close to the plastic switch box cover, and many examples have been melted by the heat of the light bulb. By 1953 Lionel had redesigned the turnout again, this time calling it

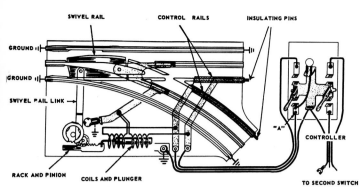

A wiring diagram as shown in the 1122 instruction sheet.

the 1122E model. Look on the underside of the galvanized base for the stamping "1122E"; these are the preferable turnouts.

The 1122E model used a rack and pinion system utilizing a nylon gear against a metal rack. It had a little lantern lens, illuminated from beneath, which plugged into a circular bracket mounted to the rack. When the turnout was thrown, the rack moved and the lantern rotated to show red or green signals. The control boxes were not changed from the earlier 1121 model; they too remained illuminated. These turnouts are very reliable and are available in excellent used condition for about the price of the new production models or a little less. The production of Lionel's O27 turnouts since 1970 is, in my opinion, inferior to the older construction. In the current O27 turnouts, neither the switch nor the controller is illuminated. The current turnouts use a highly fragile plastic drive pin attached to the switch frog instead of the older metal drive rod and rivet. If you're using O27 Gauge track, the 1122E or 1121 Turnouts are preferable to the newer construction.

One precautionary note: On the 1122E turnouts, it is important that the correct light bulbs are used in both the turnout and its controller. If too high an amperage level is present in the controller's lamp, there will be electrical "feedback" to the turnout, resulting in constant operation of the turnout's solenoid. This isn't too healthy for the turnout's life, since once the solenoid is burned out, the turnout cannot be restored without considerable labor and expense. For bayonet-based turnouts and controllers, the best bulb to use is the No. 53 (turnout) or the No. 57 (controller). Some of the earlier controllers use screw-based bulbs. These should take a large No. 430 Lamp. When you run your trains, try not to leave a train parked on the turnout's rails for too long, because if the turnout is non-derailing, the solenoid will be in operation as long as there is a car or locomotive on the insulated track.

You won't have to worry about construction differences if you wish to use O Gauge turnouts. The 022 model was made from 1938 all the way to 1969, and the current production of this turnout follows it exactly. These turnouts are about twice as expensive as the O27 models, but they are really rugged pieces of equipment which work extremely well. All of the 022 O Gauge Turnouts are non-derailing models. They use single controllers instead of the double control boxes of the O27 Gauge turnouts. They can be wired to accept constant voltage through a special plug, unlike the O27 Gauge turnouts, which must rely on track voltage. This makes for snappier operation at low voltage.

There are two great operational advantages to the 022 models. First, the operator can wire an accessory signal to them so that the signal gives the position of the turnout. For example, a 153 Block Signal can be connected to the three terminals of the 022 Turnout so that it shows red or green to indicate the position of the turnout. This is not possible with the O27 Gauge models; both signal lamps will operate at once. The second advantage to those turnouts is that the entire motor unit can be taken off the turnout and reversed so that it faces the outside of the turnout instead of the inside. This is a great advantage in "ladder- tracks" used in freight yards; the turnouts can be mounted right next to one another without spacing tracks between them. These turn-outs also come in wide-radius versions which can allow high-speed shunting of a train from one track to another. Other manufacturers besides Lionel make wide radius O27 Gauge turnouts, but the reports I have had on these turnouts have been somewhat negative as to their reliability. There is no reliability problem with the O Gauge 022 models and their latter-day successors; they are excellent turnouts. Certain manually-operated turnouts can keep your costs down if they are within easy reach of your control center, so consider them in your planning as well.

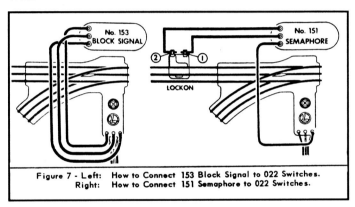

Figure 7 - Left: How to Connect 153 Block Signal to 022 Switches.
Right: How to Connect 151 Semaphore to 022 Switches.

Lionel instruction sheet showing the wiring of 151 and 153 accessories to O22 turnouts.

REMOTE CONTROL TRACKS

Over the years, Lionel has made quite a few types of uncoupling and remote-control tracks. The earliest of these, the 1019 (O27 Gauge) and the RCS (O Gauge), were simply five-rail tracks with two extra rails mounted between the outside and center rails. These extra rails would contact a shoe on the trucks of the operating cars to make them perform their functions. They featured screw terminals which connected to a four-wire, two-button controller for uncoupling and unloading functions. These early models will not uncouple cars made in 1948 or later with magnetic couplers; they will only uncouple the old coil-operated couplers.

When Lionel introduced the magnetic coupler on its rolling stock, the firm changed these operating tracks to include an electromagnet in the center rail. The 1019 became the 6019 for O27 Gauge and the RCS became the UCS for O Gauge. The 6019 poses problems for the layout operator because its wires leading to the two-button controller do not have screw terminals. Instead, they are directly soldered to the underside of the track. This means that if you want the controller's four-conductor wire to go under your layout, you will have to sever or re-solder the wires and splice them after you have led them down below the layout — an inconvenient but necessary job. The 6019 has not been reissued in later years, but good operating examples are still available. We learned at press time that it is to be reissued in 1989.

Lionel also has made remote control tracks which do not combine uncoupling with operating cars; they are simple uncouplers. The 6009 and 6029 of postwar years have two wires which connect from the underside of the track to a ground terminal and a simple push button. Later versions only had one wire which goes through the push button to a power terminal. Currently, Lionel makes the one-wire type for O27 Gauge (No. 5149) and has revived the UCS track for O Gauge (No. 5502).

Obviously, the UCS and its remakes are better remote tracks than their O27 equivalents. However, the O27 Gauge operator can combine several types of these tracks to best advantage. Where I want operating cars but do not need an uncoupling feature, I have used old 1019 models, and I have used 6029 O27 Gauge models where I only need uncoupling functions. I have used UCS tracks on my O Gauge outside loop where I uncouple cars with magnetic couplers and RCS tracks inside where I have operating cars with sliding shoes.

Great care is needed in wiring the one-wire versions of the O27 Gauge uncoupling tracks. Make sure you wire them to a power wire; they are internally grounded through the outer rails. I well remember, early in my layout-building career, a time when I outsmarted myself with these uncouplers. I did not have enough push button controllers for the six uncouplers in my layout, so I used some Atlas HO slide switches I had at hand. These slide switches had — or so I thought — an on-off position, so I wired the uncouplers through them. In reality, the Atlas switches were simple A-B slide switches, which meant the layout's power was always going through them! When I started up my train, all went well for a few minutes, but before I knew it I had six angry volcanoes in the middle of my tracks. Through my inexperience, I had "fried" all six uncoupler tracks to a crisp! The electromagnets in the tracks had become burned-out shells! As I tore out the tracks and cleared the room of the stench of burned plastic and wire, I could not help thinking about the expensive lesson I had just learned! Fortunately, I found a way to replace them with some used examples which cost just a fraction of the new ones.

As you look for used track, look also for good used uncoupler and operating tracks of all kinds. The two-button controllers are made in the form of a "stack" switch, so they are somewhat difficult to repair and rewire. To test one of these remote tracks, connect it to a transformer with jumper cables. Hold the point of a small screwdriver blade about half an inch above the electromagnet. When you press the uncoupler button, the blade should be drawn to the magnet. To test the operating car rails, connect a continuity light to one control rail. Press the "unload" button of the two-button controller and touch the prong of the

continuity tester to the control rail opposite the alligator clip connection on the other rail. If the track is working, the continuity tester should light. On models with magnets, connect the alligator clip to the lower left power rail and touch the continuity tester's prong to the upper right rail on the opposite side of the magnet. Then place the alligator clip to the upper left rail and touch the lower right rail. In both cases, the light should go on when you touch the "unload" button of the controller.

INSULATED TRACK SECTIONS

I've spoken quite a bit about insulated track sections without actually telling you how to make your own, so allow me to correct that oversight. The purpose of an insulated track section is to make the train itself the "switch" which activates track side accessories such as the operating gateman and the crossing gates. They are sold in both O and O27 Gauges by the K-Line Company, but you can save some money by making your own insulated track sections out of any regular piece of track, straight or curved. The great electrical advantage Lionel has always enjoyed with its three-rail track is the presence of two ground rails and a center power rail instead of two power rails, as is found in two-rail track. That extra ground rail can come in very handy!

To make your own insulated track sections, only a few simple steps are necessary. First, remove the metal pin from one of the outside rails. Using a medium flat-bladed screwdriver or, better yet, a tack puller, pry this outside rail from the ties. Be careful not to let the blade of the screwdriver slip! Put some short lengths of friction tape on the rail where it meets the metal ties. I often pry loose the center insulators from bent-up track pieces and save them for this purpose, but friction tape or even masking tape will do. You can also use cut-up match book covers. The idea is to prevent that rail from contacting the tie.

Replace the rail into the track ties; please be careful when you crimp down the tabs holding the rail in place! Always point the blade of the screwdriver away from you to preclude any possibility of an accident. Now, place nylon pins into both ends of the rail you've just insulated. Obviously, you'll also have to remove a metal pin from the adjacent track section.

Now you're ready to do some wiring. Insert a lockon onto the live center rail and the dead insulated rail and hook up your accessory to the lockon once the track section is in place on the layout. For some accessories, you will need a second lockon or a connection to a ground terminal underneath the layout because the accessory is lighted and has three, not two, wire connections. You certainly want to keep the accessory lighted constantly. The wire which operates the action of the accessory is the one you want connected to the No. 2 Lockon clip off that insulated rail.

Ordinarily, the accessory will not operate because there is no power in the insulated rail. However, when the metal wheels and axles of the train contact that insulated rail, something interesting happens! The ground connection for the accessory passes right through the metal wheels and axles from the other, "live" ground rail to the insulated rail. This completes the connection, and the accessory operates. This operation is a great deal better than the weight-activated contactors Lionel includes with many of its operating accessories. If these contactors are to work, the track must be free to bend under the weight of the train. This is hardly a prescription for stability, let alone ballast treatments on the track! Weight-activated contactors are fine for a temporary

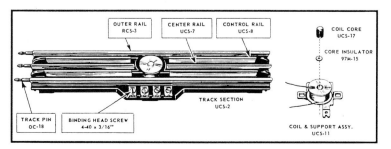

Type UCS Remote Control Track.

set-up, but the use of insulated track sections is far superior in a permanent layout.

Actually, you can do operations with insulated rail sections which you could never perform with weight-activated contactors. For example, the No. 153 Block Signal and its many successors usually alternate between red and green lights when a weight-activated contactor is used to operate them. That action is not typical of the real thing, so if you use two insulated track sections at different places in the layout, you can make the 153 operate very realistically. When my passenger train is on the opposite side of my layout on my outer loop, it contacts an insulated track which leads back to the terminal operating the green light. This remains on until the locomotive gets to the signal, where it contacts another track leading to the red lamp. The red lamp goes on about the same time the green one goes out. Then, when the last car goes over the second insulated track, the red lamp goes out and neither lamp is lit. That operation is much closer to the real thing. I also have my 45N Gateman timed so that the locomotive hits an insulated track on the opposite side of the layout, just as the caboose is going by the shack. The little man in the shack rushes out with his lantern to greet the caboose as it goes by. He then stays out until the caboose passes the insulated track, when he goes back into his shack, the little metal door closing with a tinny clank.

RECONDITIONING USED TRACK

The next topic of concern is the reconditioning of used, or "junk," track. As I've pointed out, time and labor are a great substitute for money in this hobby. You'll see more of that

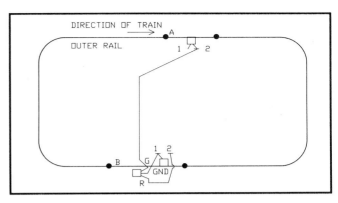

Using the two-light No. 153 Block Signal with two insulated track sections. Sequence: when train contacts insulated track (A), green light goes on. When last car leaves (A), green light goes out. When train contacts insulated track (B), red light goes on. When last car leaves track (B), both signal lights are out. Drawing by D. Dove.

philosophy in the Repair and Maintenance chapter later on. That's true of using junk track instead of new track. Used track is available in great quantities at train shows and tinplate hobby shops at a fraction of the price of new track. For example, a new section of O27 Gauge track can cost 75 cents or more. A used section of the same track can cost as little as 10 cents. When you multiply the savings in money by the number of sections of track you need for your layout, you can see that reconditioning track can save you quite a bit of cash which can be put to better use elsewhere on your layout.

Every piece of track on my own layout, including many of the turnouts, came from someone's junkpile of used track. Of course, I had to replace many of the steel connecting pins, but this is a minor expense. I even salvaged a large number of pins and insulator pieces from bent or twisted sections of track. I have demonstrated the cleaning procedure for junk track at train shows, and people cannot believe that an apparently hopelessly rusted section of track can be reconditioned until they see it with their own eyes.

There are three basic steps in the reconditioning of junk track. The first step involves a thorough sanding of the rail surfaces to get rid of the bulk of the rust and grime. Emery cloth, that black abrasive available from hardware stores, is a good abrasive for this purpose. If you have a large quantity of track to grind down, you might want to use a wire wheel on a grinder — but be sure to wear safety goggles while you operate the grinder. The best abrasive I have ever found for this purpose is called "grits paper." This substance is sold by plumbing supply houses; plumbers use it to polish brass and copper pipe. It comes in rolls of various widths. Many layout operators like to use abrasive scouring pads such as Scotch-Brite. However, never use steel wool, because little pieces of metal can come off the pad and wreck your locomotive engines! Whatever substance you use, abrade the rails until they begin to come up shiny. Be sure to sand down the track pins as well; remember that they supply contact from track section to track section.

You might think that the rail surfaces are clean after this step, but they aren't — not yet! For your second step, you should apply a good track cleaner to a clean rag and scrub down the rail surfaces. This will dissolve stubborn rust and grease if the track cleaner is any good. By far, the best track cleaning fluid I have found is an automotive solvent, CRC 5-56 Compound. This sol-

Another way of checking power in your track circuits — a continuity tester. Note my friend the Flagman just behind my hand, the Marx Ringing Signal and the Lionel 3562 Barrel Car.

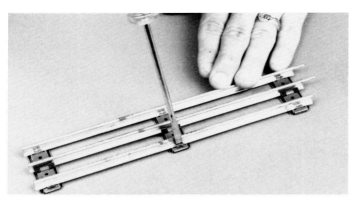

To make your own insulated rail sections, pry one of the outer rails from its ties carefully with a flat-bladed screwdriver. . .

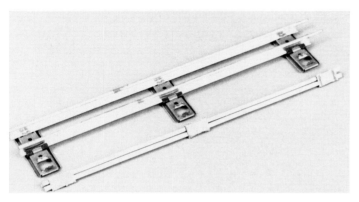

. . . and place insulating pieces (or friction tape) onto this rail where it will contact the tie. Next . . .

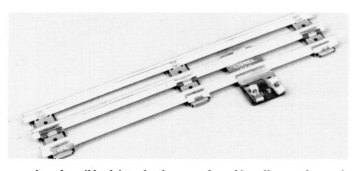

. . . crimp the rail back into the ties securely and install two nylon track pins at either end. Now hook a lockon to the dead rail and the center rail. When your accessory is hooked to the lockon, the train itself will operate the device. M. Feinstein photographs.

vent is available at supermarkets and auto supply houses; it is usually used as a starter fluid and general purpose cleaner. Since it is, after all, a volatile solvent, be sure to work with it in a well-ventilated area and keep young children away from it. Follow the manufacturer's prescribed precautions. Spray some of the CRC 5-56 onto a clean, dry cloth and rub the rails down with it. The solvent will dissolve dirt and grease readily. This solvent is also great for all toy train electrical uses such as cleaning out locomotive motors and reversing switches.

After this step, you're almost finished. However, the CRC 5-56 will leave a residue of dissolved dirt on the rail surfaces. To get this residue off, your third step is to go over the rail surfaces again with a second clean, dry rag. You will notice more dirt

coming off the track, even after sanding and cleaning. After this, however, you can run your finger over the rail surface and it will come away absolutely clean. Your apparently hopelessly dirty track can now support a train electrically on a layout! If you're going to give your track a ballast treatment, as I recommend, you will not have to worry about tarnish on the ties and lower rail surfaces. That will give your track work a realistic "used" look! A small file bit in a Dremel Moto-Tool will clean inside the rail ends for good pin contact.

You can maintain the cleanliness of your track by repeating the second and third steps above, using the CRC 5-56 to keep your layout operating efficiently. You should do this after every few hours of operation. You won't have to keep your track clean to the hospital-like standards of HO and N Gauge scale modelers, but you would be amazed at how much dirt collects on your track work after a few hours of operation! Dirt and grease are sworn enemies of model railroading. It is imperative that you keep your track work as clean as possible for best operation. A word of caution is necessary at this point. Jim Sattler, a Lionel collector and operator whose word I trust implicitly, vehemently objects to sanding down the track in any manner. He says that such sanding removes the tinplate from the rail surfaces, making it susceptible to rust in areas of high humidity. He recommends that you use a "rust eraser" type of cleaner; these are similar to pencil erasers and they are, indeed, effective cleaners. I have never encountered a rust problem on my track as long as I have cleaned it regularly, and neither have any of my friends. However, Jim lives in Hawaii, and areas such as this may indeed make track highly susceptible to rust. If you live in such an area, by all means follow Jim's advice if you experience a rust problem.

IMPROVING TRACK APPEARANCE

I've saved the most outrageous trick with track for last; it involves decorating your track work to make it look like the real thing. Lionel's track, as it comes from the factory, is pretty bleak stuff as a rule. There it sits, with its three metal ties per section. When Lionel track is laid down without decoration, I always get the feeling that something is missing from the layout. The track really needs extra ties and a ballasting treatment.

The extra ties can be purchased on the market, but it's easier and a lot more fun to make your own. Get some balsa or basswood strips from your hobby supply shop for this purpose. You could also use the thin wooden strips from old window shades, if they happen to be available. Just make sure that they are the right thickness — 1/4" for O27 Gauge and 3/8" for O Gauge. You won't have to fasten them down separately; when you screw down the track, the ties will stay in place. In any event, the hard-shell ballast treatment I'm going to recommend will keep them from moving around.

Cut the strips with a jeweler's saw into pieces about two inches long. Four such pieces per track section will look good. After you've cut the pieces, get a can of dark walnut stain. Dip the ties into the stain and set them on newspaper to dry. Once they've dried, you will have made yourself some very authentic-looking ties.

The next step in your track treatment should be some kind of ballasting work along the track. The real railroads often had rock ballast which was almost manicured to look good. You can simulate this rock in any of several ways. One way is to cut wooden templates for straight and curved sections of track. Using these templates, cut lengths of black or gray asphalt roofing shingles and place them under your track and ties. This treatment can look quite good (roofing paper is also a good substance), but it is still a little too flat, dimensionally speaking. I think it is far better to get a three-dimensional look to the ballast by using a granular rock substance for the ballast. The trick is which granular substance to use, and how to keep it from spreading all over the layout.

The Life-Like Company makes many shades of prepared rock ballast for this purpose. So does the Woodland Scenics Company. These ballast materials usually consist of very fine crushed stone in any of several colors. When I did my first ballast treatment, I used this ballast stone. It looked great, to be sure, but I had to use over ten boxes of the ballast for my layout, and this was quite expensive. I considered several substances the next time; there was aquarium sand, fine crushed stone available from craft supply houses, and several others. My solution was none of these. I discovered a substance which yielded extremely realistic ballast work at a very low price. It really is one of the oldest layout tricks in the book, but it is surprisingly effective.

Are you ready for this?

The substance I used was — CAT LITTER!!!

Now, before you think I've taken complete leave of my senses, stop and think about the possible advantages of cat litter as a ballast material for your track work. It happens to be exactly the right scale of stonework for the size of Lionel trains. It is an absorbent clay material, so the hard-shell glue and water treatment for its installation will make it surprisingly durable. Since it costs less than two dollars for a ten-pound bag, it will last you through about five layouts! If it is done with a paint-spray treatment, it can look really great on a Lionel layout!

I know, I know — what if you have a cat in the house? This situation has been the basis of countless raw jokes and cartoons in railroad magazines for a long time. The truth is that a cat won't be very interested in this ballast once you are through with it, since you'll be using glue, paint, and solvent on your tracks. You won't be limited to modeling industrial oil spills!

The installation procedure for cat litter ballast involves nothing more than plain old white glue and water. Of course, all your electrical connections must be made before the ballast is installed,

The first step in the cat litter ballasting process is to put down some white glue full-strength as a "base" for the granules of cat litter. M. Feinstein photograph.

Third, spray a mix of 25 percent white glue and 75 percent water over the ballast, saturating it completely. Get any excess glue off the tracks with a dry cloth. Allow this to dry rock-hard for 24 hours before the final step. M. Feinstein photograph.

Second, spread the cat litter over the glue with a paper cup. "Manicure" your ballast with your fingers or (in the case of curves) a metal ruler before the next step.

For the last step in the ballasting process, let the ballast dry for about a day. Then give the track a light "dusting" with flat black or dark gray spray paint to give the ballast an "aged" and dirty look. M. Feinstein photograph.

because you certainly can't change them afterwards! Once your track and ties are in place and fastened to the layout, you're ready to begin your track ballasting treatment. Keep a supply of rags handy for periodic cleanup. This is a sloppy job!

I like to work in two-foot sections when I install cat litter ballast, for reasons which will soon become apparent. First of all, apply white glue straight from the bottle, full-strength, along the sides of the rails and between the ties. This will serve as a foundation for the cat litter as you apply it. After you have done this along a two-foot section (about two sections of track), put some cat litter into a paper cup; that's the only ballast spreading device you'll need. Sprinkle the cat litter along the rail sides and between the ties; be careful not to use too much or too little. Even out the cat litter by tamping it down with your finger. For curved track areas, I like to use a metal ruler to "manicure" the ballast as I go along. Take your time; this is not a job to be rushed! Try to keep the ballast off the ties so that the dark walnut ties you have painstakingly installed will show to their best advantage.

Now comes the really sloppy part! Get a small spray bottle. Into this, prepare a mixture of 25 percent white glue and 75 percent hot water. Some layout builders prefer a substance known as "matte medium" for their bonding solution. It dries to a flat finish, unlike the gloss of white glue. Add two or three drops of dish-washing detergent to keep the nozzle of your spray bottle clean. Carefully spray this mess onto the cat litter; make sure you absolutely saturate the granules. Some people are perfectionists enough to use an eyedropper for this step, but I think this is unduly fussy. Of course, glue and train wheels don't mix too well, so wipe off the glue-water mixture from the track surfaces as you go along. You might want to attach lengths of masking tape to the rail surfaces to shield them from the glue-water mix, but this is not absolutely necessary. Now you know why I like to work with only two feet of track at a time!

The last step in the ballasting process involves giving the ballast an aged, used look for greater realism. Let the above mess dry for about a full day. It will be rock-solid by that time. Get a can of flat black spray paint and give the ballast a light dusting (not a full paint job!) to simulate wear, dirt, and grime, as you would find on the real rights of way. Once again, either shield your rail surfaces with friction tape or use a rag to get the paint off the rail surfaces right away. Here, it is wise to keep working in two-foot sections.

The result of all this strange endeavor will be a very realistic treatment of a ballasted roadbed. Every once in a while, the cat litter will chip in places. This is no problem; simply repair the chipped places in the same way you built the roadbed. My own layout has bounced around in the back of a truck for nearly five years now — surely a treatment you won't inflict on your own layout! As it goes from show to show, I am greeted with the sound of loose cat litter every time I take off the covers. However, I have been able to repair it where needed, and the bulk of the ballast work is still in place.

I had mentioned that you can't easily change your electrical connections to the track after this step is taken. However, you can if necessary chip the ballast work away for any new connections. Simply use a flat-bladed screwdriver to chip the ballast away. I once had to replace one of my turnouts; I chipped all the ballast away and re-ballasted the track once the new turnout was in place. It's as good as new today. (The 1121 Turnout I replaced had developed a loose center rail which created a voltage drop; that's a peculiar weakness of this model. Make sure the center rail is tight when you purchase used examples of these turnouts.)

Once in a while, you may suffer from a corroded center pin between two of your track sections. This will cause a voltage drop from one track section to the other and, of course, wreak havoc with the smooth operation of your trains. Your first impulse will be to complain that you'll have to rip up all that ballast to insert a new pin into the track. There's an easier way! Get your soldering iron out and clean two spots on the sides of the rails of the two sections connected by the corroded track pin. Solder a "jumper" wire on the sides of the rails so this wire connects the two track sections and by-passes the corroded pin. I even avoided taking up another turnout in this way; the turnout had a voltage drop in its center rail which slowed down my inside loop locomotives for several track sections. To correct this problem, I soldered a wire to the center rail of the track before the turnout, sent it underneath the layout below the turnout, and soldered the other end to the center rail of the track immediately after the turnout. Problem solved!

Now that I seem to have begun a discussion of wiring procedures, it is time to turn to that particular part of layout construction. In the next chapter, I'll try to show you how to keep your platform's underside from looking like an explosion in a spaghetti factory! I'll discuss the kinds of wire to use, the transformer features you can utilize, the various methods of connecting wires from place to place, and many other items. Above all, I hope to introduce you to the wonderful idea of running more than one train at a time by using a great system of wiring called cab control. With this system, you can run any engine on any part of your layout without fear of collisions. You can perform intricate switching maneuvers which add a great deal of fun to your layout operations. See you on the next page!

CHAPTER VI

WIRING TECHNIQUES AND CAB CONTROL OPERATION

"What science is more fascinating than electricity
and its principles? Think, boys, how useful the
knowledge will be to you when you grow to manhood,
the electrical and mechanical knowledge that you will
gain while playing with your Lionel Outfit; the
problems in transportation that you will be able
to solve and the many other advantages you will
have when you are ready to fight life's battle."
— Joshua Lionel Cowen, 1923 *Lionel Catalogue*

"What! Will the line stretch out till the
crack of doom?"
— Shakespeare, *MacBeth*

It's little wonder that Joshua Lionel Cowen tried to promote the wonder of electricity in his company's earliest years. In those days, electricity was the equivalent of modern-day computer technology. In 1923, when Cowen himself wrote the quote above for his catalogue, rural electrification was gaining slow but steady progress, and new uses for electricity were being found all the time. Cowen reasoned — quite correctly — that as more and more homes got wired for electrical power, his electric trains would prosper all the more.

Actually, Cowen proposed electrical power sources for his early trains which would horrify us today, especially in view of the promotion of electric trains as playthings. At one point, about 1905 or so, Cowen and other makers actually sold large glass jars and lead plates, to which the consumer had to add his own supply of sulphuric acid to produce the electric power! He also suggested wiring the trains in series with an electric light bulb socket; if the connections to the track were not correctly placed, the track would be energized with 120-volt regular household current — an extremely dangerous situation. Safety was not the issue then that it is now; as late as the 1930s, Lionel recommended cleaning track with "a little gasoline on a cloth."

The first transformers were crude affairs by today's standards, but by 1907 they had begun to solve the problem of power to the tracks. A transformer for toy trains is a very simple device; a coil which is charged with 120-volt household current passes along a greatly reduced AC power through induction to a second coil. This coil is then tapped at various places to produce a certain amount of voltage. Up to 1938, surprisingly late, Lionel's transformers sent power to the track in staggered steps with no power between the steps. When Lionel began to make locomotives with remote-control reverse, the firm put out a continuously variable separate rheostat instead of modifying the transformers. Not until 1938, with the introduction of the R, V, and Z models, did Lionel issue transformers with continuously variable voltages, as we know them today.

This isn't really the place to get into an extended discussion of electrical theory, but perhaps it would be appropriate to understand electricity's basic nature. Electricity travels in a circuit and varies in strength. The most common analogy used is to compare the flow of electricity to the flow of water in a pipe. If you turn a valve open, you send more water through the pipe; similarly, a twist of a knob sends more electrical power along your wiring. If you use larger pipe, you can send more water through it; thicker wire can carry more electrical power in the same way. If you place an operating device somewhere in the electrical circuit, it can be made to do work, just as the placement of a faucet in a water circuit can make it produce water.

Of course, there are two basic kinds of electricity, alternating current and direct current. Alternating current (AC) moves back and forth in cycles, usually measured in cycles per second. Direct current (DC) functions just as its name suggests. Your household wiring is usually 110-120 volt, 60 cycle AC current. If you operate scale model trains, this AC current is converted into DC by means of a rectifying device. Lionel trains, however, were and are made mostly to operate on alternating current. They can, in fact, operate on direct current because Lionel's electric motors are of the universal type. Lionel's reversing switches, vibrator motors, and whistle/horn relays are all made to operate on AC, so most Lionel operators keep AC as their operating current rather than sacrifice these features. Lionel's motors run a great deal cooler on direct current, but alternating current is more versatile for operation of Lionel's accessories.

Lionel's AC electric motors are marvels of simplicity. Current is transferred from the track to carbon brushes which are in contact with copper commutator plates on an armature, which is

EPOXY COATED ARMATURE FOR RELIABLE INSULATION

Diagram of Lionel AC motor from the Lionel 1977 Catalogue.

a device with many turns of fine metal wire on a double-ended shaft. The current produces a magnetic field within the metal casing around the motor; this causes the armature to rotate as it is attracted to the metal. The rapid alternation of on-off current keeps the armature spinning within the magnetic field. If the armature is fixed to a set of gears, it will do work such as turn the shaft of a coal loader or turn the locomotive wheels.

TRANSFORMERS

With this as background, let us turn to a discussion of Lionel's transformers. Lionel has produced many different types of transformers over the years, but as a rule the better transformers feature variable voltage posts for the operation of the train and fixed voltage posts for the operation of accessories such as lights and operating devices. See Chapter III for a discussion of the recommended Lionel types for your particular use. Here, we want to stress how they make use of wiring to produce the power for your train layout. I have already said that you should invest in the best Lionel transformer you can secure. Now I'll go one step further. If you can possibly manage it, secure a transformer which is capable of running two or more trains right at the outset. It will be well worth the extra money! This is more than a matter of power; it's also a matter of flexibility. Two-throttle transformers will enable you to use a wiring system called Cab Control, which will really enrich your layout operations. I'll talk more about that system towards the end of this chapter.

Which two-throttle transformers are the best ones? That's a matter of application and available money. You can get a 100-watt Type R fairly inexpensively; this transformer has two knobs and two variable voltage ranges. However, it does not have whistle and direction controls. This lack can be remedied by securing two No. 167C Controllers and wiring them into the power wire circuits of the R Transformer. The old V and Z models, last catalogued in 1947, are excellent units with four variable voltage knobs. They have 150 watts (V) and 250 watts (Z) and can control as many as four trains. The usual practice is to run two trains off these transformers and use the other two variable voltage knobs for accessories and lights. That's what I have done with my R Transformer; one circuit runs street and other lights at ten volts, and the other powers accessories and searchlights at 14 volts.

The kings of the Lionel transformer empire are the 190-watt KW model and the 250- or 275-watt ZW monster. Both of these have built-in whistle and direction controls. The KW has a

separate 14-volt pair of terminals for constant voltage to the accessories, while the ZW has four variable circuits. These transformers have become quite expensive in recent years because Lionel can no longer make transformers of this size due to Federal toy safety regulations. (However, I have never heard of shock or injury of any kind caused by these transformers.) As a result, more people are chasing fewer transformers — a sure prescription for increasing prices if ever there was one!

There are some other possibilities in the twin-throttle transformer world. For many years, American Flyer, Lionel's chief competitor, made some excellent two-throttle transformers with as much as 350 watts of power. These transformers can be used with Lionel's 167C Controllers to provide whistle and direction controls. American Flyer's voltage taps for accessories are, however, not nearly as versatile as are Lionel's. The Troller Company, usually a producer of DC transformers for scale modelers, made its Model 2001 specifically for Lionel trains; it has two throttles. Finally, the brand-new, solid-state Lionel MW transformer can be used to power two trains by using its main control and the variable control usually used for accessories. It has whistle and direction controls. Lionel also made a twin-throttle 130-watt SW in the early 1960s which surfaces from time to time.

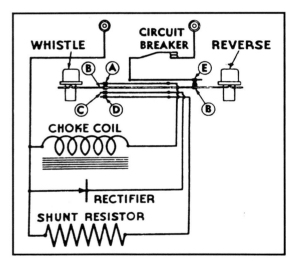

167 and 167C Controller.

If twin-throttle transformers are a little out of your reach right now, all is not lost. You can "phase" two single-throttle transformers together so you can achieve the same effect. Phasing the transformers means that you are going to have the AC current in both transformers pulsating in the same direction, not in opposition. Phasing transformers is done in the following manner: First, connect the ground posts of the two transformers together with a piece of wire. Usually, this will be the post marked "U"; Lionel's transformer plate will tell you which is the ground post. Next, attach one wire to the power post of one transformer (these are usually marked "A", but not always) and another wire to the power post of the other transformer. Move the throttle settings of the transformers about halfway up the dial so they are set approximately the same. Plug the transformers into your power supply. Touch the bare end of one of the power wires to the other. If you get a large spark, the transformers are out of phase. If you're worried about shorting out your transformers, use a light socket connected to one transformer's power lead. Touch the socket's

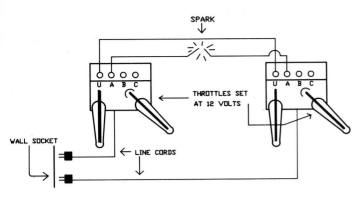

Phasing two type 1033 Transformers. Drawing by D. Dove.

other wire to the second transformer's power post. If the light shines, the transformers are out of phase. In either case, simply reverse one transformer's power cord plug in the wall socket. Now your transformers will be in phase. Leave the ground wire connecting the two transformers in place and mark off the cord plugs so you will know how to insert them. I'd suggest a power strip with its own on-off switch to avoid unplugging the transformers every time you run your trains. Hook up your two-train operation normally from this point on and split the auxiliary operations between the two transformers to even the load. Actually, you can connect four or even more transformers in this way to give you an awesome amount of power. Four 90-watt 1033 Transformers will cost you less than one ZW Transformer, give you considerable wiring flexibility and 85 more watts of power as well! However, if you happen to be running prewar locomotives, remember that these old motors were designed to run on 18 to 20 volts. The top voltage output of the 1033 is only 16 volts.

Even the inexpensive small transformers such as the many types included in inexpensive sets have many practical uses. These transformers, which usually have just two wire terminals and range from 25 to 50 watts in power, are excellent for use in powering lighting systems and accessories. They take the load off your main transformer so it can run trains more efficiently. The best bets for auxiliary transformers may be the ancient B, T, and K types made in the 1920s and 1930s. Believe it or not, these transformers are still around in shops and at train shows. They were very well made, but they are not really suitable for running trains because of their click-stop construction. However, these old transformers feature as many as six voltage ranges and many taps for constant voltage use, so they are excellent as power sources for lights and accessories. Check the integrity of the power cord before you purchase one of these old transformers. If it is worn or frayed, you can pry the cover off the transformer and solder a modern power cord onto the primary coil windings where the old cord is attached. It's also a good idea to place a circuit breaker into your main leads off the old transformers. Lionel's No. 91 is perfect for this job. If you are going to use an auxiliary transformer, I recommend keeping the circuits for this transformer entirely separate from your main transformer. In other words, do not use a track-activated accessory on your auxiliary transformer. Use the auxiliary for constant voltage to lights and accessories which operate independently of track contacts. This will eliminate the necessity for phasing the two transformers because the auxiliary transformer will have its own separate ground circuit. For accessories which require a track clip, use the main transformer's auxiliary circuits.

It is quite desirable to have a transformer with whistle and direction controls, even if you do not operate the older whistle and horn units in some of Lionel's postwar trains because of their age. Nowadays, Lionel's diesel horns and steam engine whistles are electronic, but like the older units, they are designed to be activated by a burst of direct current from the whistle controller. When you move the whistle controller, you activate a copper oxide rectifier disc which sends a burst of DC called "pickup voltage" to the track, activating either a DC relay in the older models or a special circuit in the newer models. Moving the controller further up reduces the DC into a "holding voltage," which keeps the whistle or horn operating. The older diesel locomotives used a dry cell for power to the horn unit; if you purchase any of these locomotives, be sure to check for damage from battery leakage.

Lionel's reversing units operate either mechanically or electronically. The mechanical units, by far the most common, operate through a rotating drum and pawl system which changes the position of the electrical contacts to the motor every time the current is interrupted. Some of these E-Units, as they are known, have only two positions, forward-reverse. The better locomotives have a three-position reversing sequence, forward-neutral-reverse-neutral, etc. The neutral position is needed for the operation of cars which need current from the track. Obviously, the locomotive has to be stationary for these cars to operate.

The majority of Lionel's transformers have a built-in direction control button or lever which interrupts the current. For those which do not have this button, you'd have to turn the throttle back to its off position all the time — a decided nuisance. The 167C Controller has a direction control as well as a whistle control, but if you decide that you can use a separate diesel horn shed or steam whistle shed, two of Lionel's most popular accessories, there is another possibility. Lionel's old No. 88 Controller is readily available. This is a button control which allows current to be normally on, unlike many of Lionel's control buttons, which supply current only when the button is pushed. When you push the button of the No. 88, you interrupt the current and activate the locomotive's reverse mechanism. Simply install these button switches into the transformer's power lead, and you'll have your direction control.

Most of Lionel's transformers are protected by circuit breakers. These are devices which protect the transformer and wiring from damage by cutting off the power from the trans-

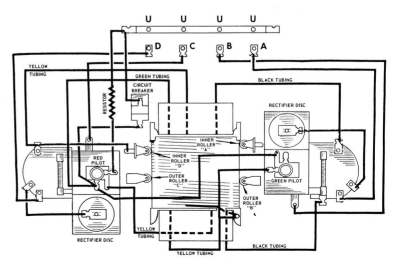

Pictorial Wiring Diagram of ZW Transformer Model R.

TRANSFORMER TROUBLESHOOTING

PROBLEM	SOLUTION
Transformer hums normally; loco does not light; loco does not run.	Check wires to track. Check power on track with test bulb or lighted car. Change loco E-unit position. Check loco bulb. Push train on track.
Transformer is THROBBING and not humming normally; loco does not hum and does not run.	Short circuit. Operate transformer 10 seconds or less. Check for derailed cars. Find source of short!
Transformer hums normally; loco lights, but does not run and does not hum.	Change loco E-unit position.
Transformer THROBS; loco lights dimly, loco hums but does not run.	Short circuit. Operate transformer 10 seconds or less. Check for derailed cars. Find source of short!
Transformer hums normally; loco runs but does not light	Check loco bulb.
Transformer hums normally; loco runs only one direction; loco lights.	Change loco E-unit position.
Transformer hums normally loco lights and hums; loco does not run.	Change loco E-unit position.

former in the event of an electrical overload such as a "short circuit." Short circuits occur mostly when any substance which conducts electricity contacts both the center and the outside rail of the track. Sometimes locomotives develop internal short circuits, but this is an infrequent occurrence. The most insidious cause of a short circuit I can recall is a shifted piece of insulation in the center rail of a piece of track. This allows the center rail to touch the metal tie and short out the system, and it is very difficult to find and repair. Care in selecting your track should prevent this nasty problem. The most common cause of a short circuit is derailment of a locomotive or a car on the tracks. If the circuit breaker is operating properly, it will snap open and, on some transformers, a red light will go on, indicating the short. When the cause of the short circuit is removed, the circuit breaker will snap back and the transformer will again send power to the rails.

Most of Lionel's transformers use a chip-type circuit breaker. There is a specific problem with this circuit breaker which seems to occur in the big ZW Transformers. Once I was operating my layout at a show, and the ZW's circuit breaker began to snap open at very low voltages. I would push the button of my Operating Milk Car and see the red light go on! After borrowing another transformer for the rest of the show, I examined the chip-type circuit breaker. It had opened and closed so many times over the life of the transformer that it had developed metal fatigue; that allowed the points of the breaker to open far too easily. The solution to this problem is to replace the chip-type circuit breaker with a more durable Bakelite-encased unit now made by Texas Instruments. This unit is an exact replacement for the first circuit breakers used in the ZW models in their first few years of production. Detach the wires from the chip-type breaker, take it off the transformer, and attach the wires to the two terminals of the Bakelite-type breaker. Push the Bakelite breaker down into the lower left corner of the transformer casing near the base so it will be out of harm's way. After I replaced the chip-type breaker with this model, I got flawless performance from my ZW. I would advise replacement of the chip breaker as soon as it develops problems.

One more element of circuit breakers is worth mentioning. For transformers which do not have a built-in circuit breaker, Lionel at one time in the late 1950s offered a No. 91 Adjustable Circuit Breaker for installation into the transformer's power line. These units are still easy to find, and they work quite well. They can be tested by adjusting the knob under load until the circuit breaker snaps and the light in the unit goes on. The No. 91 is reset by pushing a rectangular button which closes the electrical points.

WIRING YOUR LAYOUT

The wire you use for wiring your layout should be determined by its appropriateness for a particular use. Lionel trains are designed to operate on low voltage from the transformer, usually between 8 and 16 volts. As a result, you will not have to use heavy wire for your trains. Wire is measured by gauge; the lower the number of the gauge, the thicker the wire. Ordinary lamp cord, which is designed to carry normal 120-volt household current, is 16- or 18-gauge stranded wire; this is really too heavy for your use except on very large layouts. For the main leads to your transformer and the ground wiring (off the U terminals of your transformer), I would recommend stranded audio speaker wire of 20-gauge thickness. This should be ample for the heaviest current draw you are likely to encounter. For the rest of your electrical connections, secure both solid and stranded wires of 20-gauge thickness. Solid copper telephone wire is excellent for many toy train applications; this wire is 20- or 22-gauge in thickness. Some wire comes as thin as 24-gauge; this wire is difficult to work with.

The insulation on the wires should come in several colors so you can use one particular color for each circuit. For example, I have six circuits on my layout, four from the ZW Transformer and two from the auxiliary R Transformer. I use black wire for the ground "U" post off the ZW, orange for the ZW-A circuit, white for the ZW-B circuit, green for the ZW-C circuit, yellow for the ZW-D circuit, black again for the R ground circuit, purple for the R-B (10 volt) circuit, and blue stripe for the R-F (14-volt) circuit. I use red wire for all the power leads from the insulated cab control blocks. In that way, I know which wire leads to which circuit, and I can track down trouble much more easily than with random coloring of the wires.

Stranded and solid wires each have particular advantages. Stranded wire is much more flexible than solid wire, so I use this wire to reach difficult spots where the wire has to be bent to reach a terminal. I also use this wire when I have to solder wire to a track because it holds much better than a solid wire. Solid wire does not have the flexibility of stranded wire, but it is better to use when it has to be attached to the Fahnstock clip of a track lockon or an accessory. These Fahnstock clips are all-time fingernail breakers! To attach a wire to one of these clips, you must press down on the clip while you insert the wire through a projection. When you release the end of the clip, spring tension holds the wire in place. Personally, I much prefer to work with the posts and knurled nuts of transformers and some accessories, but often you will have no choice but to work with Fahnstock clips. If you use stranded wire, twist the ends tight before insertion into the clip.

I have found it advantageous to use spade lugs on the ends of wires which fasten to screw terminals or knurled nuts and posts. These little lugs, easily available at electrical supply houses, prevent bare wires from unraveling at the posts and screws, and they simplify connections readily. They come in insulated and non-insulated varieties. To attach these spade lugs (also available in circular and hook shapes), you'll need a crimping tool. Strip the insulation off one end of the wire, leaving about 1/4" of the wire bare. For stripping wire, I've found linesmen's pliers very valuable. Some train dealers offer several varieties of wire strippers which will strip the insulation off as many as five wires at once; these strippers are very valuable for work with three- and four-wire cables. Next, place the spade lug into the crimping tool, insert the wire through the spade lug, and crimp the lug onto the end of the wire. You should secure spade lugs which are designed for wire gauges 18 through 22. Then, simply insert the spade lug into the screw or nut terminal and tighten. These wires should stay put!

There are also quite a few varieties of lockons for attaching power to the track. By far the most common is the Lionel CTC type, which snaps onto the track and uses two Fahnstock clips for wire attachment. Lionel has also made larger UTC Universal Lockons which can be useful. For some operating accessories, there is an OTC Lockon with operating blades to contact operating shoes on some freight cars. The best of the Lionel lockons is the illuminated LTC Lockon, which can be expensive but is useful in a cab control wiring setup. The LTC Lockon lights when power is applied to the track. As a result, you can check each separately wired block for power. Additionally, the LTC features good old post and nut wire terminals rather than the Fahnstock clips.

Other manufacturers have made similar lockon devices. I have made it a point to secure some of the old Marx lockons because they attach to the track differently than the Lionel CTC type. Sometimes the Lionel lockons work themselves loose and cause problems. The Marx lockons attach to the track from underneath; they have two metal blades which are inserted into the gaps where the rails are crimped together. This arrangement is shielded from dirt and grease much better and does not work loose.

Of course, you can bypass the use of lockons altogether in many instances by soldering the wire directly to the track. Many people prefer to do this because of the positive connection to the rails. Clean off areas on the center rail and one of the outside rails to be used for the connections. For soldering applications to tinplate, use resin-core solder, never acid-core solder, which can cause corrosion and bad connections. I highly recommend the gun-type soldering iron with a separate hand-held trigger over the cheaper pencil-types, which are slow to warm up and corrode too easily. The better pencil-type irons are very handy for locomotive and accessory repair, where precision is needed. Of course, be careful not to let the tip slip onto your finger or hand! You should heat both the surface of the rail and the end of the wire before you attach the wire. Once that is done, let the solder flow over the heated surfaces, withdraw the iron, and allow the solder to cool before you move the wire. It is wise to use a glove on the hand holding the wire; remember that metal conducts heat and blisters hurt! As an alternative to soldering, you might also consider inserting the wires right into the ends of the track rails as you assemble your track. Another method involves jamming a spade lug into the gap on the underside of the rails.

You will soon find that wires have a tendency to proliferate as you add more and more accessories. For example, each turnout requires three wires, and I have eight of these on my layout. (The ground wire from the controller can be connected right to the transformer ground wire instead of the turnout itself.) Some accessories require four-cable wire as well. Each remote track needs anywhere from one to four wires. Many of the accessories require three wires. Add all this to your main operational wiring, and you've got quite a bit of wire! If you don't have some system for keeping it all under control, you'll wind up with quite a mess at your transformer terminals!

I've devised a system for extending the terminals of the transformer all around the layout. I call it the Bus Bar System because it uses commercially available strip terminals with as many as a dozen screw attachments. I have no fewer than 45 of these little terminal strips under my layout, and I have found that they not only simplify the wiring process, but also save wire in

the long run. These terminal strips with flat-headed screws are commonly used in electronic applications and are available in many sizes from such places as Radio Shack. Purchase several sizes of these bus bars, enough for all your transformer circuits.

To prepare the bus bars for your layout, you must first interconnect all the screw terminals. I did this by using some uninsulated fine doorbell wire. Attach one end of the wire to one screw terminal at the end of the bus bar and wind the wire around the bar so it touches all the screws. Then fasten the other end of the wire to a screw at the other end of the bus bar and clip it off.

Now you are ready to install the bus bars under your layout. This step should be done before any track is put down on the platform. (See why I wanted you to read all of Chapters IV, V, and VI before you began your construction?) Install a short row of four-screw bus bars near where your transformer will be. There should be one four-screw bus bar for each of the transformer's circuits. Use a marker and mark the platform near the bus bars with the transformer circuit they will service. For example, my bus bars are marked with the transformer and its circuit, such as ZW-U, ZW-A, R-F, and so on. When you are ready to install your transformer, all you will have to do is run one wire per circuit up to the transformer terminals themselves.

Now you should install the remaining bus bar terminals all around the layout. Begin with the ground, or U terminals, since these will be the most numerous. Install several of these ground terminals all around the perimeter of the layout, being sure to label them as you go along. Interconnect each of the bus bars with black wire (remember your color coding). Connect the last of the terminals with the small bus bar leading up to the transformer. For uniformity of the circuit, you should connect each of the two bus bars around the perimeter with the transformer's lead-in terminal.

For the rest of the transformer's circuits, install bus bars in a straight line from one end of the layout to the other. Label these as you go along, interconnect them with the proper color-coded wire, and attach the nearest one to the transformer's lead-in terminal. This is admittedly a tedious job, but it will pay dividends when you start wiring your layout. Use spade lugs to attach the wires to the screw terminals; wires will have less of a tendency to work loose. As you're working from the underside of the layout, you might want to put a blanket on any cold concrete garage or basement floor for your own comfort. An automotive mechanic's creeper would be an excellent device to use in this operation as well as a portable extension light for good vision. Safety goggles are essential for overhead soldering.

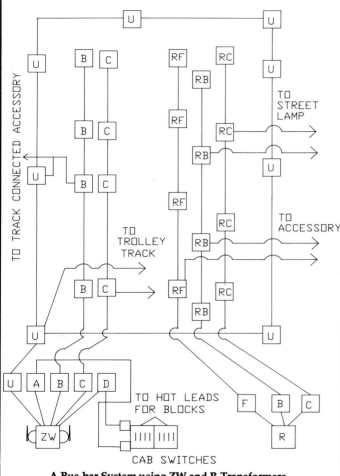

A Bus-bar System using ZW and R Transformers.

The ZW Transformer has four available circuits. One circuit is used for accessories (Posts B and U), another circuit for a trolley (Posts C and U), and two circuits for two trains operating under cab control (A and U) (D and U). The ZW has four U posts which are internally connected. All four circuits require a hookup to U. Each circuit can be hooked up to any wire running from the U post. Consequently the layout includes a single heavy copper wire called a bus-bar from U running around the layout to facilitate hookup. This substantially reduces the amount of wiring under the table. The R Transformer is hooked up to two circuits, one circuit is used for accessories (Posts B and F set at 14 volts) and one for street lamps (Posts B and C set at 10 volts). Note that a wire (a bus-bar) from Post B is used for both circuits and reduces under table wiring. Drawing by D. Dove.

A wide assortment of Lionel and other controllers, buttons, and lockons, all of which have specific applications on a tinplate layout. The two lockons flanking the Lionel lighted LTC model are American Flyer models for S Gauge. M. Feinstein photograph.

Once all this is done, you've extended the terminals of your transformer, and your wiring of the layout should be much easier. For example, when you're installing a street light, all you have to do is install one wire to the nearest "U" bus bar and one wire to the nearest bar on the circuit you'll be using for constant voltage operation. In that fashion, the only long wires you'll have to deal with are those used for turnouts at the far end of the layout and those used for buttons for the operating accessories. This system really does bring your wiring under control!

Jim Sattler has suggested stringing uninsulated copper wire all along the perimeter of the layout and soldering the connections for accessories, etc. to these wires. While this is certainly less expensive, it involves soldering wires from beneath the layout. Not many beginners are adept at this practice, which carries certain safety hazards.

Inevitably, you'll have to splice wire underneath the platform for some applications. This task occurs most frequently with turnout wiring and street lights. To splice wires, you can use double-ended crimping connectors or plug connectors, but this isn't really necessary. Simply strip the ends of the wires to be spliced, securely twist them together, and apply twist connectors or electrical tape to the bare connected ends. Be sure your connections are absolutely tight. When properly done, these splices should hold up with no trouble. You'll certainly get plenty of practice as you go along! Make sure that your electrical tape covers the bare wires completely so there is no possibility of a difficult-to-detect short circuit.

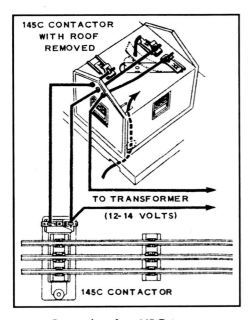

Connections for a 145 Gateman.

Of course, each accessory, lamp, and track connection has its own specific circuitry. That's one excellent reason to secure a fine repair and operator's manual before you build your layout. These manuals not only give schematics for repair purposes, but also wiring diagrams for the correct connection of the accessories to the transformer and/or track. Additionally, the new accessories are always sold with an instruction sheet, and even the older ones have instruction sheets available. Make sure that you follow the individual item's directions and use the correct operating buttons or switches and recommended voltages.

Once you have done all your wiring, you should have no real maintenance problems with it except possibly for the corrosion of center-rail track pins over time. You'll know about this when your locomotives slow down over a particular piece of track. To check this, use a voltmeter or continuity tester. If there is a drop between two sections of track, simply solder a "jumper" wire between the two tracks to bypass the center rail pin. In this way, you won't have to wreck your ballast treatment to replace the pin.

A few more basic matters should take you through basic wiring techniques before I introduce you to Cab Control, one of the best ways to run any layout. Many of you will use trestle work on your layouts to elevate one or more of your track loops. I'll discuss the use of trestles and bridges in the next chapter on scenery, but one operational problem will be inherent to trestles and grades on your layout. Your train will always slow down on an upgrade and speed up on a downgrade, thanks to good old gravity. If you're operating a heavy train or using a locomotive designed for lighter service, your upgrades may slow your trains down to an unacceptable degree. On your downgrades, your train may even speed up to the point where it is in dire peril at the next curve on your layout. Since you don't want your trains to act anemic — or like the reincarnation of an Olympic platform diver as they fly off your layout — some method of controlling speeds on the up and downgrades will be necessary.

There are two basic ways to solve this problem. One of them — perhaps a little difficult — will solve the downgrade problem but not the upgrade problem. Block off the downgrade area by inserting nylon pins into the center rails where the beginning and the end of the downgrade will be located. Then, use a lockon to hook up this insulated block to the transformer as usual, but purchase an adjustable resistor (potentiometer) from an electrical supply house and insert it into the power line. This resistor will cut down the power to the insulated block slightly if it is adjusted properly and allow your train to slow down on the downstroke of the trestle work.

That still leaves the upgrade problem, however, and I think there's a better answer for both the downgrade and the upgrade. For this answer, make an insulated block for both the upgrade and the downgrade. Now, instead of wiring these blocks to your main transformer, wire them to two small 25-50 watt transformers. Remember when I said that Lionel's smaller transformers can make terrific auxiliary power units? Here's one example of that! When you're running your train, increase the voltage from your upgrade transformer until your train goes up the trestle satisfactorily; of course, this transformer has to deliver higher operating voltage than you're normally using to run the train from your main transformer. Similarly, adjust the throttle of the downgrade transformer below your normal train operating voltage until your train slows down enough on the downgrade to operate safely.

There are many advantages to hooking up your accessories to constant voltage instead of track voltage. For one thing, Lionel's newest locomotives often use a "can-type" motor which operates much more efficiently than Lionel's big universal motors. If your train runs around the track at a good speed at, say, 10-11 volts, track voltage may not give enough power to lower crossing gates or activate ringing signals. The procedure for constant voltage is very simple. If, for example, you're running a crossing gate off an insulated track, connect the first post of the gate to the No. 2 clip of the lockon so that the train will activate it. However, instead of connecting the second post of the gate to the No. 1 clip of the lockon, run a wire from it down to a connection to a constant voltage line of your transformer. In the case of the ZW, this might be the B or C circuit which will be set at a snappy 14 volts. Now your accessory will operate crisply no matter what voltage is in the track. It also means that you'll have more available voltage to run the trains themselves. Many of Lionel's accessories feature alternative wiring diagrams which make use of constant voltage; make use of it whenever you can. If you're using an auxiliary transformer, make sure that you wire track-activated accessories to constant voltage posts on the main transformer. The auxiliary transformer by its very nature is a constant voltage device, and it can be used for many track side accessories which do not depend upon a track connection.

CAB CONTROL SYSTEMS

Now, let us discuss one of the universal truths of Lionel railroading. Every Lionel operator agrees that it's a great deal more fun to operate two trains at once — or more — rather than just one train. All along, I've been steering you in the direction of a two-train layout. Now I'll detail a terrific system of operation which will make this operation possible and greatly increase the potential complexity of the switching moves you can perform — without danger of collisions! This is the Cab Control System, and to me it is the best way to operate a small to medium layout.

There are many ways to run more than one train on a layout. Some operators have designed complex relay systems so they can run more than one train on the same track without fear of collisions. These systems can be designed to operate from AC relays or from insulated track sections in one insulated block which cut the power from the block immediately preceding it. The reversing switches of the locomotives have to be set so the locomotives can only go forward, an easy procedure. This is a very good way to run trains on a large layout, but the wiring is such that the beginner may not have a very easy time setting it up. Other operators have blocked off their trackage into insulated blocks and wired each one to an on-off switch so they can "stall" a train in one block while a second locomotive proceeds onto the first train's right of way for switching. That's not bad, but simple on-off switches have limitations because the operating train will have to bridge any voltage gap between the two loops; otherwise, the reversing switch will activate and the train will stall out. There's a better way which uses single-pole, double-throw switches with A, B, and center-off positions. Along with blocking off the track into separately wired sections, these special switches are the heart of the Cab Control System.

To understand the idea of cab control, think of the transformer as being connected to the locomotive, not the track. The track is simply the medium of power transfer and steering for the locomotive. If you have constructed a smaller layout, it is highly likely that you have made a track plan with two loops, possibly connected by four turnouts which provide you with an interchange track on the inside loop with an uncoupler track located between the turnouts on that inside loop. The secret of cab control, of course, is to separate your connected loops electrically into separately wired sections which we call blocks. If you can do this, you can turn the power on and off at will in each block, just as you can with simple on-off switches. However, with the use of single-pole, double-throw switches with a center-off position, you can assign each throttle of your two-throttle transformer to a particular engine and use that throttle to control it no matter where it is on the layout. You can't do that with a simple on-off switch.

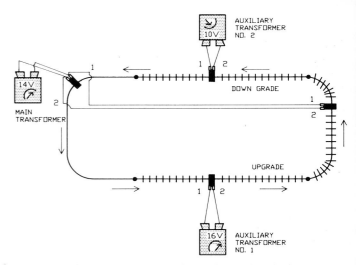

Controlling train speed on grades with auxiliary transformers. Drawing by D. Dove.

This arrangement enables you to use the interchange track so one locomotive can place a car on that track and the other locomotive can pick it up and put it into its train.

Now you can see why a two-throttle transformer (or two separate transformers wired in phase, as described earlier) is so desirable for a small to medium layout. You will also need those single-pole, double-throw switches with a center-off position. Fortunately for all of us, the Atlas Company, a manufacturer of electrical equipment for HO and N Scale trains, makes these switches as its Model 215 Selector Switch. These switches come in units of four which can be connected to each other; they are inexpensive and they work very well with Lionel layouts. Keep a generous supply of the proper nylon insulating pins and lockons handy as well.

To wire your layout for Cab Control operation, divide all your track into blocks by inserting a nylon pin into the center rail of your track at either end of the block. I have seven blocks in my system, three on the outside loop, three on the inside loop, and one on a spur siding where I can keep a locomotive as "reserve power" and activate it when I want to change locomotives on one of the trains. Try to find a way to mark the blocks visually so you will know where one block ends and another begins. In my case, I used lighted LTC Lockons on the first track of my blocks running right to left. In that way, I know just where to place my engines so I can get them out of the way.

Now, attach a lockon to each one of the blocked sections of track. Run a wire from the No. 2 lockon clip (outer rail) to the nearest U, or ground wire, under your layout. Next, run a wire from the No. 1 clip of the lockon (center rail) to one of the little screw terminals on the top of the Atlas 215 Switches. Label these slide switches 1, 2, etc. to correspond with your desired block numbers. My Block 1 covers the turnouts leading to the interchange track and all the track between them on the outside loop, for example. Blocks 2 and 3 split up the rest of the loop about evenly. My Block 4 does the same thing to the inner loop's part of the interchange track and two track sections beyond the turnouts in that loop. Blocks 5 and 6 split up the rest of the inner loop, and Block 7 controls the spur siding with the relief locomotive.

Now, attach the Atlas switches to the transformer by running one wire from the screw terminal at the top left of the switch box to the outside throttle circuit of the transformer. When the

Atlas slide switch is thrown to the top "A" position, that throttle will control the block. Attach another wire to the screw terminal at the bottom left of the Atlas switch box and run this wire to the inside throttle circuit of your transformer. When the Atlas slide switch is in the down or "B" position, that throttle will control the block instead of the outer throttle. When the Atlas slide switch is in the center position, all power to the individual block will be turned off. The Atlas switch boxes can be connected to each other by means of little metal "tangs" on the left side of the switch boxes. Be sure to interconnect all the switch boxes in that manner.

After this wiring is done, you're ready to operate the layout. It is simple and pleasurable to do this because of the fancy interchanges you can perform. Let us assume that you have Train A running in the outer loop, which has three cab control blocks which you have numbered 1, 2, and 3. Meanwhile, another train, Train B, is running on the inside loop, which also has three blocks labeled 4, 5, and 6. The normal position of the Atlas switches will be as follows during normal running: Switches 1, 2, and 3 will be in the top or A position controlled (in the case of the ZW) by the right-hand throttle lever. Switches 4, 5, and 6 will be in the bottom or B position controlled by the left-hand throttle lever.

Let's assume that you have the Fort Knox Mint Car with a shipment of gold bullion on one of your inside sidings, and you want to put it on your outside train, which is a fast (relatively speaking, of course!) passenger express train. You want to have your express engine go inside to pick up the car, but your inside peddler freight is in the way and will collide with the express engine. How can you get your express engine into the siding to pick up the bullion car? It's easy with Cab Control operation! Here's how it's done:

STEP 1: Stop the inside train in the block just before your siding turnout. Just for the sake of argument, let's assume that this section of track is located in Block 6. Turn the Atlas switch for Block 6 to its center-off position. This will cut off all power to the peddler freight.

STEP 2: Blocks 1, 2, and 3 for the fast express are already in the A position. Now, move the Atlas switches for Blocks 4 and 5 from the B position to the A position. You have now enabled your express locomotive to go into the siding by transferring the

These are the Atlas No. 215 Selector Switches used in a cab control application. The wire at the left top side leads to the inside handle of the ZW Transformer, which controls the inside train in Blocks 4-7. The one at the bottom left side leads to the outside handle for the outside train in Blocks 1-3. The switch at the far right isn't used on my layout, but for illustration purposes it's in the center-off position. The wires at the top lead to the center-rail terminals of each block lockon. M. Feinstein photograph.

power for those blocks to the throttle which controls the express engine.

STEP 3: Using the same throttle, perform your switching operation. Run the express locomotive into the inside loop, pick up the bullion car in the siding, come out of the inside loop, and couple back onto the passenger train.

STEP 4: Simply return Blocks 4 and 5 to the B position, activate the train in Block 6, and resume normal operations! It's that easy!

If you have an interchange track, as I've suggested, you can have your inside locomotive take the car out of the siding, drop off the car on the interchange track, and move your blocks so the outside locomotive then picks it up from the interchange track. If you have insulated a block which controls a siding with a relief locomotive, you can maneuver the blocks so the engines are exchanged very realistically. You could become a mad scientist in a Frankensteinian laboratory with all the switching maneuvers you could devise with this system!

There's another big advantage to having Cab Control wiring on your layout; it has to do with locating a short circuit. Sometimes short circuits are troublesome to locate. In an ordinary layout, all the track work would have to be checked to find the source of the short circuit. In a Cab Control layout, it's easy to narrow down the location of a short. All you have to do is turn the power on with one of the throttles and move all the Atlas slide switches to the center-off position. Then, one by one, move the switches to the position powered by the open throttle. If the block does not have a short circuit, there will be no dimming of the power light on the transformer or activation of the circuit breaker. Try all the blocks, one by one, until you have located the block with the short circuit. You will then know the location of your problem without having to search through your entire layout.

What's that, you say? You want to run three trains instead of just two? Can Cab Control be adapted to a three-train system? Yes, it can! It's quite a bit more complicated to wire, but it can work very well. Obviously, you'll need three block switch positions instead of two. You would need single-pole, triple-throw switches for this, but even if such complex switches might be available, they are likely to be somewhat expensive. (Someone at an electrical supply house can advise you about this.)

Unfortunately, since the Atlas 215 Selector Switches are all interconnected, you won't be able to use them in a three-train Cab-Control layout. However, you can make use of individual single-pole, double-throw switches in pairs. You would run one wire from the first switch to the throttle of the single transformer. The other wire from this switch would be connected to the second switch in such a way that only if the first switch is in the down, or B, position would the second switch of the pair be activated. This second switch would have two wires running to each of the throttles of the twin-throttle transformer, and its position would determine which of these throttles controls a given block. You will need a pair of SPDT switches for each block on your layout. It's complicated, but it works!

If you're really ambitious and you have a large layout with three trains or more running, you might also wish to construct a remote cab layout. Basically, this type of layout would involve the same set-up as the three-train operation described above, but an extra transformer would be located at a different part of the layout — or even totally duplicate controls! By interconnecting all the blocks between the given transformers and then separating the main power leads of the transformers with a simple A-B two-position switch, you can turn over the controls of the layout from one operator to another at a completely different location!

My own experience with Lionel trains does not extend to complex remote cab operations or computer-controlled train operation with special operating programs, but if you're more experienced with electronics than I am, you could devise some really complicated operating schemes, all based upon the Cab

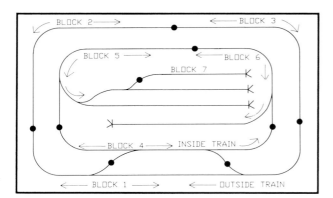

Cab control blocks and settings for two-train operation. The symbol "•" denotes an insulating pin in the center rail. Note that Block 5 controls two inner sidings; Block 6 controls the outer siding; and Block 7 controls only a "spare locomotive" siding. To move inside locomotive onto outside track, "store" outside train in Block 3 with power off and set Blocks 1 and 2 to inside throttle. To move outside locomotive into switch yards, "store" inside train in Block 6 with power off and set Blocks 4 and 5 to outside throttle. Normal operations: Blocks 1, 2, and 3 at "A" setting. Blocks 4, 5, and 6 at "B" setting. Block 7 at center-off position. Activate when changing engines. Drawing by D. Dove.

Control principle. Many books on operating Lionel trains describe such systems, so I will leave the details to them. I would suggest trying a simple two-train Cab Control operation at the outset until you feel confident enough to use more intricate operating systems. A word about Cab Control and Lionel's new RailScope system is in order here. In RailScope, a video transmitter in a locomotive sends a pulse wave through the track, where it is picked up by an electronic unit which sends it to a television, giving you an "engineer's eye" view of your layout. Although it eats up 9-volt batteries at an alarming rate, it's quite spectacular. If you've insulated your center rails, however, as you would in Cab Control, you'll only get a picture from one small layout segment. Instead of hooking the transmission leads to the track, hook one lead directly to the "U" post of your transformer. Attach the other lead to the side of the Atlas 215 Selector Switch on whichever terminal leads to the throttle controlling the RailScope locomotive. Put the end of this lead on an alligator clip so you can switch from upper to lower connections. Then you'll get the RailScope picture from all the blocks which are in the position corresponding to the wire connection.

Now we have your platform built, your track work down, your wiring in place, and your trains running. That's several big steps forward! There is more to come, however, since you would be looking at vast expanses of bare plywood without a discussion of scenery and decorations. This is an area where your imagination can really come into play. Good scenery and decorating effects — trees, buildings, human figures, etc. — can make your layout riveting and interesting to the viewer. One of the great things about using scenery on a Lionel layout is that many times you can build something out of simple junk around your own house! It is time to toss around such terms as "kitbashing," "scratch-building," and many others. Let us now turn our attention to the finishing touches for your layout. Keep your glue, paints, model knives, and tools handy!

Above: An early summer afternoon, the trees are in full leaf and a thunderstorm has swept through tearing branches and leaves from trees. Everyone is going shopping and the streets are crowded with cars. Jones, a collector of old trucks, is taking his classic vehicle out for a ride. Greenberg's 48-foot layout, M. Feinstein photograph.

Below: A view across one of the 4-foot wide center sections of the 48-foot layout. Walthers scenic background paper provides an illusion of great depth. The Daylight locomotive engineered by Bill Dyson provides regular passenger service. M. Feinstein photograph.

CHAPTER VII

SCENERY AND DECORATIONS

"In my beginning is my end.
In succession
Houses rise, crumble,
Are gone."

— T. S. Eliot

"Let your eye stretch down that expanse of steel rail,
farther than it can see physically, far enough to reach
the city, where the four-track main line becomes open
expanses of railroad yards and terminals ... Here, the
commerce of a nation rests on its journey to its final
destination, sitting on long tracks nestled between
block after block of dirty dilapidated houses and
soot-filled patches of barren ground."

— Robert Carper, **American Railroads In Transition**

These days, Lionel trains are depicted in the catalogues by themselves, as if they are just another product waiting to be packaged. Actually, there has been a concerted effort in the last few years to change that "merchandise" look, but I can't help but compare the modern Lionel catalogues to the ones issued in the prewar and postwar years, when Lionel was king of the toy world. In those days, Lionel trains were more than pieces of merchandise; they were part of the dreams of children. To be part of those dreams, the trains had to be depicted against a backdrop of reality —which meant railroad workers, cars, roads, villages, mountains, and so forth. Talented artists were often employed by Lionel to achieve this illusion of reality. I know that when I was young, many of my elementary school classmates and I brightened up otherwise dull lessons with clandestine looks at smuggled catalogues! We imagined ourselves right inside those engines, piloting the trains of our imagination through a complete and realistic backdrop of imitative reality. (With Lionel's new Rail-Scope, it may be possible to achieve that effect literally!)

Just for one example, take a look at the 1954 Lionel Catalogue, one of the very best. On one page, there is an artist's beautiful rendition of the 2356 Southern A-B-A Triple Diesels available that year. The locomotives are pulling a train of Lionel freight cars past workmen alongside a dockyard scene. In the background is a sleek one-stack ocean liner which is a dead ringer for the Italian Line's magnificent ships plying the Atlantic at the time, the *Cristoforo Colombo* and the ill-fated and better-known *Andrea Doria*. Now, that's a dream scene!

Toy trains are not an entity unto themselves. For the full magic of Lionel trains, your locomotives and cars must be seen against a convincing illusion of reality, not just languish as objects in a display case on a shelf. Only when these trains are part of that illusion do they work their full wonder upon you. The way to create that illusion is, of course, through the skillful construction of layout scenery. Do you remember that in the first part of this book I said that you would create an empire over which you would be the absolute monarch? Can you imagine your empire without trees, grass, roads, cars, and all the other realities of everyday life, except in miniature? Of course not! Carefully constructed scenic effects can create the illusion of a real world in miniature, and that's what you should be after!

The famous writer and critic Samuel Taylor Coleridge once said that "the razor's edge is a jagged saw to the armed vision." By that he meant the vision of the poet. Poets see everything twice, unlike most people. They see objects in their world for what they are, and they also see them for the concepts and visions they suggest rather than literally represent. In a way, I am asking you to try to be poets of scenic design. Look very carefully at the ordinary "junk" around your house. Those plastic soda straws over there — maybe they can make a pipeline if I paint them silver or black. Excuse me! Don't throw out the plastic flashing on that model airplane you're building! Those extra plastic pieces might be useful as complex piping for the oil refinery I'm building! See what I mean? You are limited only by your imagination! Maybe you can be as imaginative as the fellow I read about in one of the railroad modeling magazines not too long ago. He built a miniature drive-in, the Passion Pit Drive-In Theatre, but this one had a real difference. He mounted a movie projector under his train platform and, through an ingenious system of mirrors similar to a submarine's periscope, actually projected miniature movies onto a screen! You could do the same thing with a small-screen television set.

To get started, let us discuss a few general principles about scenery and decoration. These principles aren't exactly etched into concrete, but they have generally worked for me and have led to much enjoyment for many other Lionel railroaders I have known. After that, we will turn over the earth, plant trees and grass, construct buildings, invite some people into our miniature world, tote barges, and lift bales!

First of all, I think it's more fun to avoid using commercially prepared kits and materials as much as possible. To be sure, there are many outstanding aids to scenery construction in the model train world. However, there's nothing quite like creating something out of nothing! In Chapter X, you'll find an article by one of my modeling friends, Jack Robinson. Jack is one of the best miniaturists I have ever met. He's not a train man; Jack constructs exquisite dollhouses and furnishings with an outstanding eye for detail. It was Jack who gave me the ideas for the soda straws and plastic model flashing above. He has many more great suggestions for you, including some highly creative uses for twigs from your back yard. Would you believe that you can even do something with the little plastic container of Jet-Dri dishwasher rinsing agent? This kind of creativity is also found in the fine arts of kitbashing and scratch building, which I'll explain when we get to buildings and structures later in this chapter.

Whatever buildings, structures, and other features you place onto your layout, they should be grouped together into areas which would make sense in the real world. Now, I've violated this rule more than once. I took an unmerciful ribbing from my friend Tom Rollo in Milwaukee when he saw pictures of the layout I operated before this one. I had a roadway on that layout which led to the side of a plate girder bridge. I tried to "shadow" the roadway to give the illusion that it disappeared under the bridge, but my effort did not work, and the sudden terminus of that road at the girder bridge was a blatant mistake I haven't repeated! In the real world, you wouldn't find a school house in the middle of a freight yard. It would be located within a town center, perhaps with a little cyclone fence made of wooden stakes painted silver and some fine mesh. That's the way it should be with your layout; various sections of your scenery should have unified themes.

Remember, too, that it's the little, imaginative things which really make a layout come alive, especially if they have a sense of humor attached to them. I've tried to do this in a couple of places. I made a "graffiti caboose shed" by taking a beat-up Lionel caboose body off its frame, painting it black, and scribbling all over it with white paint — "Kool Boys of 87th Street Rule!", and other

statements like that. My K-Line Diner has a slightly altered sign on its roof. The original read, "K-Lineville Diner". Bor-ing! Mine reads, "Wise and Heimer Diner ... Fast Food At Fast Prices". Elsewhere on my layout, I have a little Tonka cherry-picker truck parked next to one of the street lights. The globe is off the light, a miniature "supervisor" stands below it, and in the cherry-picker's bucket there is a workman going up to change the light bulb, a scale-gigantic screw-base bulb half as large as he is crammed into the cherry-picker bucket with him. My diner even has two miniature trash cans next to it — a small touch, but a good detail. Take every possible opportunity to put your personal touch on your layout! John Allen had mining cars pulled by dinosaurs on his pike!

If there's one thing I believe in for layout scenery, it's lighting. Professional photographers know that a touch of light in the right places can make the difference between a great photograph and an ordinary one. So it is with lighting on a layout. I have a few spotlights focused on places I want to highlight. Street lamps and searchlight and floodlight towers are plentiful on my layout, too. Some companies sell little blinking signs for diners, traffic lights, etc., and these add a nice touch in the right places. I use as many lighted accessories as possible and, when an accessory isn't lighted by its maker, I try to find a way to make it lighted. I'll have more specific suggestions about this topic a little later on.

Finally, you should try to choose colors for harmony and realism. Try to find exactly the right shades of grass and earth for your platform, and since neither grass nor earth is the same color everywhere, mix the colors a bit. Try to avoid abrupt shifts in colors; instead, blend in your scenic colors so they complement each other smoothly. Balance the colors of your accessories so you get bright splashes of color in places which need sprucing up. If you give your buildings a weathering treatment, blend in the dirt and aging as smoothly as possible. Pay attention to the details; it's amazing how good a little simulated rust on a pile of iron pipes looks!

Now that these general suggestions for scenery and decoration are in your creative repertoire, it is time to get specific about some of the elements of scenery. Like the real world, we will try to build scenery from the ground up — in this case, the layout platform itself.

GRASS, EARTH, AND TREES

In the beginning, many model railroaders make use of paper-backed grass mats available at many hobby stores. For a not-too-permanent layout, I suppose that these grass mats are better than a bare platform, but not much, in my experience. These mats have some serious disadvantages for the permanent layout. In the first place, they are absolutely uniform in color, and the real world is not that way. After time, they have a tendency to fade; your grass gets rather unsightly, and there's no easy way to replace the mat once your track work and wires are laid down. If the paper backing of these mats gets ripped, as is inevitable, it will leave an unsightly mess. My advice is to avoid the use of these mats, even though you'll have to do some painstaking work instead.

The best strategy for ground cover is to apply grass and earth by hand with ballast cement. This cement is available ready-made through the Life-Like Company, but you can just as easily make your own with the same good old white glue mixture you used on your track ballast. Prepare a mixture of 25 percent white glue

It is a busy day at the old horse corral as we load up the horses for their journey to the Kentucky Derby. Note the Marx floodlight towers and Lionel 2318 Control Tower in the background. A separate Marx spotlight illuminates the corral. Maybe there's been a terrorist threat against the horses, judging by that mean-looking soldier sitting on the bench.

Left: Lionel prewar equipment such as this green 253 Passenger Set are often run on the Greenberg 48-foot show layout. However, because of differences in wheel flange thickness, this equipment is run on track that does not include switches. The 253 Set is from W. Miller and M. Sager Collection. B. Greenberg photograph.

Below: The industrial section of the Greenberg 48-foot show layout includes a 362 Barrel Loader, 30 Water Tower, 397 Coal Loader, and a 3462 Milk Car Platform. Accessory power is supplied by a prewar T Transformer powering two sets of buss bars, one with 18 volts and one with 10 volts. Skyline HO paper and wood buildings were placed behind the layout for this photograph. B. Greenberg photograph.

The little details really count on a train layout, especially if they're a bit whimsical. Here, a worker in a cherry-picker bucket is about to "replace" a burned-out street lamp, while presumably his supervisor watches from below.

So many times the little details can add life to your layout. This prototype, a little three-truck narrow gauge Shay-geared steamer, is on the Pine Creek Railroad in Allaire, New Jersey. Note the wheel sets and junk metal in the foreground. Author's photograph.

and 75 percent water again, but this time put it into an old coffee can instead of a spray bottle. Using a one-inch paint brush, daub a small area with the glue-water mixture. Place your grass and/or earth material into a paper cup and apply the material smoothly by hand, a pinch at a time. Try to make your ground cover as even as possible, although some irregularities will add to the real-world illusion. Once the platform is dry, use a small vacuum cleaner to take up the excess grass and earth. I have found it helpful to use the old glue-water spray-bottle treatment on ground cover after the bottom layer has dried.

There are some excellent commercial grasses available from Life-Like, Woodland Scenics, and many other companies. Use more than one color of grass and earth over the surface of your layout, and add some depth to the ground cover by adding some ground foam, which is nothing more than finely cut-up sponges. Every so often, cement some coal around the track work to simulate a coal spill. For earth, concentrate along the track ballast and simulate a few bare spots on the layout where it would look the most realistic. For the sides of roadways, sprinkle gray ballast

Lionel has been criticized by prewar collectors for making its scenic plots a little too "perfect" to mimic the real thing. Not so — compare Lionel's scenic plots to this real-life scene on the long-vanished Atlantic City Railroad near Tuckahoe, New Jersey. Note the old track side signals and the station roof details, too. Lots of good modeling ideas here! Photograph taken by the Reading Railroad in 1922, courtesy Mr. Robert Long of the West Jersey Chapter, NRHS.

To put any scenic material down permanently, all you have to do is spread a weak glue-water mixture onto your surface with a brush . . .

. . . and then sprinkle your dirt, grass, etc. onto the glue with a paper cup. I happen to be using coffee grounds here. Vacuum off the excess after the glue-water mixture dries. M. Feinstein photographs.

stone and give it a glue spray-bottle treatment to keep it in place. One great substitute for commercially prepared earth is, believe it or not, coffee grounds! Even used coffee grounds can be dried out and used on a train layout.

Don't be in too much of a hurry with this decorating process; it takes time and effort. However, when you step back from your completed layout, you will see that the results are well worth the effort. You could gild the lily a bit by applying real dried weeds from your own back yard in places where you would want to represent scrub and brush. Additionally, most hobby shops sell boxes of prepared lichen, a rubbery bush-like substance which is simply placed along the layout to simulate undergrowth. I use these mini-bushes to cover up electrical connections and occasional neglected spots; I have found that lichen is handy for covering up a number of decorating flaws. Be patient, and you will be amply rewarded.

Perhaps you will not want your layout to look exactly flat, and this is understandable. There are several ways of achieving the illusion of rises and falls in the terrain without the formality of hill and mountain building, which I'll discuss later. Simply apply your grass a little thicker in some spots to simulate little ridges in a field or back yard. If you want more defined hillocks, I would suggest troweling on a few irregular gobs of spackling putty. Make sure you let this putty dry before you apply grass or earth to it. Real stones, especially irregular ones, can make interesting-looking boulders when they are simply placed on a layout and grass and earth is blended with them.

Some people like to simulate lakes and rivers on their layouts. While I have never tried to do this myself, I would take advantage of two basic ways to achieve this effect. You can make a pond by painting the surface of your board a light blue with white streaking, applying crumpled cellophane to the painted area, and placing a pane of glass over its surface. However, there's a better, more realistic way. First, define the pond, river, etc., with its depths and banks by painting it onto your layout. Build up the banks of your water body with grass, and earth-covered putty or plaster. Then, secure some resin casting material from your hobby shop and mix it according to the package directions. Apply the resin material between the banks of your water body. Before it dries completely, "ripple" the resin material with a nail end to simulate water ripples and motion. You could also ripple the surface by blowing a hair dryer onto it before it dries. Great-look-

ing water can be achieved, according to Pete Riddle, by using the stippled 2' x 4' covers for fluorescent lights in suspended ceilings. These covers, when cut to size, would have just the right texture. I like this idea! The result of this effort will be a very realistic approximation of water. The ultimate in this area is, of course, real water. Due to the difficulty of this project and the dangers of electrical problems, I wouldn't recommend this process right away. However, some railroaders have used real water in cast plaster sealed basins, even using little aquarium pumps to make waterfalls and fountains.

How about the side of a cliff for something a little more spectacular? If your permanent layout is against a wall in your home, you can simulate the side of a cliff very easily. Secure a few tiles such as the ones used to make acoustically dampened drop ceilings. These white tiles measure about a foot square. Break off the edges of the tiles to leave a jagged surface on the side you want to show. Then, mount them on top of one another to the desired height, using white glue to fasten them together. After you have mounted your cliffside in place, simply paint it, using browns, blacks, greens, and grays to represent real cliffside markings — study some pictures. You'll be amazed how realistic the jagged edges of these tiles look. Maybe you can even suspend a couple of human figures from ropes to suggest mountain climbers!

Trees are a special case. Here, you might want to save some time by getting some of the many commercially available trees in all kinds of colors. Some of these trees do not have bases. In these cases, drill small holes in your platform and insert the "trunks" of the trees in them. For those which do have bases, use modeling cement to attach them to the bare platform wood before you lay down your grass and earth. The plastic bases of some commercial trees do not look very realistic. In such cases, carry your grass and earth ground cover over the tops of the tree bases after you have fastened the trees down. That way, only the trunks will show. I have found that trees look best when they are planted in groves instead of singly. Many of the commercial trees look a little too perfect to be totally realistic. In those cases, a little judicious tree trimming with wire cutters or scissors will give them an imperfect, real-world look.

You might want to make your own trees, too, and there are several ways to do this. Try some inverted pine cones in groups spray-painted green. Wooden dowels painted a dark brown and scored to resemble bark make good tree trunks as long as the top of the dowel is hidden by the brush. Fine furnace filter material wound around these dowels can simulate the tree's foliage if it is spray-painted various shades of green and brown. (If you use this material, wear gloves because this fibrous material can irritate skin. Do not use any fiberglass because of the obvious safety hazard associated with this material.) Fine cotton painted or dyed green and brown can also simulate the foliage on trees and shrubs very well. Even brown-painted soda straws can make acceptable tree trunks, although I believe wooden dowels to be better. Many layout and scenery books have more detailed instructions on the making of your own trees.

TRACKSIDE STRUCTURES

In the real world, railroads made use of a good number of odd track side structures for many different purposes. Many of these structures showed creative uses for old, worn-out rolling stock. You can duplicate what the real railroads did by looking through junk boxes of old Lionel or Marx freight cars and securing old cabooses, boxcars, and tank cars for very little money, sometimes as little as a dollar apiece. These old cars can be redecorated to simulate track side sheds and many other buildings. For example, old passenger car shells make great roadside diners!

My own preference for this job is old caboose bodies, since I can really detail these for a realistic look. First, take the caboose body off its frame and trucks, either by unscrewing it or by prying loose the attachment tabs. Don't throw the frame away; you never know when one of the wheel sets will come in handy! Sand down some of the lettering on the caboose body to simulate its removal; then, spray-paint the caboose body flat black both inside and outside. Next, either saw off the steps on the end platforms with a jeweler's saw or attach black-painted balsa wood pieces to the caboose body so it will fit onto the platform with no gaps underneath the sides of the caboose shell. Glue unpainted balsa wood pieces into the cupola and a few of the side windows to simulate windows which have been "boarded up." Additionally, glue a few clear plastic pieces onto the remaining caboose body window openings to simulate the remaining glass. Using chalk and a damp cloth, smudge some brown and gray streaks onto the caboose to simulate dirt and grime. (In my case, I applied some white-painted graffiti!) Now, cut a piece of asphalt shingle, pebble side up, to simulate a gravel platform; edge the shingle with loose gravel.

If you want a lighted shed, go to your hardware store and get a supply of ceramic or plastic round light bulb sockets with two screw connections. Make sure they are of the right size to accept a screw-base Lionel bulb such as the No. 430 (large globe) or 1447 (small globe). The old low-voltage conical Christmas tree lights are also correctly sized for these sockets. Attach the socket on the asphalt shingle at a convenient place where the light will shine through the windows. Then wire the socket to a constant-voltage 14-volt circuit, and you will have the nicest lighted track side storage shed you have ever seen!

For cabooses, there's another touch you can add, although it's not very easy. Secure an old plastic smoke unit from an inexpensive Lionel postwar steam locomotive. You may be able to get a working smoke unit as part of a "junk" locomotive. The Seuthe Company makes a good smoke generator; these are available at most hobby shops. Mount this smoke unit, which has a simulated stack, inside the caboose so it projects through the hole originally meant for the decorative caboose stack. In most cases, you'll have to drill out the stack hole in the caboose body. Connect the two leads from the smoke unit to a 14-volt circuit and add a little liquid smoke down the stack. Now you'll have a lighted, smoking track side shed! This treatment can also be used with factory smokestacks; American Flyer railroaders have actually mounted the entire chugging mechanism from locomotives inside the structures so smoke puffs out the stacks!

Cabooses are not the only pieces of old rolling stock suitable for use as track side structures. Boxcars taken off their trucks can be used as storage sheds. Once again, mount the boxcar, suitably weathered and painted, onto an asphalt shingle base. Sometimes you can add to the realism of these sheds by mounting the boxcar body onto a balsa wood platform, including little steps leading up to the doors. Tank car bodies can be painted silver or black and mounted in groups on asphalt shingles. Connect the valves on the tops of the tank car domes with plastic flashing from model kits to simulate complex piping, and you'll have an instant tank farm on your layout.

Besides these retired rolling stock pieces, common household items can be used to build some interesting track side structures. The cardboard center rolls of paper towels and toilet paper can, with a little imagination and paint, become the cracking towers of an oil refinery. Oil tanks can be made out of cardboard oat cereal cartons cut down to size, painted silver, and decorated with oil company symbols cut out from advertisements. The best source for these ingenious structures was Lionel's own *Model Builder Magazine,* published from the 1930s until the early 1940s. The pages of the *Model Builder* articles have been reprinted many times in other publications since then. These pages include ideas for wash racks, track pits, trestles, and just about any track side structure imaginable.

BUILDINGS

There are, of course, many commercially available buildings for your layout, most notably Lionel's own kits, the famous Plasticville offerings, both new and old, and K-Line's structures, not to mention many others. These buildings are mostly made of rather durable plastic which either snaps together or can be glued together. Some of these buildings can be painted and super-detailed. Some buildings, such as the metal lithographed offerings of Marx, Colber, and Skyline, are no longer made but are still available; the lithography on these buildings can add its own special charm to a layout. In addition to the buildings themselves, many details such as fencing, farm animals, human figures, road signs, telephone poles, etc. are available from all these manufacturers; they will help to give your layout that detailed look which can be so desirable. Don't forget that most of these buildings can be lighted by the simple use of one or more ceramic or plastic light sockets fastened to the layout and wired to a 14-volt circuit. The buildings are then simply placed atop the lights.

There's really only one trouble with all these layout structures; they are almost too perfect. All one must do is snap them together, and they're ready to use. Mind you, that's not really a flaw, but if you really want to have fun with your buildings, it would be better if you made a few modifications of your own. After all, you want to make your layout a personal statement, don't you? That's where the two fine arts of building construction, kitbashing and scratch building, come in, and each should be explained at this point.

Above: The industrial section of the Author's layout has many operating accessories including the 362 Barrel Loader, the 30 Water Tower, and 2787 Freight Station in the background. B. Greenberg photograph.

Right: A busy scene from the Author's layout. The Lionel trolley provides frequent service for the people who work in the commercial-industrial sector. M. Feinstein photograph.

Above: The usual observation car is missing today from the Overland Limited. Passengers anxiously throng forward, even before the traps are opened. The narrow platforms are hazardous in peak periods, not unlike those in the Chicago Union Station. Consequently, the station managers attempt to confine visitors to the main station building. Railfans frequently ignore the warnings as they seek photographs of the deluxe streamliners. W. D. Hakkarinen, M.D. layout, M. Feinstein photograph.

Below: An example of good road and street work on the 48-foot Greenberg show layout. Note the Plasticville Hospital and the uneven coloring of the roadways — not to mention the great die-cast old car models. M. Feinstein photograph.

Kitbashing is a rather colorful term which applies to the selective use of two or more building kits to create a new structure. The simplest form of kitbashing involves placing buildings atop one another or side by side to form larger units. The Bachmann Company, the maker of Plasticville structures, makes an expandable apartment house which can rise one, two, or many stories high. You can place Lionel's No. 157 Station sheds together and connect them with extra fencing pieces to form a long roofed-over passenger platform, complete with billboards on the fences. More creatively, you can use parts from one kit along with parts from another kit to form an entirely new structure. In one case I know about, several Bachmann Plasticville freight stations were placed one atop the other and provided with a flat roof. The stations thus became a large apartment building, complete with bay windows on one side at least four stories high. I've also seen Lionel's gigantic Rico Station kit expanded into a super passenger terminal by the addition of the long piece of building from a second Rico Station kit.

Scratch building applies to the construction of a complete structure without resorting to any part of a ready-made kit — in other words, you construct a building or other structure entirely from your own skills and plans. Obviously, this is more demanding than kitbashing, but with a little imagination, you'd be surprised how easy it can be. Many years ago, when I was ten years old or so and running my American Flyer trains, my father decided to make a water tower for my layout. He used an old metal salted peanuts can for the tower body. Then he secured a circular piece of metal and cut a slot into it which reached to the exact center of the circle. He bent the metal so it formed a conic section — a pointed tower roof — and cut off the excess metal, soldering the edges together. After he soldered the roof to the tower body, he bent parts of two old curtain rods to form the tower supports, soldering these to the bottom of the can. After the structure was painted black and a little "RCA" emblem was added from an old radio, the thing looked surprisingly realistic, considering its construction. Popsicle sticks, tongue depressors, and little railroad ties can be glued together and painted to form trestlework, lumber platforms, and small structures of almost any description — all it takes is patience. Many of the model railroading magazines feature articles about scratch-built structures which can give you ideas. You can also look around the railroads in your own area for ideas for scratch-built structures.

I haven't tried it yet, but I have an idea for a scratch-built Union Station I'd like to build someday. I would use quarter-inch Lauan board — the same board I used for my train platform — to construct large walls for this station. It would be a relatively simple matter to draw outlines of windows and doors and then cut them before assembly. However, the roof would be my most daunting challenge. I'd like a glassed-over roof, such as the ones used by the great train stations of a bygone era; London's Victoria Station comes to mind. To do that, I would cut apart plastic two-liter soda bottles into half-sections so I would have some arched "glass" structures. I would glue these together, probably three segments wide and two segments long, and fasten them to my building to form an arched glass roof. The glass structure would rest upon balsa wood cross members stretched across the building and painted gray. A little black drafting tape (not paint, which won't adhere to the plastic) would simulate the supporting girders, and some half-moon shaped pieces of wood could close off the open ends. All I would need is some paper brickwork to complete the illusion of a great metropolitan train shed! Someday!

That's not all there is about buildings, either. You can certainly alter the plastic or metal ones you secure from commercial sources. Fortunately, styrene plastic takes to painting very well, and with a little patience you can make your buildings look like anything but Plasticville. Glue some auxiliary items onto or around the buildings, such as human figures, barrels, logs, oil drums, etc. Spray them with Testor's "Dull Coat" — a very handy substance — to take off the plastic shine. You can also age them with chalk dust and a damp rag; simply put a little chalk onto the edge of a rag slightly dampened and rub it along the building to create streaks of dirt and rust. Rooftop treatments especially look good when this weathering treatment is used. A small paint brush can also be useful in applying the chalk to the buildings.

The placement of your buildings depends upon the themes you want to use on your layout. I would suggest selecting the buildings you want before you do your landscaping. Simply pencil in the outlines of your buildings and structures, label them, and landscape the layout appropriately; if a building is going to fit onto your layout, obviously landscaping is unnecessary where the building will hide the layout. If you are going to light your buildings, you might want to glue clear or opaque white plastic pieces into the windows for a more realistic look.

ROADWAYS

There are several ways to place roads and highways onto a layout. Obviously, one effective method is to paint the road directly onto the layout board itself. That can be very effective with the right paint job, but it has the serious disadvantage of immobility in case you want to change your layout a little later. Two other methods have a little more promise, depending upon which type of road you want to create.

The attachment of good old asphalt shingles, black side up, can be very effective in creating a roadway, especially since the black side of the shingle is usually uneven in color, like a real roadway. Attach the shingle sections with black upholstery tacks; make sure your curves are cut evenly. There will be seams to hide, but that's not a difficult process. A little fine gravel stone glued to the seam can suggest a recent road repair. You can even gouge a hole or two in the shingles to suggest unrepaired potholes. With gray and white paint, you can draw little streaks on your roadways to suggest oil dropping, skid marks or the latest "patchout" done by the local hot-rodder in his '68 Pontiac GTO. For the edges of the roads, use glued gravel or long, narrow painted cardboard pieces to suggest curbing. For the lines and markings on the roadway, I've found that paint is ineffective. White or yellow crayon is a little better, but the best solution of all is to get a supply of drafting tape from an artists' supply house. This tape is used in the preparation of overhead visuals for sales; it usually comes in a kit with several dispensers of various kinds of tape. The most useful tape for you will be the narrow white or yellow border tape. Apply this tape to the roads as needed. If you have trouble making it stick, get out that glue spray bottle again! With a shingle road, you can create a grade crossing by using wedges of wood cut to fit and installed under the shingle where it abuts the track. Dark brown-painted balsa wood sections between the rails will complete the illusion.

Another way of applying roadways is to apply glue-sprayed gravel or earth directly onto the layout. This method might be best where you want to create a dirt road in a rural area or a gravel road in industrial areas. It has the significant advantage of being highly three-dimensional, as a high-crowned back road might be in real life. The same method can be used to build pathways to houses or other buildings. Sidewalks can be constructed simply of thick gray cardboard which has been painted with lines and fake cracks. Use gray-painted balsa wood strips or folded heavy cardboard to give the illusion of curbs.

Other roadway-related items are easy to secure and set up. Little road signs, easily available commercially, can be glued directly onto the layout at strategic points. Lionel and others have made many kinds of billboards over the years; the standard billboards are colorful and attractive, but you also have the option of drawing up your own billboards and inserting them into the Lionel frames. (I can see it now ... "Old Frothingslosh Beer, The Beer Of Choice For Famous Fullback Rodney Rocknoggin ...") Obviously, that's a more creative approach for you. Lionel even sells a blinking billboard light which attaches directly to the billboard frame. Life-Like's O Scale Scenics include little mailboxes, telephone booths, trash cans, and even little red fire hydrants. Telephone poles are plentiful and colorful; for these, fasten the poles securely onto the layout and then string fine black cloth fishing line between the insulators to create power and telephone lines.

"LITTLE STUFF"

I've often said that it's the little things on a layout which can make a tremendous difference to the realism of your little universe. Besides the examples I've already given, there are several more little touches you can apply to your layout to give it that finished look. Human figures, for example, can be secured from firms such as Life-Like and Bowser ready-painted for your use. These figures are correctly sized in O Scale, and they are mounted on little clear plastic squares so they can be glued to the layout. Use rubber cement so you can change their locations easily. You can have a mother and her two children waiting at the train depot for your fast express, or you can have a road crew out on the highway busily attacking a hole in your roadway. (I try to have four guys digging the same hole!) Other figures such as a jogger in warm-up clothes and a conductor are also available in these little figures. The more, the better — you want your universe to be decidedly human!

I've already mentioned other little elements such as mailboxes, fire hydrants, telephone booths, and highway and railroad signs, but a word should also be given to you about cars and trucks. Be sure you choose these vehicles to proper scale. The Matchbox, Corbi, and other little metal cars are more properly scaled to HO than to Lionel, so choose cars a bit larger. They need not be expensive models, either; a little paint in the right place can dress up a cheap automobile so it looks quite acceptable. K-Line sells an assortment of inexpensive automobiles which look fine when they are painted a bit with detailing. Some of the smaller Tonka metal cars and trucks are very effective for Lionel trains as well.

For the bare spots on your grass and earth world, you're not limited to trees. Aside from commercial lichen, you can simply collect real twigs, weeds, and other debris from your yard and apply them strategically to your layout. A stack of miniature twigs inside a fine wire hoop makes a convincing pile of firewood next to a house. One of the most clever ideas I've ever read about

concerned a novel use for an old bristle scrub brush. The railroader cut a hole in his platform the exact size of the brush and mounted it so the wooden part of the brush where it met the bristles was level with the layout surface. Then he cut the bristles about halfway and carefully camouflaged the seams with grass and earth. He continued the camouflage of dirt inside where the rows of cut bristles were. The result? The most convincing small wheat field you'd ever want to see! All it takes is a little imagination ...

LIGHT IT ALL UP!

I must confess that I'm an absolute nut on lights and illumination on my layout. When I am operating a passenger train on the outside track, I estimate that there are over 60 individual light bulbs glowing on my layout. That's one of the main reasons why I need two transformers to supply power to my layout! Each light bulb takes a certain amount of power, of course, and if there are just a few lighted accessories and lamps, there isn't much of a problem. However, you'll find that the cumulative effect of many little light bulbs means an absolutely hellacious power draw out of your transformer!

There are a few ways by which you can alleviate the mammoth power draw these light bulbs take from your transformer. Certain bayonet-based light bulbs are designed so they draw far less power than others. In Lionel's case, these bulbs are the No. 53 (small globe) and the No. 57 (large globe). Each of these bulbs will save you about two-tenths of an ampere of power over other bulbs. That doesn't sound like much, but every fraction of an ampere you save is available to run your accessories and trains. The more power you drain from your transformer, the more heat you create in it as a by-product, and I am certain that you did not purchase your transformer as a cooking implement! In addition, the hotter your transformer gets, the less efficient it is in sending power to the tracks. Obviously, it is in your interest to save as much power as possible.

The low-amperage lamps Nos. 53 and 57 are fine for bayonet-base sockets, but what about all those screw-base sockets you will also have on your layout? There is also a lamp for those applications, but it is very hard to find except at specialty electrical supply houses. This screw-base lamp is No. 52, and nowhere in Lionel's literature is it ever mentioned! These lamps are excellent for lighted older turnouts, screw-base street lamps, the ceramic sockets for your buildings, and many other uses. If you can find these No. 52 Lamps, stock up on them!

You will have an incredible variety of street lamps for use on your layout. Lionel has made a staggering number of these over the years. For a formal (but expensive) look, use Lionel's metal No. 58 from prewar and early postwar years. This gooseneck lamp looks great in urban settings. Lionel's all-metal No. 71 is usually available used for very reasonable prices, since it was made in great quantities. The later green plastic street lamps are also good bets, but be sure to use a relatively high-capacity lamp, at least 14 volts, to avoid excess light bulb heat which can warp the plastic lamp globes. Some of these lamp posts accept a double pin-base bulb, but the most recent lamp posts take a subminiature foreign-made light bulb which can be a little difficult to find.

Fortunately, Lionel's lamp posts are not your only choices. Both the Colber and Marx Companies made very durable plastic lamp posts for many years, and these can be secured for very reasonable prices. They usually take a screw-base bulb. Some of

Above: The 623 Santa Fe NW-2 Switcher emerging from a tunnel on Neville Long's railroad. Note the detailed brick and stonework around the tunnel portal. N. Long photograph.

Below: A derailment on a main line curve. The big hook has been called; the Pacific Fruit Express reefer will soon be on track. However the load of tomatoes is likely much worse for wear. N. Long layout and photograph.

Above: Multiple levels add much to a layout and create opportunity for bridges and trestles. Note the effective background paper which dramatically enhances the visual perspective. N. Long layout and photograph.

Below: The arched bridge spans a steep valley and provides a level train right of way. Note how the bridge rests on a stone base. N. Long layout and photograph.

the Marx models even came with little mailboxes, police call boxes, and fire alarm boxes attached to them. I've seen a set of three Marx lamp posts selling for about ten dollars recently, so you can put quite a few of these lamp posts on your layout for minimal expense. Other, more obscure companies also made some good lamp posts. One firm which comes to mind is the Latrobe Company, which made some fine all-metal lamp posts in the 1950s. These lamps show up quite frequently at train shows and hobby shops.

In the case of used lamp posts, the sockets and their wires should be checked before purchase. Many times, the wiring to the sockets is badly corroded and it must be replaced. If you can get the socket out of the lamp post, you can rewire the socket by soldering one wire to the outside of the socket shell and the other wire to the center of the lamp shell's base. If the lamp post is inexpensive enough, it's worth the rewiring. If you have used a bus bar wiring system, it is a relatively easy matter to splice the lamp post leads with electrical tape to wire extensions which lead down to a 10-volt power source. (Many railroaders illuminate their lamp posts at 14 volts, but I prefer a softer glow, longer lamp life, and less risk of lamp heat distorting the globe, so I keep the voltage at 10 volts.)

Floodlight and searchlight towers can give your railroad a very busy look, especially if you have your layout in a place where you can turn off the room lights and illuminate the layout with just its own lights. That, in fact, is another reason for using a great deal of lighting on your layout. Just think of the red, green, and white reflections off the little lamps of your miniature world at "night!" Lionel has made a good variety of these floodlight and searchlight towers. I am partial to the old four-light 395 Floodlight Tower and the 494 Rotating Aircraft Beacon. There are also blinking water and microwave relay towers available from Lionel. The eight-light floodlight towers issued over the years by Lionel are pretty good, too.

Despite Lionel's excellence with light towers, I must confess my preference for the astonishing number of light towers made by the Marx Company, which are somewhat prominent on my layout. Many of these Marx towers were all-metal, and when they can be found in good shape they are quite rugged and reasonably priced. Some of the single-light towers had thick optical glass lenses which really diffuse the light over quite a distance. The later Marx two- and four-light varieties are good, too, but the screw-base light bulbs are difficult to replace inside their rigid metal sockets. Some Marx searchlights are mounted on a simple square pedestal; I use one of these as an extra light for my horse

corral. These smaller searchlights can be mounted lower down on the layout to illuminate features of your layout strategically.

Add up all of the lighting tips I have given to you — the specific models of street and other lamp posts, the ceramic or plastic lamp holders for building illumination, the blinking sign lights, and so on — and you will have a very lively universe! Nothing fascinates people who watch layouts like clever, imaginative lighting. You can even do some special effects with a little creative lighting. One effect you can make is a series of lightning flashes against a distant mountainside on your layout edge. Get an old rheostat, or even an old Lionel transformer of the type which has click-stops instead of continuously variable voltage. Hook up one light socket to each of about six or seven of the connections available on the rheostat. When you move the rheostat lever quickly from one end to the other, each lamp will flash in sequence as the lever contacts its stops, giving the impression of lightning traveling along a hillside!

Some people have told me that they've designed their layout lighting to take full 120-volt household current. My advice: DON'T DO IT! There is simply too much risk of severe electric shock, especially with small children. Think about safety above all else and keep your lights low-voltage!

MOUNTAINS, BRIDGES, TRESTLES, AND TUNNELS

Due to the fact that my one and only layout must survive the rigors of transportation to many train shows, I decided that building it on more than one level was too great a risk. Therefore, my trains and railroaders live in Flatland. You, of course, are under no such strictures, especially if you have a good amount of room for your layout. It certainly is wise to investigate the addition of mountains and tunnels to your layout as well as bridges of all kinds and trestles. Since trestlework is more or less the easiest way to add another level of height to your layout, let us begin there.

Generally speaking, Lionel's trestles are very sturdy when they are properly assembled. However, proper assembly requires a great deal of care. If you purchase a used No. 110 Graduated Trestle Set or a No. 111 Trestle Extension Set, make sure that the set includes a packet of the required screws and attachment plates. If you are using O27 track, the attachment plates will be long, narrow indented brackets. If you are using O Gauge, the attachment plates will be smaller hexagonal brackets. These attachment plates connect the track by fitting down over the track ties where their bases are bent upwards. The track you use on your trestles must have straight tie edges which have never been bent or kinked. The newer trestle sets include little plastic brackets which slide onto the trestle pieces themselves. The track is then screwed directly to the plastic pieces. My fellow railroaders tell me that both types work well, but the older metal brackets seem a little more stable. Since trestle sets are plentiful, it might be wise to secure an older set. The graduated trestle set should have 24 pieces, including two small flat plastic plates to begin the track's rise to meet the trestles. Many times, these pieces have become lost; check before you buy. Individual pieces are usually available at train shows and hobby shops, too.

The graduated trestles rise from platform level to a height of four and a half inches over the platform. The extension set includes ten more 4-1/2" trestle piers to lengthen the elevated

No. 71 Lamp Post.

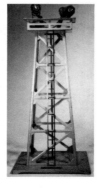

395 Floodlight Tower

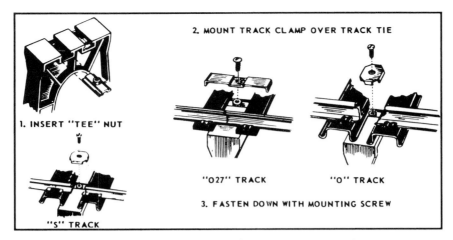

1. INSERT "TEE" NUT

2. MOUNT TRACK CLAMP OVER TRACK TIE

3. FASTEN DOWN WITH MOUNTING SCREW

"S" TRACK

"O27" TRACK

"O" TRACK

How to mount various types of track on No. 110 Trestle.

section of the layout. There is also a large bridge available, Lionel's No. 2122. This is a large and fine-looking bridge which can easily be combined with your trestlework. Some layout builders have elevated the entire loop of track on their layouts; this is a good idea because such trestlework saves space for more tracks on the platform level. It is also relatively easy to make the trestlework into an embankment once it is built by using some of the hill and mountain making methods I will discuss a little later.

When you fasten the trestles to your platform, make sure that they are placed and angled precisely; the slightest deviation from proper placement will weaken the structure or — worse — kink the track so you run the risk of diving your train off the upper track. Build your trestle work one section at a time by fastening your track piece to the previous section and then penciling in exactly where the next section should be placed. You should use sturdy screws to fasten the trestles to the layout board, too, and since these trestle sections will vibrate with the train, it might be wise to use small bolts with lock washers instead of screws for your fastening. Refer back to the wiring chapter for some advice on powering the upgrade and the downgrade sections of the trestle section.

Tunnels can add a great deal of fun to your layout if you build them yourself. Of course, there are quite a number of commercial styrofoam tunnels which simply are placed right onto the track work, but I would avoid these because they are very fragile and they don't, as a rule, look very realistic. If you make your own tunnels and mountains, you could get much better results. The only drawback to building your own mountains and tunnels is that you have to do an extremely messy, sloppy piece of work! After you clean yourself and the layout, you'll be quite pleased, however.

You can achieve some rather spectacular special effects with mountains and tunnels, especially on a large layout. In 1950 the Lionel Corporation introduced its new Magnetraction feature, whereby the locomotive wheels were magnetized to grip the track better and achieve more pulling power. To demonstrate this new feature, the company built some special display layouts for its larger New York store accounts. These layouts featured a Magnetraction steam locomotive pulling a long string of specially colored gondola cars. The train was made to go into a special tunnel, where a truly spectacular effect was achieved. The train appeared to vanish into a two-foot long tunnel, only to have the locomotive reappear just as the caboose was entering the first

tunnel portal! The effect was startling; it was as if the entire eight-foot train had been compressed into two feet inside the tunnel. The train really proceeded around a hidden loop beneath the layout which carried it around to the second tunnel portal; the tunnel hid the depression and elevation needed for the optical illusion. You could achieve this effect by hanging curved train board cut for the purpose and attached by wooden brackets to the underside of the layout. However, your curvature would have to be absolutely precise for the effect to work!

A railroading friend, Lou Bargeron, works with American Flyer trains, and his layout incorporates a fine illusion with a mountain and several tunnel entrances. The high mountain is

Broken pieces of ceiling tile are used to simulate a cut in the rocks that leads to a tunnel portal. C. Weaver layout, M. Feinstein photograph.

built into one corner of the layout, and three train loops enter it, all at different heights in the mountain. The tunnel portals are angled so none of them is exactly parallel to one another. When Lou runs his three trains, he achieves an effect which convinces the onlooker that there must be at least six trains running, even though he can see only three. The spectator's eye follows one train into the mountain, but his eye is immediately arrested by a different train emerging from it. This rapid diversion of attention prevents the onlooker from concentrating on the progress of just one of the trains, and since attention rapidly shifts from one of the trains to another, it is possible to be convinced that many more than three trains are running. It is the irregularity of the entrances and exits in the mountainside which creates this effect.

The basic method of building a mountain-tunnel arrangement for your trains is first to build a framework which will support the mountain material you'll be using. To do this, visualize the general size and shape of your tunnel, especially the height. Using 1 x 2 pieces of wood, cut vertical supports and attach them to your layout with L-shaped brackets. These vertical supports must be sturdy. Then, attach horizontal supports to the vertical supports with wood screws until you have a rough framework. If you're going to use Lionel's tunnel portals, measure where they will be and run framework around them after you have attached the tunnel portals to the layout itself. While you are building this framework, run a locomotive and a larger passenger or freight car through the framework to be sure that you have maintained proper clearances for your track.

The next step is a little easier, but it still requires patience and care. Find a supply of aluminum screening. Stretch a piece of this screening across your mountain framework, attaching it to the framework with a staple gun as you go along. The screening should not be exactly uniform over the framework; allow for some irregular rises and falls for the illusion of an irregular mountain surface. Cut the excess screening away with a small pair of metal snips or scissors, and cut it away from the tunnel portals. Some modelers prefer a cardboard web with long 1" wide strips.

Once you have your framework and screening in place, you're ready for the really sloppy part of the mountain building process. The oldest way to build a mountain is to use papier-mache tactics; that is, old newspapers or paper towels soaked in a papier-mache mix which are then draped over the screening and framework and allowed to dry before painting and decorating. Plaster of Paris is a little heavier than papier-mache, but it too is very effective. One tip on these two materials, however: If there is a little chip in the papier-mache or plaster of Paris after you have decorated the hillside, it will show up as an unsightly white spot. To avoid this problem, toss a little brown paint, varnish, or even food dye into the papier-mache or plaster of Paris mix before its use. Excess newspaper can be cut away later before the mixture thoroughly dries with an X-Acto knife. Another material which could be used for mountain building purposes is dentist's plaster; even the plaster hospitals use for casting broken limbs is suitable. However, these materials can be expensive. They do have the advantage of being molded to desired contours more easily than are papier-mache or plaster of Paris. Paper towels dipped into a 50-50 mix of water and plaster of Paris can be very effective. Before the towels dry, paint them with a 50-50 mix of water and earth-colored latex paint, which will form a hard shell.

The above materials are not the only ones suitable for mountain building, however. There is a product called Mountains In Minutes available from hobby shops which works extremely well.

This is a special plaster which takes very well to paper towels soaked in it and draped over the hillside framework. Another material may be the best of all; it is sold under the trade name Hydrocal. It has the advantage of much faster drying than plaster or papier-mache. Basically, the Hydrocal is mixed in a flat container such as a tub used for automotive oil changes. Paper towels soaked in Hydrocal are quickly draped over the framework. I say quickly because Hydrocal hardens very rapidly. Therefore, mix the Hydrocal in small batches and have your paper towels close at hand — you'll have to work fast! If the Hydrocal does harden in the plastic pan, it can be removed by bashing the pan from the bottom with a rubber mallet. Hydrocal is an excellent building material which will take to the contours of your screen framework very readily. Just be sure to mix only as much as you will use for one part of the hillside.

Peter Riddle has suggested a good alternative method of mountain-building. He uses 4' x 8' sheets of styrofoam, in thicknesses ranging up to 2", which can be layered and carved into beautiful mountain shapes with a kitchen knife. No supporting structures are needed, the results are extremely lightweight, and they deaden sound inside the tunnels. The stuff is very easy to carve around tunnel portals, and cliffs and overhangs are a cinch. Straight cuts make very convincing cement walls; by breaking instead of cutting, you get a fine representation of a blasted rockfall. Best of all, cleanup is by vacuum cleaner, quickly. Carpenter's glue is all that's needed to hold it all together, and wallboard crack filler can be used to texture the surface if you want. It takes paint well, is easy to detail with scenery material, and if you want to change the layout, there's no problem with screening and plaster and supports — just chop it off and chuck it!

Whatever method of mountain and hillside building you have used, once your newspapers and/or paper towels soaked in your building material have dried, it will be time to decorate your mountainside. Use the same techniques for scenery building you have used on the layout itself — grass and earth attached with ballast cement, brown, gray, and green spray paint, and perhaps a little commercial snow near the summit of the hillside. Carefully

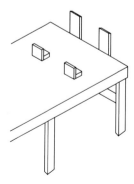

A diagram showing 1x4 vertical supports for a screen mountain process. To support the low mountain end, take a 2x4 block, 4" long or thereabouts, and nail a 1x4 piece to it. On the floor start the nails in the 2x4 block to nail it to the platform. Have a friend hold a 2 lb. mallet under the table where you are nailing the 2x4. Assuming that your mountain reaches its peak at the end of the table, nail 1x4's to the table end to support its peak. Start your nails in the 1x4 on the floor, then nail the board with nails onto the table end. To support the table end, use the mallet held inside the frame while nailing.

sand off a small area of the hillside and attach lichen or trees to give it a three-dimensional look. You can also attach some real pebbles from your yard into some interesting rock formations along the sides of the slope. At the tunnel portals, smudge a little black paint along the top where a real tunnel portal might be stained by diesel exhaust or steam engine smoke.

Bridges can add a nice touch to a layout, too, but here a word of caution is necessary. Many beginners simply place their bridges flat on a layout, especially the smaller bridges. That isn't conducive to the creation of an illusion of realism. Bridges should span something — a road, a river, or a brook. Lionel has made many bridges for this purpose, and so have other manufacturers. If you're lucky enough to own one of the magnificent No. 313 Bascule Bridges in working condition, you've really got something special. With this bridge, when you press the operating button the train stops before the bridge, which then raises its span to the accompaniment of a powerful motor. The span then lowers, re-connects the track circuit, and the train starts on its journey again. The Marx Company made a hand-crank girder bridge at one time which operates much the same way at far less expense. Not too many years ago, Lionel also made a fine operating drawbridge (No. 2317) which is complex to wire but very effective as an operating accessory.

The non-operating bridges come in many shapes and sizes. Lionel has made some fine truss bridges as well as an arch-under style. Marx, Colber, and several other manufacturers made these bridges, too, some of which are quite large. They look best when they are combined with trestlework, a relatively simple operation. To span a brook, for example, all you would need are the beginning sections of the graduated trestle set to make your track rise about an inch over the brook's surface. The small 214 Plate Girder Bridge and its many successors is ideal for this operation. It can even be used in multiples for a longer girder bridge. Incredibly, you can also install these bridges upside down for use as a deck girder bridge (although, of course, the bridge's lettering will be upside down unless it is installed with the girder lettering facing inside, an easy process).

If the readily available bridges do not suit your purposes, you can always build your own trestlework bridges out of such items as popsicle sticks, tongue depressors, and model railroad ties. All you would need is a piece of wood suitable for the train platform part of the bridge. Study some photographs of trestlework on real railroads and build your trestlework with model cement. It's painstaking work, but the results can be spectacular, especially on mountain railroads where the wooden trestlework really shows well.

Finally, you can do some terrific backdrop work if your layout is situated along the walls of your attic, garage, or other room. Some commercially available backdrop materials for deserts, mountains, plains, and the like can simply be tacked up along the walls of your room where they meet the sides of your layout, but this is the least imaginative approach to this situation. You can paint your walls themselves with specific scenery if your abilities are good enough; this looks more realistic than artistic backdrop paper. Sometimes you can scratch-build some corner buildings for a backdrop in such a way that they look three-dimensional but are really false fronts for perspective, just like a Hollywood stage set. Strategically placed mirrors can enlarge the apparent size of your layout if the edges of the mirror are camouflaged with scenery and your lighting is made so reflections are avoided. For further ideas along these lines, consult the many scenery building articles in magazines such as *Model Railroader* and *Railroad Model Craftsman*. Even better, study the relevant scenery chapters in *Model Railroading With John Allen*. Allen was a master at realistic scenery and the uses of mirrors; his tactics were clever and well worth an extensive study. Another fine book is Dave Frary's *Realistic Model Railroad Scenery*. Frary's techniques are considered more modern by scale modelers.

We're getting there! Now your little universe has been decorated with the right scenery, and your trains are up and running. There couldn't possibly be anything we've forgotten, have we? Yes, there is! The one feature which we haven't discussed is the feature which makes Lionel railroading different from any other model railroading — animation! That's where the many varied, clever, and altogether charming Lionel action accessories come into play. In the next chapter, we will discuss some of the more popular Lionel action accessories in three categories: track side signals and accessories, operating freight cars, and operating industrial accessories. No one chapter can cover all the accessories Lionel has produced, but a survey of the more available and less costly ones can lead you to some interesting choices. That lumber and coal, those mail sacks and barrels, have to move around to complete the illusion of your railroad as a busy little place. That is exactly what we must now add to your scenario of magic. Great fun awaits!

Chapter VIII

LIONEL'S OPERATING ACCESSORIES

"The reasons for Dad's interest are very understandable. Lionel trains have an endless variety of nonrepetitive movements, all directed by means of remote controls operated selectively by the user... It requires a degree of skill and coordination and, above all, it is not an automatic cycle brought about by merely pressing a button."

—Laurence Cowen

"A few minutes of that [children running trains in circles], and the little nippers will wander off and squeeze out some toothpaste or set fire to the curtains. They've got to be in on it!"

—Joshua Lionel Cowen

(Both these comments are as quoted by Ron Hollander, *All Aboard!*)

"Control of a Lionel train today... Control of his life tomorrow." That was the message of Lionel's advertising in the late 1950s and early 1960s, even as the company's fortunes had begun to sour with the advent of television and slot car racing as newer diversions. Actually, such messages had been an important part of Lionel's pitch to consumers ever since the 1920s, and people were more than willing to listen to it even when cold logic contradicted the statement to some extent.

Whatever the case, the educational value of Lionel trains is excellent, as I've pointed out in a previous chapter. Part of that educational value does indeed involve control, and Lionel's message was far more important psychologically than it was philosophically. You see, in the early part of a child's education, that child is well aware of the control adults exercise over the world he or she inhabits. It seems to me that all children have an innate desire to have total control over at least a part of the adult world. I see this phenomenon all the time in my position as an eleventh grade English teacher, and I am quite sure that it is also true for younger children.

As far as Lionel trains are concerned, that phenomenon of control does not just come from a child's manipulation of a transformer handle. The main exercise of a child's control of a train layout — and thus a little world — is in the action of Lionel's accessories. When I do a demonstration at a train show, I am continually amazed at the simple thrill experienced by children

when they push the whistle or diesel horn buttons or, better yet, push the buttons which control the Barrel Car, which operates together with a second button working the Barrel Ramp. There are, significantly, two little adult "men" on the car and the accessory. Those representations of adults are now at the command of a child — the usual authority of adults over children has had its tables turned in a highly constructive way!

Animation and attractiveness aside, I am sure that Lionel's accessories have sold extremely well over their many years of production for important psychological reasons. In addition, their designs, both electrical and mechanical, show tremendous ingenuity, reliable operation, and considerable aesthetic value. No wonder, then, that a little accessory like the Automatic Gateman was produced for fifty years in several forms, from 1935 to 1984! It began production again in a new model in 1987, and that too is selling well, in spite of the existence of thousands upon thousands of these little Gateman Shacks, most of which, even the oldest, still work well. What a remarkable production record this is in an industry where a toy is fortunate to have even a two- or three-year span of production!

If you add the animation provided by Lionel's accessories to your layout, you will go a long way towards completing the illusion of a miniature world which we have been stressing from the first page of this book. You certainly have a variety from which to choose! Lionel has made an absolutely incredible number of clever operating accessories in its long and illustrious history, beginning with operating track side accessories very early and adding electrically operated cars and structures later on. Only a major book all by itself could give you comprehensive coverage of all the Lionel accessories produced, and this chapter cannot begin to cover all that ground. However, we shall discuss the types of operating mechanisms shared by most of the Lionel accessories and then give some capsule summaries of many of the most easily obtained and popular ones. We can categorize these accessories into three more or less consistent groups: track side accessories, operating rolling stock, and independently operating accessories.

There are three basic types of drive mechanisms used by most of the Lionel accessories. First of all, there are accessories such as the 282R Gantry Crane and its successors which work by universal electric motors, just as the locomotives do. The older electric motors in these accessories are serviced in much the same

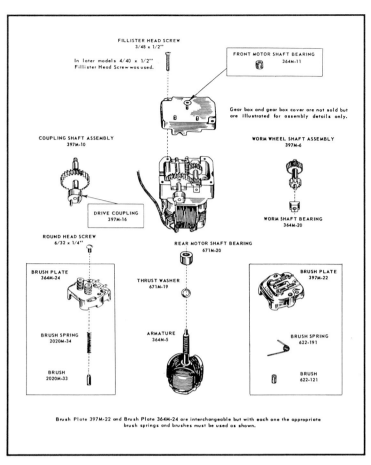

Diagram of the motor and gear assembly for the 397 Coal Loader.

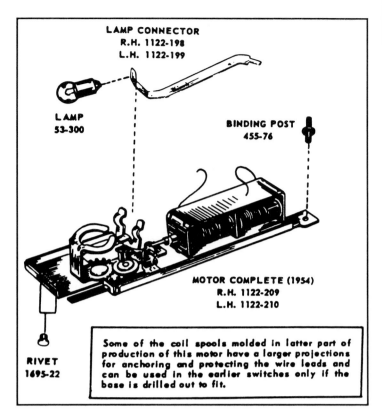

Diagram of a solenoid for the 1122 E Turnout.

manner as the locomotives — a topic we will explore in the next chapter. These motors can be made to drive a driveshaft (No. 397 Coal Loader), a system of gears (No. 165 Magnetic Crane), or a worm gear drive (No. 313 Bascule Bridge). In the last few years, these motors have gradually been replaced by DC-style "can" motors which are lubricated for life, less expensive to manufacture, and quite dependable. They are also much more quiet than their heavy predecessors, and they use far less current. If they do break down, however, they are just about impossible to repair, and the whole motor is best replaced — a relatively simple job.

The second type of drive system used in Lionel's accessories is an old and reliable electrical device, the solenoid. A solenoid is made by placing a cylindrical metal bar inside a long coil of wires. When an electromagnetic field is induced into the coil by an electrical current, one side of the coil repels the bar inside the coil and the other side attracts it. Thus, the bar is made to move, and if a device is attached to the bar, it can be made to do work such as opening the door to the Gateman house and sending out the Gateman, raising the arm with a flag on the outrageously oversized No. 1045 Flagman, or opening the doors of the 3462-72-82 Automatic Refrigerated Milk Car so the little milkman can push his milk cans onto his platform.

The third type of operating mechanism commonly found in Lionel's accessories is the vibrator mechanism. When electricity is introduced into an electromagnet, it vibrates a bracket suspended over an air gap, which in turn agitates the surface of anything to which the vibrator mechanism is attached. When such disparate objects as barrels, cattle, horses, or station carts are placed upon the vibrating surface, they will move, even uphill. One variation of the vibrator mechanism has it tied to a string wrapped around a reel adjusted with spring tension. This apparatus can drive a belt or a cable, as it does in the No. 464 Lumber Mill, the 128 Animated Newsstand, the 3435 Aquarium Car, and the 3444 Animated Gondola and their successors. The air gap can be adjusted simply by bending the mechanism's bracket, adjusting the spring tension on the pulley, or adjusting tension screws.

All these mechanisms are relatively simple, very dependable, easy to adjust and repair, and rather effective. Only a few accessories are finicky to keep in adjustment; the 342 Culvert Pipe Loader and 345 Unloader come to mind. No matter which of them you select, you're bound to introduce some rather fascinating action to your layout. Some accessories are very expensive to acquire, but most are quite reasonably priced; the track side signals are especially attractive in terms of price.

In the following capsule comments, I have listed many of Lionel's most popular and most obtainable accessories according to the three categories of track side structures and signals, operating rolling stock, and independently operating accessories. The first number listed is the number of the accessory as it was produced in Lionel's best and most productive years, 1945-1969. Other numbers are those of its modern day successors, if the accessory has been reissued in the years from 1970 to 1988. There may be slight variations among the numbers for a given accessory, but most of the time all the varieties operate similarly. If there are any special operating or repair problems inherent to any of these accessories, I will mention them as I go along.

PART 1:

TRACK SIDE STRUCTURES AND SIGNALS:

Roughly speaking, this category includes any accessory designed to send signals to trains or motorists and any accessory which is closely associated with the track itself, as opposed to independently operating accessories, which can work anywhere on the layout regardless of track placement. Quite a few of the accessories in this category are designed to work with operating cars.

2145 Gateman.

• **45/145/2145/12713 AUTOMATIC GATEMAN:** This incredibly popular accessory has been made for many years. When the train activates a contactor or piece of insulated track, the door of the shack swings open and a little Gateman figure rushes out of the shack to warn motorists. He retreats back into the shack after the train has passed. I much prefer the older 45/45N versions, which were made of stamped-steel painted in bright white or ivory, green, and red colors. In this version, the Gateman swings a lantern which is lighted from a bulb concealed under the platform. I particularly like the little "clank" made by the metal door when it shuts! Later versions with separate interior illumination were made in the form of a plastic clapboard shack on a metal base. All of the Gatemen operate extremely well, and usually little attention is needed to keep them operating. This is a charming and inexpensive accessory which belongs on anyone's Lionel layout. Marx and Colber also made versions of the Lionel gateman, but these did not operate nearly as well.

• **125/2125/2126/12737 WHISTLE SHACK AND 2127/12735 DIESEL HORN SHED:** If your locomotive does not have a whistle or a diesel horn, you can equip your layout with these features very easily by the addition of these little track side shacks. The whistle shacks have a motor mounted on a whistle box and attached to the bottom of the shack. When the motor turns, it drives an impeller (fan) which forces air through the tuned whistle box, producing the whistle sound. Typically, the 125 and the scarce 2125 versions sound a little better than the later 2126 and new 12737 versions because the later versions contain a much smaller can motor which does not drive as much air through the whistle box. The whole whistling apparatus is mounted to the underside of the shack by double-sided adhesive sponge tape. On older versions, this attaching tape deteriorates and the whistle box and motor fall off the shack, destroying the airtight seal needed for the sound. To fix this, purchase some double-sided stick-on adhesive material, cut it to fit, scrape off the old adhesive, and apply it to the whistle box. The 2127 Diesel Horn Shack has a somewhat nasal sound; it is powered completely independently of the layout by a nine-volt dry cell. There is a little slot underneath the cardboard sounding horn to adjust the pitch of the horn. (Older versions made thirty years ago operate by a standard "D"-sized battery, but I don't recommend these because they are often damaged due to battery leakage and unreliable due to their age.) The new 12735 model is fully electronic, and it sounds a great deal better than the 2127.

There's a very interesting story behind the production of the 2125 Whistle Shack, which was only produced in 1971. By 1969 the original Lionel Corporation was in serious financial trouble, and General Mills was looking to add toy lines so it could play the then-new business game, "Turn Into A Conglomerate." The two firms struck a deal whereby General Mills secured the right to manufacture Lionel trains, and the new Lionel licensees moved the whole operation from Hillside, New Jersey to Mount Clemens, Michigan. Part of the General Mills inheritance was a monstrous warehouse full of train parts. Quite sensibly, the firm decided to assemble these parts and sell them. After finding a number of good whistle motors and casings and spare houses for the old 125 model of the whistle shack, General Mills had bases and roofs made in new colors.

Before the accessory was produced, however, someone had (you should excuse the terrible pun) the bright idea to light up the shack; the old 125 model had never been illuminated. The new and inexperienced engineers forgot something when they attached the light. If you want an operating accessory to operate and be constantly lighted, you will need three attaching clips — one for a ground, one for the light, and one for the accessory button. The light for this whistle shack was simply attached between the two existing wire clips. As a result, the shack would light up only when the whistle was blown! I estimate that there are only about 1,000 of these engineering mistakes in existence. I have purchased three of the four I have seen in my train collecting years. It's an interesting little curio, to say the least!

2133 Freight Station.

• **132/133/2133 ILLUMINATED FREIGHT STATION:** This large building is a good-looking plastic accessory which, in its simplest version (the 133/2133) is simply connected to a 14-volt source for illumination. However, the 132, which has not been reissued, is a special case because it features a thermostat which can stop and restart the train. After the station is connected, disengage the locomotive's reversing switch so it will operate only forward. The thermostat will cut off power to the train once it gets to the station and then trip and restart it at a predetermined interval, thus giving the illusion of a station stop. Some of the track side block signals also use this thermostat switch for the same purpose. Used examples of the 132 should be tested before purchase.

• **30/38/138 WATER TOWER:** This massive water tank is a very good-looking accessory which is connected to a push-button enabling you to stop the steam engine at the tower and push the button to lower the tank's spout, thus simulating the steamer stopping to take on water. I prefer the No. 30 because of its metal

30

2140

148

151

152

base and above-base electrical terminals, but the 138 is brightly colored and very attractive. The 38 model is a special case with a great story behind it. Just after World War II, plans for this water tower were drawn up by Frank Pettit, Lionel's brilliant design engineer, and shown to Mr. Cowen. Cowen insisted that the tank be designed so it would use real water! Undaunted, Mr. Pettit came up with one of Lionel's most cleverly engineered products. The 38 model had a double-walled tank. The purchaser was supposed to fill the space between the inner and outer walls with water. Little vegetable dye tablets were even supplied so the colored water would be visible through the amber walls of the tank. When the button was pressed, the spout lowered and a little pump motor inside the tank sent the water through a series of hoses to a hidden reservoir just under the tank's roof. The illusion was that the water looked like it was draining out of the tank and into the tender, and it worked spectacularly well! Unfortunately, the tank was made of plastic joined with seams, and these were excessively prone to leakage. Soon, a flood (excuse the pun!) of consumer complaints about leaky water tanks came to Lionel's offices, and after two years of production, the No. 30 replaced the No. 38. It looked the same, but — no water! Perhaps it's just as well. The No. 38 in good condition fetches at least $300, sometimes more!

• **140/2140/12709 BANJO SIGNAL:** When this little track side signal is activated, a little vibrator coil spins a pegged cap in a circle, and a plastic sign through which the peg fits wags back and forth, exposing a red light. As with the crossing gates, this accessory is best hooked up to a constant 14-volt source and activated by an insulated track section instead of a contactor. The older and newer units are identically made; the latest version is colored tuscan instead of black. The Marx Company made a fine banjo signal in the 1950s which I think operates better than Lionel's because it is spring-loaded. However, the Marx version lacks a light and is quite over-sized for Lionel trains.

• **148/2115/12704 DWARF SIGNAL:** These little two-light signals are mounted at track level and look great in a freight yard. The older version came with a special switch and was manually operated; if you buy the 148, be sure it comes with the proper controller. There's no such problem with the newer versions; they are wired to work like any other set of signal lights. If you use a series of these signals, wire them with one insulated track outside

the switch yard so an approaching locomotive turns them all on at once. Better yet, wire them so they operate in concert with your turnouts if you use No. 022 O Gauge Turnouts.

• **151/2151 OPERATING SEMAPHORE:** This is one of the rare instances where the construction of the postwar model totally differs from the newer one. Both have operating flaws. The 151 sometimes operates very sluggishly and, for best results, really has to be connected to constant 14-volt power instead of track power. The newer 2151 operates somewhat more smoothly, but it lacks the durability of its 151 predecessor and can burn out more easily. Both versions of these signal devices add a nice touch to a layout; I prefer the older 151 because of its metal construction. Fundimensions has also made a strictly mechanical version of the semaphore which operates by the weight of the train, but I don't recommend this No. 2311 version because the track under it must bend. That, of course, precludes any track ballast and introduces instability.

• **152/252/2152/12714 CROSSING GATE; 262/2162 CROSSING GATE AND SIGNAL:** This is certainly the most common track side sight on a real railroad, and it is no different with Lionel. These crossing gates were made by the thousands upon thousands; they operate by means of a solenoid which pulls down on the rear end of the gate, forcing it into its downward position. The gate returns to its vertical position by means of weights in most versions. The two red lights in the crossing gate with signal illuminate but do not flash alternately as does the 154 Highway Flasher (see below). The older 152 model came with a troublesome pedestrian gate which usually jams the gate in its downward position and is removed by most operators. Later versions operate much better. My personal favorite is the old prewar 77N Crossing Gate, which is larger than the newer versions but works the same way. Wire these gates to an insulated track and a constant 14-volt power source for best operation.

• **153/2117/2163 TWO-LIGHT BLOCK SIGNAL; 253/353 TRAIN CONTROL BLOCK SIGNAL:** This track side twin-light signal has a long history dating back to prewar years. Although all of these signals operate well, I prefer the very common 153 model because of its all-metal construction. Make sure you get the 153 model which has bayonet-based bulbs instead of the old screw-based bulbs. The older version used 8-volt screw-based bulbs connected to a resistor which is frequently burned out.

154

161

192

182

Besides, try to find 8-volt red and green screw-based lamps! The newer versions work well, too, but if the lamps are lighted too long they can warp the plastic lamp hood. There's a 163 Single-target Signal available as well. You should hook these signals up with two insulated track sections for true-to-prototype operation; see the chapter on wiring for details. The 253 model incorporates the same train-stopping thermostat used in the 132 Freight Station; see that entry above for operation of this feature.

• **154/2154 HIGHWAY FLASHER SIGNAL:** This accessory has been produced more or less unchanged since its introduction all the way back in 1940. When the train passes over a special 154C Contactor, each of the red lights flashes on and off alternately. The special contactor is really clever; it features a split clip which fastens over one of the outside rails. As the train wheels pass over each half of the clip, contact is made to each of the two lamps in succession by wires running from each side of the clip, producing the flashing effect. This clip has to have straight edges to operate properly; many have been bent through hard use so they will not fit properly over the track rail. Sometimes the paper which insulates the clip from the rail is missing or worn. If that's the case, use some masking tape carefully cut to fit the clip; this will restore the insulating property.

• **161/12719 MAIL PICKUP SET:** The postwar 161 version of this accessory is very scarce, but Lionel Trains, Inc. has just introduced a fine remake. You are supposed to attach a magnet to one of your pieces of rolling stock, preferably a U.S. Mail Boxcar (the 3428, 9301, and 9708 models are appropriate). When you push the accessory button, a swinging arm rotates into the path of the train, and a mailbag which has a magnet is attracted to the magnet on the car, which pulls the mailbag off the rotating arm. Don't push and hold the button for too long, because this accessory is more sensitive to operating heat than most. It's a cleverly designed accessory which adds good action to a station setting.

• **192/2318/12702 ANIMATED CONTROL TOWER:** The constant action of this lighted tower is attractive, if a little too hectic for reality. A vibrator mechanism spins two little men around the control tables in the center of the tower interior. The 192 version is very scarce, but the two newest versions are not very hard to find. However, there are several operating cautions with this accessory. You may have to take the roof off to center the rotating disc into its square hole properly. When you do this, pry the roof off very carefully, because it is attached by two very fragile tabs, and the tower structure itself is very delicate. Insert the rotating disc by holding the metal pole and aligning it with the square centering washer inside the vibrator mechanism. Test its insertion by manually rotating the disc; if the little men clear the lamp

bracket, the disc is inserted properly. Often, the light bulb is too close to the roof, and there is no way to bend the lamp bracket down, since it will interfere with the rotation of the figures. To protect against the lamp burning a hole into the roof by heat, replace the 14-volt lamp supplied with the accessory with an 18-volt bayonet-base lamp, which will burn less brightly but with less heat. In addition, tape a piece of aluminum foil to the roof, shiny side down, where it fits over the light bulb. This will reflect away the light bulb's heat. The 12702 model already has a roof reflector, but the large-globe bulb supplied with this version should still be replaced with a small-globe one.

• **165/182 TRACK SIDE MAGNETIC CRANE; 282/282R/12700 MAGNETIC GANTRY CRANE:** One of the greatest operations you can perform on a layout is the operation of a scrap iron yard. Lionel realized this by introducing the 165 Magnetic Crane in 1940 and, later on, the Gantry Crane models which straddled the track instead of being placed at track side. Through a complex system of strings and gears, you can swivel the hook with the magnet by turning the cab, lower the magnet to a scrap steel pile, turn the magnet on, hoist the load aloft, and transfer it to a waiting gondola — all with a single three- or four-button or three-lever controller. The earlier models used a big and rather noisy AC motor for all operations; this motor requires periodic servicing. On the older models, there was a lock-in feature for the magnet, and on the 165 a red light would shine in the cab when the magnet was activated. Unfortunately, the 282 and 282R versions omitted the lighting feature, resulting in burned-out magnet coils when operators forgot to unlatch the holding feature on the magnet lever. (The 282 and 282R versions differ in their gearing; the revised 282R version works better.) The latest version, the 12700, works by two small can motors instead of one AC motor. This is a quieter, much better arrangement. The 12700 also omits the magnet-lock feature; it's awkward to hold the magnet lever on while operating the crane's other functions, but at least you'll never burn out the magnet. The older versions of this accessory are somewhat difficult to service and repair, but the new can motors remove some of the aggravation. When you swivel the cabs of any of these cranes from side to side, be sure to leave some slack in the line holding the magnet because this line will shorten as the crane cab swivels around. I recommend the newer version if you can find it. Unfortunately, the newer version is scarce, and even the older versions of this spectacular accessory are expensive if they are in good condition.

• **352/2306/12703 ICING STATION:** This accessory imitates an old-fashioned custom of loading ice into the bunkers of refrigerator cars about seventy years ago. You pull your train up

356

364

352   450

to this station so a special icing station car has its door next to a little chute. When you push the accessory, a solenoid operates a little man with a paddle who pushes a plastic ice cube off the station ramp and into a bunker built into the roof of the car. The cubes are retrieved by opening a bin on the side of the car. Track placement is crucial to this accessory, but otherwise it is quite reliable. Make sure that used versions have a man who possesses the arm and paddle assembly; this piece is sometimes missing and it is hard to find. Replacement ice cubes are readily available.

• **356/2323 OPERATING FREIGHT STATION:** Many layouts had the 356 Operating Freight Station in the mid-1950s because it was a fine operating accessory. When a switch is activated, two little baggage carts move along a vibrating metal oval built into the station base. There is a trip mechanism inside the station which alternates the carts one at a time; when the first cart enters the station, it releases the second cart for its turn. The station is also lighted. Sometimes this accessory can be difficult to adjust. If you purchase a used version, make sure it has the proper adjustment screws for the base. Mine did not have these screws, but I improvised them by substituting two round-head bolts with nuts and cushioning them with little lengths of aquarium hose. The newer version has brighter, more attractive colors, but it doesn't work as well as the old one. Some production pieces from the early part of the run had warped bases; check the new versions by pulling them from their boxes and placing them on a table until you find one which doesn't "rock." In addition, the dark green carts from the newer version were built differently; the upper plastic piece which contacts the trip mechanism is shorter than on the older carts, and it sometimes misses the mechanism. I've found it best to use the new station with the old carts. If the station platform buzzes too loudly, tighten the adjustment screws until you get good platform vibration without the noise. These cautions aside, the accessory works quite well, and it adds good animation to a layout.

• **364 LUMBER LOADER:** This is an old favorite among Lionel operators which has not been revived yet. It is an all-metal, long and narrow ramp which takes logs to a different car once they are unloaded at the bottom of the ramp by an operating log dump car. The accessory is designed to work only with the small diameter logs which came with the 3361 Log Dump Car; fortunately, these are easily found. The larger logs of later model log dump cars are too wide for this accessory. When it is made to work, the newly-dumped logs are worked onto a long red cloth belt which brings them onto the top of the ramp, where they are shunted and dumped into a waiting car. Operationally, sometimes the belt is worn, chafed, or even broken, and the large AC motor at the top of the ramp has a nasty tendency to freeze up. Replacement belts are easy to find. This is a plentiful accessory,

so test a used example before you purchase it. If you have a long, narrow space between sidings, the 364 will fit into it just fine, and when it is working it is fun to watch. If the belt slips, there's an easy cure. Take the back panel off the accessory and install a large rubber band around the takeup drum — the type of rubber band used for celery or broccoli. When you reinstall the belt over the rubber band, it won't slip any more.

• **415/12701 DIESEL FUELING STATION:** This accessory is essentially like a Gateman without the housing shack. When a button is pressed, a man rushes forward along a slot in the accessory's base with a hose in his hand leading to a fuel tank. He thus is made to appear to "fuel up" a diesel locomotive parked on the adjacent track. Although a little shed is lighted and the accessory has action, this accessory has never been popular, perhaps because the fueling action isn't perceived as very realistic. It does, however, work well.

• **445/2324 OPERATING SWITCH TOWER:** This accessory was a very popular one during the postwar years; its successor operates the same way, but has different colors. When a track contactor or insulated track is activated, a man on the top platform goes inside the tower while another man with a little lantern rushes down the stairs towards the train, presumably bringing orders to the train crew. A solenoid operates a two-ended arm; one end has the upstairs man, while the other end has a string which is connected to a bracket supporting the man on the stairs. The weight of the man on the stairs is supposed to pull him down when the solenoid releases the string tension. Sometimes the man on the stairs sticks at the top. This situation can be cured by a little wax on the string and graphite lubricant at the point where the string passes through the station wall. Hook up the ground and the light clips to a 14-volt source and the action clip to the No. 2 terminal of a lockon on an insulated track for best results. This is a relatively inexpensive action accessory which has amusing action.

• **450/12724 TWO-TRACK SIGNAL BRIDGE:** Basically, this is two two-light signals mounted on a double-span metal bridge which is wired the same way as two No. 153 Block Signals. You can change the positions of the light hoods so they face opposite directions. For the most realistic results, wire each lens hood to two insulated track sections so the green light goes on when the train is at the opposite side of the layout, the red light goes on and the green light goes out when the train reaches the bridge, and both lights go out when the last car passes the bridge. I like the massive look of this accessory; be aware that Marx, Colber, and several other manufacturers made bridges like these and K-Line still makes another version of it. All of them work well, so your purchase should depend upon the best buy and the most visible lighting.

456

• **456 COAL RAMP:** This accessory was designed to be used with a special hopper car. It has not been reissued, and it will not work with the newer operating hopper cars because they will not uncouple at the top of the ramp. The operation of this long, narrow accessory is complex and very interesting. The ramp is placed at the end of a siding. Your locomotive pushes the operating hopper up the ramp; the hopper has to be at the end of at least two cars because the ramp tracks are not electrified. The hopper couples to a knuckle coupler built into the top of the ramp. When another button is pressed, a magnet in the ramp track pulls down a disc in the hopper car, opening two bay doors which allow the coal in the hopper to dump into a tray or into a No. 397 Coal Loader. After the hopper is unloaded, another press of a button uncouples the hopper car from the ramp coupler and allows it to roll back down the ramp for pickup by the locomotive. Alignment of the ramp is critical to its successful operation, and since the ramp's incline is steep, you had better do your switching with a powerful locomotive. The Standard O trucks on the newer operating hoppers will allow the car to unload at the top of the ramp, but since the uncoupling magnet is in the wrong position for the armature disc, these hoppers won't uncouple at the top of the ramp except by hand. Otherwise, this is an attractive accessory well worth the acquisition. You'll need a long siding to situate it properly.

• **1045 OPERATING FLAGMAN:** Although this accessory was last produced in 1949, it is quite plentiful and inexpensive, and I find it a charming accessory despite its outlandishly oversized human figure — he's actually taller than the trains he waves down with his flag! The human figure is hand-painted and mounted on a colorful red base. When an insulated track or track contactor activates the accessory, the fellow raises a big white flag which he holds in his right hand. A half-section of insulated track would make the figure wave the flag up and down quite realistically. If the accessory is working and the human figure is intact, it will give you very little trouble. I like its old-fashioned look; it's a big favorite with children at my layout, where from their perspective the conductor figure is waving his flag right at them! This accessory will also work very well with its original 1045C contactor, which is like the 154C Highway Flasher contactor, except that the blade is not split into two sections. The comments I made about the 154C Contactor also apply to the 1045C version.

PART 2:

OPERATING ROLLING STOCK

• **3356/9224 HORSE CAR AND CORRAL:** An updated version of the older 3656 Cattle Car, this operating set adds a great deal of animation to your layout. When a switch is turned on, vibrator mechanisms in both the car and the corral make horses proceed around the corral, into one door of the car, and out the other side. There is a blocking device attached to one of the car doors to keep the horses inside the car, presumably for a spin around the layout. In addition, there is a little door in the corral runway to allow horses to detour to a watering trough in the center of the corral. The horses (and Lionel's cattle) move by means of little rubber fingers on the underside of their bases, but Lionel has adopted American Flyer's old procedures and is now recommending the placement of little felt pads under the miniature animals, making them move far more effectively. These pads can be retrofitted to older horses and cattle if the rubber fingers are cut off and the pads glued onto the underside of the bases; the same would hold true for the 356 Freight Station's carts. Occasionally, a horse or a cow will get stuck inside the car chute due to some plastic flashing on the chute's inner surface or to slight warping of the chute itself. The horses seem to move better through the car chutes, but they are also more prone to tip over. You should make sure you have connected the wires to variable voltage posts because this accessory is quite sensitive to changes in voltage. Ordinarily, you shouldn't have to adjust the vibrators, but if you must do so, the corral's vibrator mechanism can be reached from underneath, and the car's vibrator and solenoid can be reached by taking the body off the frame. Be careful not to bind the operating doors when you disassemble the car. With these precautions, you should have a trouble-free accessory.

• **3357/7901 COP AND HOBO BOXCAR:** This is a clever little boxcar with some amusing operating action. You assemble and mount a little trestle bridge over the track upon which the car operates. The car comes with an elevated platform and two figures with magnets. One of these is placed atop the car and the other placed onto the bridge. When the car goes under the bridge, the two figures exchange places though a slotted runway. Of course, the trestle bridge limits the height of any other operating cars you have in the train; the crane and giraffe cars will imperil the bridge and the figures. The bridge itself must be perfectly aligned with the track; this is made relatively easy by a special bent mounting screw. One wise precaution is to put friction tape on the underside of the screw and the bracket for the bridge to prevent any possibility of a short circuit. Additionally, if you run the train too fast through the bridge, the leading figure on the bridge can be knocked off the car's ramp as the exchange takes place. By adjusting the screws holding the hydraulic platform to the car, you can get the height just right. If the accessory is operating properly, you've got a somewhat unrealistic but rather amusing railroad chase.

• **3359 TWIN-BIN DUMPING CAR:** This car may look a little fanciful, but it actually had a prototype on the New York Central and was a popular item in the mid-1950s. Although it hasn't been reissued, it is fairly easy to find at a reasonable price. It differs from Lionel's other dump cars because of its operation and its length. To set up this car, you must use two OTC Lockons instead of a remote-control track. Make sure both lockons come with the car or are at least available to you. When you push a button, you rotate a cam underneath the car which gradually raises the bins, one at a time, rather realistically. It takes seven pushes of the button to make the bin rise from a flat position, dump, and return to its start. Further pushes of the button transfer the action to the second bin. A sliding lever on the car locks the bins into place while the car goes around in the train so accidental dumping of the car's gravel or coal load is prevented. When you find a good used example of this car, make sure the cam rotates properly and the lever locks it out; some cars have had their lockout levers bent over the years. Use a test track to make sure the car works before you buy it and to get experience with its unusual operation.

3361-55 Log Dump.

• **3361 LOG DUMP CAR:** This log dumping car looks like the more recent versions produced by Lionel; it has a little log cradle and three small logs. However, in operation it is more like the 3359 Twin-Bin Dump Car described above. One push of the button on a remote track causes the cradle to lift up a little at a time due to a rotating cam until the logs are dumped; then the cradle retracts to its horizontal position. As a rule, this car is a little more tedious to operate than the earlier or later log dump cars, although it is generally a reliable operator. The newer log dump cars, including all those produced since 1970, use a cradle attached to a large metal disc which is released by the magnetic action of an uncoupling track. The cradles on the newer cars are spring-loaded and dump their loads all at once. On these new cars, the logs have trouble staying on the cars in sharp turns around the layout. For that reason and several others, I prefer the older units; see the 3451-3461.

• **3376/3386/7904, 7913 (etc.) OPERATING GIRAFFE CARS:** Of all the operating cars I have on my layout or in my trains, this little car is the best crowd-pleaser when I do a demonstration at a train show. In real terms, it's an incredibly fanciful car; out of a slot cut in the roof of a short stock car, a giraffe's head and neck protrude grotesquely. Inside the car, the giraffe is held aloft by a tension spring. The giraffe's neck is attached to a weighted shaft with little extensions which jut from the car between the trucks at the car sides. When one of these extensions rides up on a cam plate, the weight pulls the giraffe's head down into the car, and he ducks under the fringes of the telltale pole mounted onto the plate which holds the sprung cam. I must admit that the action of this car is really cute!

The fringed telltales have a story of their own from the earlier days of railroading, and it's worth relating. Before the invention of the air brake, railroad brakemen had to stop the train by walking along catwalks at the tops of the cars and turning brakewheels by hand. This was no job for an amateur or anyone faint of heart! Can you imagine someone performing this hazardous duty at night in a snowstorm? At any rate, if the brakeman were facing the rear of the train, he might not be aware of a bridge or tunnel until it was too late for him to lie flat on the car top. To avoid brakemen becoming smeared all over bridge trestles and tunnel portals, the railroads invented fringes of rope which hung from poles aside the tracks. The brakemen were trained so that if they felt those ropes on their backs, they were to duck immediately to avoid getting injured — or worse!

The giraffe car is a rather reliable operator. All you really have to do is make sure that the cam plates are set up properly and that the spring for the giraffe is working inside the car — no real problem. This is a great operating car for the kids!

• **3410/3419 HELICOPTER LAUNCHING FLATCARS:** These are interesting flatcars with winders which launch such devices as satellites and helicopters, but I would not recommend them around young children because the winding springs are simply too powerful. I once had a satellite launching car, and at one show

I put it on my layout. The winder was capable of sending the satellite twenty feet into the air! However, I soon realized that I couldn't control the up and down flight of the satellite, and since I was afraid someone might get hurt, I stopped using it. On your layout, be careful not to wind the spring more than six clicks — anything more, and the satellite could threaten to bore a hole in your ceiling! As a rule, the helicopters on some of these cars do not fly very well or accurately. Since these cars are somewhat scarce, break easily, and have the potential for injury when misused, I do not recommend them for your use on a layout. They are, however, fine collector's items.

• **3424 OPERATING BRAKEMAN CAR:** It is a shame that this car has not been reissued, because it is really a fine operating car. A little Brakeman stands atop the blue Wabash boxcar. As the car approaches a track trip, the Brakeman ducks to a prone position on the car roof when he contacts the telltales supplied with the car. At a second track clip, the Brakeman stands up once again. The ideal operation of this car has the placement of two telltales and their track clips on either end of a tunnel. In that way, the Brakeman can duck when the train goes into the tunnel and stand up when the train emerges. Many times, the original telltales, poles, and cam plates are missing when this car is found today. These original telltales are very scarce and costly. However, since Lionel has been so kind as to reissue the Giraffe Cars, you have a solution. The special two-bladed clip (one for O Gauge and one for O27 Gauge) will fit right into the track clip which holds the Giraffe Car's telltale and pole. That way, you can operate the Brakeman Car off the same track clip which operates the Giraffe Car; obviously, these telltales and track plates are common and easily available. So is the track clip for the brakeman car. By itself, the Brakeman Car is quite common and readily available at reasonable prices; I highly recommend this car as an operating accessory. Inside the car, there is a manual lever for lowering the Brakeman for storage. Beware of trying to force the Brakeman into a prone position by bending him down onto the roof; you may do damage to the retaining clip, which is brittle plastic. If you have to operate the Brakeman manually, use the inside lever.

• **3428/9301/9217 (etc.) OPERATING MAIL BOXCARS:** These clever little cars, several of which have been produced over the years, operate by means of a plunger which is pulled down by the magnet in a remote-control track — the same one which is used for uncoupling. The door of the car flies open and a mailman tosses out a little plastic mail sack which is attached to his body by a magnet contacting a little pin in the sack. Mostly, the Mail Car works well. However, the doors of the versions with plastic upper and lower door guides sometimes bind, so each example should be checked for freedom of motion before the car is purchased. The biggest problem is the loss of the mail sack; have you ever tried to look for a gray mail sack on a gray rug? Instant Bifocals! The sack is easy to replace, but you can make your own somewhat cruder version of the mail sack out of a small lump of Play-Doh to which you've added a little nail head so the magnet in the mailman's body can hold onto the sack.

• **3434/9221 POULTRY DISPATCH CARS:** This long and substantial lighted stock car is irreverently referred to as the "chicken sweeper car" by many collectors because of its action. Two interior lights illuminate three rows of chickens on their way to market. (Sometimes the chicken inserts are placed upside down, especially in the newer version.) When the button of a remote track is pushed, the magnet attracts a plunger which opens the car door. A man with a small broom is mounted on a hairspring; he sways back and forth in the door opening as if he is sweeping the chicken feathers (etc.) out of the car! Lighted versions of this car have also been made without the operating human figure. The hair spring mechanism of this car is very delicate and easily broken. I prefer to leave my car's door open as it travels around the layout; the differential action of the curved track will provide the man with his sweeping motion just as easily as the remote track. In its own droll way, this car is quite amusing, and it's certainly colorful!

• 3444/9307 ANIMATED GONDOLAS: Of all of Lionel's operating cars, this is one of my favorites! The car has packing crates in its middle which conceal its operating mechanism. Two human figures, a fleeing hobo with his rucksack and a policeman with a raised nightstick, chase each other around and around the packing crates when you pull a lever which activates a vibrator mechanism. The crates conceal two spools at either end of the car; around these spools is wrapped a continuous loop of 16 mm. movie film. The figures are attached to the film by means of L-shaped brackets which slip under the crates, and the vibrator mechanism turns a disc which is adjusted for tension by a length of string attached to a little spring on a bracket. Periodically, this string must be tightened in its grommet — a tricky operation best performed by a trained (pardon the pun!) serviceman. For some reason, the older version works a little better than the newer one; the film loop has a tendency to bind on the crate sides in the new version. This is a really amusing car to watch!

3461 Log Dump.

• 3451/3461 LOG DUMP CARS: This older, all-metal log dump car was made from the late 1940s into the early 1950s before it was supplanted by a larger version, the 3361. It has a rugged die-cast base and stamped-steel lifting platform and is meant to operate on a remote track which will activate the sliding shoes. The only difference between the two is that the 3451 has the older coil-operated couplers, while the 3461 has magnetic-couplers. The coil couplers of the 3451 tend to open when the unloading button is pressed to activate the car; for that reason, I prefer the 3461 with magnetically operated couplers, though the two versions work equally well. A solenoid on the car bottom lifts a metal pin which in turn tilts the stamped-steel log platform. The metal side stakes pivot downward and allow the logs to roll off the base onto a platform or into a dumping bin. You should take care that the side stakes stay straight, or else they will jam the lift platform. Other than that, this car works very well. The 3451/3461 cars are natural companion pieces for the 364 Lumber Loader or the 464 Sawmill.

• 3462/3472/3482 SHORT OPERATING MILK CAR; 3662/9220/19802/19810 O GAUGE OPERATING MILK CAR: The short 3462/72/82 version of this operating car was the most popular operating accessory ever issued by Lionel. During its time of production from 1947 to 1955, Lionel sold two and a half million of these little white cars! Even when the short car was replaced by the larger O Gauge 3662, this accessory continued to

sell very well, and all the newer versions have been highly successful as well. It isn't hard to figure out why once you've seen this car in action. At the touch of a button, a little man dressed in spotless white emerges from the car's double doors and pushes a little metal or (later on) plastic milk can out the door onto the platform. The cans load through a clever little chute built into the car's roof and concealed by a hinged hatch. Operationally, the earlier short version has always worked a little better than the larger versions produced later on, even though the solenoid and plunger mechanism was substantially revised and improved beginning with the 3482 version of the car.

Once the Milk Car is in good operating condition, it needs very little service. The milk can chute will jam if anything but Lionel's milk cans are used; fortunately, replacements are readily available. Even Lionel's cans will jam inside the chute once in a while if the car is shaken by accident. To take apart the older 3462-72 versions of the car, you must pry loose two bail wires which hold the car body to the frame. The 3462 version has little aluminum doors which are part of the car body, but easily bent; however, on the 3472 and 3482, you must carefully pry off the door sets from the car frame. These doors are very delicate because the springs which hold them closed are separately mounted, very small, and easily lost. The door frames become brittle with age and sometimes snap; here again, replacement doors and door frames are readily available on the parts market. The 3482 disassembles conventionally by a slot and screw arrangement, as do the larger cars. The chute cover must be unscrewed to clear any cans jammed sideways in the chute before the car will operate again.

The larger O Gauge Milk Cars have problems of their own, though they too are pretty dependable. Occasionally a piece of plastic flashing in the chute (the chutes in the older cars are metal) will block the soft plastic milk can from traversing the chute and landing on the platform for ejection by the attendant in the car. Simply clear this from the inside of the chute and your problem should be solved. The older metal milk cans will work in the newer cars, by the way. Be careful of the door springs once again; though their design is improved over the small Milk Car, they too are rather delicate. For all the milk cars, be sure you have the platform adjusted to the right height for your track. The lower slots in the rear of the platform frame are meant for O27 operation; the upper slots are for O Gauge. Since the screw terminals for the older operating tracks are exposed, there is also the danger that the screw heads will contact the metal underside of the milk platform, causing a short circuit. Merely insulate the screw heads from the platform base with a piece of friction tape to prevent this occurrence.

One puzzling problem for layout operators is how to get the larger O Gauge Milk Car to operate on O27 track, since it is too long for the O27 remote track. On this car, both sliding shoes must be in contact with the operating rails for the electrical circuit to be complete. That leaves the O27 operator in a quandary, but it is solvable. Look at the operating track for your O Gauge Milk Car; on the O27 1019 Track (the one without the magnet) or the 6019 Track (the one with the magnet), determine which of the soldered wire connections meets with the operating blades. Using a second O27 operating track, solder the wire connections of both power blades of the tracks together from the undersides of the tracks. The idea is to get both tracks to operate even though only one of them is connected to the two-button controller; all you are doing is extending the operating rails to a second track. Now the car should operate when the button is pressed; you will have to live with the door being off-center on the platform. This tactic will probably work with an OTC Lockon as well; merely solder connections from the operating blades of the OTC to the corresponding power blades of the remote track. Then insert your OTC Lockon where the car's sliding shoe will contact it.

For the smoothest operation of all these Milk Cars, be sure to spray a little CRC 5-56 solvent into the cylinder of the solenoid once in a long while, and try a little WD-40 lubricant where the plates of the operating mechanism slide out with the human figure. With minimal care, these little Milk Cars will operate darn near forever, and they're really attractive on a layout — especially considering their illustrious history!

• **3459/3469 COAL DUMP CAR:** This is the earliest of Lionel's postwar Operating Coal Dump Cars; there was an earlier 3559 model with a little red bin, but it is a less reliable prewar design. When the button of an operating track activates this car's sliding shoes, a solenoid lifts a dump bin from the die-cast platform, causing the hinged side of the bin to open and release the ore load. This arrangement is very similar to the 3451/3461 Log Dump Car discussed earlier, including the coupler distinctions between the 3459 model (coil-operated) and the 3469 model (magnetically-operated). The car is usually a very rugged and reliable piece of equipment, but it does have a weak spot — the toothed gear on the end of the car which opens the side of the bin. Sometimes this gear is out of adjustment; to realign it, hold the gear steady with a screwdriver blade in the slotted screw which holds the gear onto the car. Then push the bin down until the bin is flush with the base and the bin side is in the closed position. This should move the gear setting so the bin side opens and closes properly. Of course, check the side gear for wear and stripping; many examples are damaged. The newer Coal Dump Cars are not nearly as rugged as this one. These feature a bin mounted atop the same cradle used for the newer Log Dump Cars. They operate by the same plunger mechanism, and in my experience these newer Coal Dump Cars are limited in capacity and very fragile in operation. They do not look as good to me, either; I would recommend that you find one of the 3469 models for your layout. This car is plentiful, and most of them have lasted quite well, even though they are as much as forty years old by now. Of course, the Coal Dump Car is a good companion for the 97, 397, or 497 Lionel Coal Loading Accessories, which I'll discuss a little later in this chapter.

• **3562/9240 OPERATING BARREL GONDOLAS:** This car is a very reliable, relatively inexpensive (in its most common gray version), and picturesque operating car for your layout. When the sliding shoe contact of one end of the car is atop the power blades of an OTC Lockon, a push of the control button activates a vibrator mechanism which sends little wooden barrels up a metal ramp in the middle of the car. At the top of the car, they fall off the car into a dumping bin or (better yet) a 362 Barrel Ramp which vibrates them to another destination. The barrels appear to be "kicked off" the ramp by a human figure which is mounted on a little metal bracket atop the car. The intensity of the vibrator mechanism is easily adjusted from beneath the car by sliding the vibrator along a slot and tightening a screw. The only operating problem I have experienced with this car concerns the barrels, not the car itself. Six varnished wooden barrels were supplied with the newer versions of this car; the older models came with plain wooden barrels. Of course, the varnished barrels look much better, but the varnish is so slippery that the barrels cannot get enough traction

to vibrate up the car's ramp! The older barrels work much better than the newer ones. Your 3562 model should come with a 364C Controller, six plain smaller wooden barrels (not the ones used with the standard 6462 Gondolas), a 160 Dumping Bin, and an OTC Lockon. Test used examples before purchase and insist on these components.

Naturally, every operating car is more impressive when it is used in conjunction with an operating accessory, and the 3562 Barrel Car is no exception. Secure a 362 Barrel Ramp and install it next to your track siding so the barrels will dump off the car and onto the ramp. You'll need a special clip which attaches to the side of the 362 Barrel Ramp for this purpose. The barrels will dump off the car and onto the ramp, where they can be sent up the ramp to dump into a second gondola immediately behind the Operating Barrel Car — all without the assistance of the human hand! This car and its ramp are nice pieces of electromechanical engineering, and young people never get tired of operating them together.

• **3656 OPERATING CATTLE CAR:** Next to the Milk Cars, this accessory was one of Lionel's biggest sellers. It consists of a short orange stock car with opening doors and an all-metal platform. When the car is aligned with the platform, the control button activates vibrator mechanisms in both the car and the platform. The doors of the car open upwards (newer versions open downwards) and cattle move around the chutes of the corral (more or less stubbornly) and through the car. When you get a used example of this car, it should be fully set up and tested before purchase, or at least have an operating guarantee, because there are many potential trouble spots in the accessory. Lionel's assembly and operating instructions are written exceptionally well in an eight-page leaflet; make sure you have this instruction leaflet and follow it very carefully. The accessory should come with a 364C Control Switch, a box of cattle, and the proper grounding blade for O Gauge or O27 Gauge track.

In general, the stock car itself has few operating problems. The metal chute inside the car is cushioned by little rubber bumpers, and sometimes these deteriorate. They can be replaced easily by little pieces of felt cut and glued onto the base. The same holds true for the platform, where most of the problems occur. The platform is also cushioned by rubber pads subject to deterioration.

Two pieces of this accessory can be particularly troublesome. One is the door set in the car, where the rod connecting them can be bent if someone has tried to force the doors open. Check for smooth up and down operation of these doors. The small ramp extensions on the platform which meet the car doors are far worse offenders in this regard. These little metal ramps are pulled down by a shaft connecting to a rod joining both ramps. If the corral solenoid doesn't pull the shaft down all the way, the ramps won't descend to their horizontal position and the cattle will be blocked from entering the car. Make sure the shaft is free to pull down the ramps. Worse, sometimes the ramp rod has become bent with use. If that has happened, you can try to bend it back (I can't resist this!) 'till the cows come home, but the ramp still won't descend. It has to be absolutely straight. Parts dealers sometimes have replacement parts to correct this problem, and the ramp and rod combination is easily replaced.

This isn't an easy accessory to keep in good operating condition, but when it does work properly it is a lot of fun to watch — even more than its larger successors, which are more trouble-free. The bright enamel paint on the all-metal corral is much more

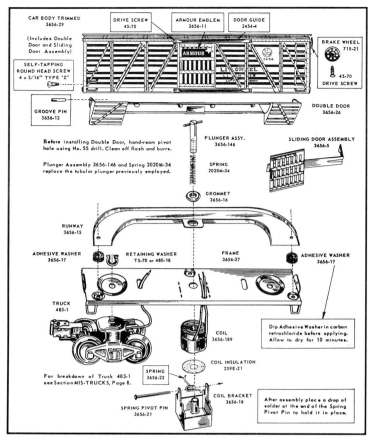

Schematic of 356 Operating Stock Car.

attractive than the plastic corrals of later units. If you can find a boxed example of the 3656 in excellent condition, it is worth paying a slight premium because it is much more likely to work properly. I would avoid the purchase of a heavily used example because of the potential maintenance and repair headaches. There's no denying the charm of this little accessory, however, and you should add it to your operating repertoire if you can. The new 19802 model operates more like the 3356 Horse Car and Corral than this accessory, and it comes with cattle equipped with felt pads instead of little fingers, so it operates much better.

• **6470/6480 EXPLODING BOXCAR:** Don't worry — I'm not telling you about a boxcar that literally explodes! In the late 1950s and early 1960s, Lionel brought out a large number of military and space-related train items, all of which were somewhat fragile but quite popular at the time. Some of these cars and accessories involved flying missiles which came off a spring-loaded ramp mounted on a car or a platform. Naturally, these missiles had to have targets. One was a sinister-looking squat green enclosure known as an ammunition dump. There was a spring-loaded mechanism inside the dump which would scatter the dump walls if a missile hit the building. It wasn't long before Lionel also built a target boxcar to perform the same function. You must carefully prop up the sides of this flimsily-built car and push down a rod connected to a powerful spring until it is held by a bracket — somewhat similar to an adapted mouse trap. The sides and roof of the car will only fit one way. When the car is struck by a missile — or anything else — the spring will release and scatter the sides and roof of the car to the four winds. During the times the car is traversing the layout, accidental operation of the sprung rod is prevented by a long aluminum pin which fits down through the car roof across the spring trip and into the metal car base. This pin is often missing when the car is found today, but a good old flat-headed nail will perform the same function. I'm very hesitant to recommend this car around young children because of its flimsy construction and, more appropriately, because the spring-loaded rod is very powerful. It can snap back like the spring of a mouse trap and inflict a painful sting on a young child. When this car is found today, the side pieces are often warped so badly that they will no longer fit into the slots designed to hold them. I view this car more as a collector's item than an operating piece. I'm also leery of the idea of missiles flying overhead because of the potential for abuse, even though the missiles are rubber-tipped.

• **6557/19807 SMOKING CABOOSES:** The old postwar 6557 Smoking Caboose wasn't produced for very long, but it has become a popular item among collectors. It is very hard to obtain now, but I'm including a discussion of it here because Lionel Trains, Inc. has produced a new model of it. The smoke unit in the older model was troublesome. For the 6557, Lionel used a No. 55 Light Bulb to produce the heat which vaporized the smoke; this bulb was a 7-volt pin-based lamp which is extremely hard to find today, since the smoking caboose was its one and only application. The lamp was also made to function as a resistor in the circuit, so no other lamp can be substituted. The model railroader lifted the cap of a chimney stack in the roof of the SP-style caboose and put a few drops of smoke fluid down the stack. Smoke would then curl out of the stack in thin wisps, as if someone were cooking breakfast inside the little car. The smoke was just about invisible when the caboose was in motion, so most operators left this car on a siding, where the smoke could be seen to greater advantage. The smoke generator for the new 19807 model is a newly designed convection-type unit which works much better than the older version. It looks better, too, because it is a Pennsylvania model of the big extended vision caboose.

PART 3:

INDEPENDENTLY OPERATING ACCESSORIES

• **97/397/497/2315 et al. COAL LOADERS AND STATIONS:** Coal has always been a big industry in Lionel Land. Over many years, Lionel has developed structures by which little plastic simulated coal can be moved into and out of cars, chutes, and conveyors. All of these coaling devices work reasonably well, but some are more difficult to maintain than others. It is best to talk about the three basic types of coal loaders chronologically. See Part Two for a discussion of the 456 Coal Ramp, another great coal accessory.

The big, tall No. 97 Coal Tower was a predominant accessory of the late prewar and early postwar period. It was made up to 1950, when it was replaced by the much smaller and less dramatic 397 model. This Coal Tower stands on a large black compression-molded plastic base with a receiving tray on one end. The model railroader brings a remote-control Coal Dump Car up to the tray and dumps coal into it. Perhaps several cars can be used this way; back in 1940, Lionel even made a special freight train of Coal Dump cars just for this accessory! The touch of a button on a controller activates the big AC motor hidden in the base; a string of little buckets on a conveyor chain dips into the coal and carries it up a metal girderwork path to the top of the tower, where the

97 Coal Elevator.

buckets dump the coal into a reservoir concealed inside a yellow tower house with a red roof. After the coal is put into the tower, the operator brings a coal car to the other side of the tower so that it is below a chute at the base of the tower house. Another button is pushed, and a solenoid opens the reservoir and allows the coal to slide down the chute and into the waiting car. The 97 can still be found in fine operating condition, since it was a very rugged accessory to begin with. It's noisy enough to let your neighbors know you're in the miniature coal business! There aren't many operating problems, but sometimes the little buckets have a tendency to work loose from their chain and fall off. Merely tighten them around the chain with needle-nose pliers. The bottom coal tray has to tilt slightly to lead the coal to the buckets, so make sure the rod attached to the tray is operating properly. Coal pieces can also jam the chute door open.

The 397 Coal Loader isn't nearly as spectacular as the 97, but it can be combined with the 456 Coal Ramp by means of a special chute with thick metal rods which attaches to the back of the 397. Then you can have a really complex operation which is plenty of fun to operate. As it is, the 397 model is a fine piece to have on a layout. Coal placed into the back of a tray is carried up a toothed rubber belt by a motor attached to a rotating rod with a universal joint. The motor is hidden by a generator housing. At the top of the belt, the coal is ejected off a scatter shield downward into a waiting car ... and sometimes onto the living room rug or floor if the voltage is too high. Meanwhile, a large tray is positioned over a cam which kicks it up and down, vibrating dumped coal back up the tray and into the receptacle at the rear of the belt. At least, that's the theory; in practice, you'll probably have to help the coal along with a brush from time to time. Every once in a while, the belt will jam, especially if you've tried to use some other substance besides Lionel No. 206 Coal or its replacements. (The coal comes in a little cloth sack and is readily available.) Lionel advised the operator to dust the underside of the belt with talcum powder every once in a while for smooth operation. If the belt still sticks, remove it from the track and apply Scotch tape along the track to keep coal from jamming the belt. The motor is a big AC unit which needs servicing only once in a while. Simply remove the generator cover for access to it. Be sure to try out a 397 for operation before you buy; it should operate briskly at no more than 14 volts.

The 497 Coal Tower straddles a track and operates quite a bit differently from either the 97 or the 397. A coal car dumps its load off to one side into a large plastic dump bin. This bin is attached to two strings which act as pull cables. When you press the operating button, a motor pulls the dump bin up by reeling in the strings. When the dump bin reaches the top of the tower, it dumps the coal into a reservoir above the track. After the dump

bin is lowered to the surface of the layout, the operator brings a hopper car underneath the accessory and pushes another button, which releases the coal out an opening in the reservoir and into the waiting car. This accessory works well, but great care must be taken not to overwind the strings, or the bin lifting mechanism will be misadjusted. Of course, the strings which lift the bin can be tangled or otherwise fouled if the accessory has been stored and tilted. Check the takeup reels beneath the coal reservoir to see that they have taken up the strings evenly. The latest production of this accessory substituted Lionel's new can-type motor for the older AC motor; the new motor is much quieter and it will operate on lower voltage, but it can't lift quite as heavy a load.

• **128/2308 ANIMATED NEWSSTAND/12718 ANIMATED REFRESHMENT STAND:** This little roadside accessory was one of Lionel's best accessories for animated action. It consists of a little flat-roofed Newsstand, complete with little paper magazine decoration, which rests on a light gray base made to resemble a sidewalk. Through a complicated system of rack and pinion devices moved by a vibrator mechanism, when the button is pressed the news vendor moves to the front window of his lighted cubicle, a newsboy turns on a rotating disc and raises a newspaper held in his hand, and an inquisitive little canine circles around a little red fire hydrant on one corner of the sidewalk! When Bruce Greenberg and I visited Frank Pettit a little while ago, Mr. Pettit, who was the designer of this and many other accessories, showed us his original mockup for this accessory. He also showed us a photograph of his dog, a little black and white terrier; this little animal has been immortalized as the model for the accessory's hydrant-circling dog. Few animals have become more familiar to Lionel train operators and collectors!

This accessory works by means of a drive spring system which is adjusted by spring tension. If the tension is wrong, the vibrator will not move the lever and sliding gear which works the man and the newsboy. The sliding lever usually stays positioned inside the slotted lever, but once in a while the nylon fitting which attaches one lever to the other will slip out of its socket, disabling the accessory. If you maintain the spring tension tightly enough, the accessory will work fine. See the operating diagrams in the fine Greenberg printing of the Lionel repair manual for further information about the working of this and other accessories.

The Newest version of this newsstand uses a redesigned drive mechanism, and the features have changed. The 12718 Refreshment Stand is decorated in very bright colors, right down

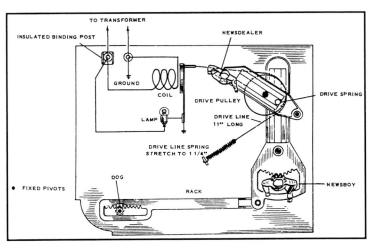

Schematic drawing of No. 128 Newsstand.

to a checkerboard color scheme on the stand counter. A huge rotating ice cream cone replaces the dog and the hydrant, while a boy and girl on roller skates now stand on the rotating disc once occupied by the newsboy. The counterman moves from front to back, as the newsman did before him, but his white uniform is more appropriate to the new version of this fine accessory. All of these accessories should be run slowly, at about 12 volts, to keep the operating mechanism in proper alignment and adjustment. You'll like this little piece in either of its forms!

342

345

• **342/345 CULVERT LOADER/UNLOADER:** This pair may be the most spectacularly operating accessories in the whole Lionel repertoire — when they are working in proper adjustment with a really steady hand on the voltage throttle! They can operate independently, but in practice they are often found together, and they are a great deal more attractive that way. Each piece comes with a special gondola car with an inclined ramp. This gondola contains cylindrical metal pieces of culvert pipe. The Unloader starts the action. When a button is pushed, culvert pipes in a waiting gondola are picked up by a magnet on a boom assembly which is controlled by strings attached to a drive belt operated by another vibrator mechanism. One end of the drive line is attached to a counterweight and the other end is secured to the drive belt. The magnet picks up the pipe section from the car and moves it across to the ramp on the accessory. Once the pipe section is over the ramp, it is "brushed off" the magnet by the edge of the platform.

If the Unloader is connected to the Loader by a special bridge section, the pipe section rolls across that bridge all the way down to the bottom of the Loader's ramp. When this accessory's button is pushed, a traveling crane with sliding jaws moves toward the waiting culvert pipe. The movable jaws grab the pipe, carry it back across its boom assembly, and drop the pipe into a waiting gondola.

If this all all sounds like Lionel's version of the famous board game *Mouse Trap*, you're absolutely right! I believe these two accessories to be the most complex operating devices ever issued by Lionel, and the trouble is that the more complex an accessory, the more likely something is to go wrong. The drive line and spring tension line on these pieces have to be at exactly the right length and tension. Every piece must be in absolutely perfect alignment. The voltage going to each accessory must be very, very carefully regulated. Finally, the culvert cars must be positioned precisely on the track, which also must be exactly aligned with the Loader and Unloaders themselves. Is it worth all the trouble to maintain and set up these two pieces? You'd better believe it is! No other Lionel accessory features such incredibly complicated action when these two companion pieces are working together! These pieces are a real study in precision and a terrific challenge

to operate. You'll need considerable practice in adjusting the operating voltage just right; no two operating pieces take the same voltage due to mechanical tolerances! Unfortunately, they are also quite expensive in excellent or better condition, and well-used pieces usually require considerable work and patience to get them operating again. If you want these accessories on your layout, either spend some extra money to secure truly excellent pieces or wait until you have experience repairing and maintaining vibrator-equipped accessories before you purchase one or both of these intriguing pieces.

455

• **455/2305 OPERATING OIL DERRICK:** Want to put a touch of J. Paul Getty onto your layout? Install one or more of these magnificently appointed and colored Oil Derricks. This accessory has a large metal base and tower with a crank hook suspended from the top of the tower by a piece of string. (It can be raised and lowered on a takeup drum with a little crank built into the drum.) When power is fed to the accessory, a thermostat operates a grasshopper-head pump every few seconds, and heat from a light bulb mounted underneath the base makes the liquid in a glass tube illuminate and bubble, just as the old Noma Lites of many Christmases ago once did in holiday displays. Just a few precautions are needed to make this a great addition to your layout. The electrical connections for this accessory are perilously close to the metal base; it might be wise to insulate them with a little friction tape once the wiring is connected to a constant 14 volts. Sometimes the lamp works loose and slips downward in its bracket. This causes it to lose physical contact with the bubble tube and fail to transfer its heat. Tape the bracket shut, and you will have no problem. Carefully position the bubble tube in its socket until it just barely touches the light bulb. If by severe mischance you break the tube, replacement tubes are available through parts dealers. The thermostat which operates the grasshopper pump adjusts by means of a small screw. If its action isn't fast enough, or too fast, turn the screw until the pump action satisfies you. Be patient; the adjustment is delicate. Make sure the little brass counterweight for the grasshopper pump is inside its little hole in the pump holding bracket. Both the sound and the appearance of this accessory add great action to your layout. This accessory is one of my stronger recommendations.

• **464/2301 OPERATING SAWMILL:** This long and imposing piece is cleverly designed to add a little illusion to your layout. When a Log Dump Car puts logs into the base of this accessory, they roll onto a belt with sprockets which pulls them into a building. However, they don't emerge from the other side of the building, as you'd expect. Instead, a little piece of cut and sawed lumber comes out the other side of the building and falls onto the base, ready for delivery to the lumber yard! Is there a little buzz saw inside the building? Not on your life! The round logs actually fall off inside the building into a hidden compartment where they can be retrieved later, totally intact. The little boards are separately loaded into a slot in the top of the roof, where they are grabbed by the same sprockets which brought the logs into the building. The belt is driven by a vibrator mechanism attached to a pulley and drive line; as with all the accessories powered by this apparatus, the drive line will need periodic adjustment — a relatively simple procedure. If the logs catch onto parts of the building, adjust the screws which hold the building together, and check for clearances. The old and the new versions of this accessory are identical except for their numbers. This accessory creates a great illusion for those who do not know its little secret!

• 2301 AMERICAN FLYER OIL DRUM LOADER: In the late 1960s, Lionel purchased the assets of its arch-rival, American Flyer, even as toy trains themselves were going into a serious decline. Now, twenty years later, this purchase has resulted in the reissue of many new American Flyer trains and two of Flyer's best accessories which will also work well with Lionel trains. One of these accessories is the American Flyer Oil Drum Loader, a very amusing piece which takes a great deal of concentration to operate. Five oil drums are loaded onto a little ramp. A little lift truck with wheels is placed onto a pin protruding from a sweep arm hidden beneath the platform; it is free to pivot on this pin. At the touch of a button, the lift truck scurries over to the ramp edge, where its end tilts the edge holding one of the barrels downward. The barrel transfers onto a little circular platform mounted onto the lift truck. The truck carries the barrel across the platform over to a waiting gondola, whose edge contacts a little hinged rest which holds the oil drum. This rest tilts the drum into the gondola and falls back to its horizontal position on the lift truck, and the whole operation begins again. I've found, much to my frustration at times, that the voltage needed to operate this accessory has to be very carefully precise. If the voltage isn't high enough, the drum rest on the truck will not fall back into the proper horizontal position, or the drum on the ramp will not tilt enough to stay on the truck platform. If the voltage is too high, the truck will knock

over the oil drum and fail to pick it up. It's a challenge to operate this little accessory, but its action is great and it works extremely well. It needs very little maintenance because of its sweep-arm operation; just make sure the lift truck is properly positioned on its operating pin. For the challenge, I heartily recommend this accessory.

• 2321 AMERICAN FLYER SAWMILL: This is the second American Flyer accessory reissued by Lionel to operate with Lionel trains, which it does very well. When the button is pressed, a little plastic saw blade rotates, and a man on a carriage rides back and forth on two rails. When he reaches the lumber house, two metal rods grab a piece of sawed lumber. The overhead carriage proceeds to a position over a waiting gondola, where the holding rods are made to tip the piece of lumber into the car. Here again, the operating mechanism is very simple and rugged, requiring very little attention. This accessory doesn't feature the illusion of the Lionel Sawmill (see 464 entry above), but it works very well and is quite amusing. We can look forward to the reissue of other American Flyer accessories in the future, it seems.

That, briefly (though it may not seem that way!), is a synopsis of some of the many Lionel accessories designed to add action to your layout. I can't begin to cover them all, but the preceding discussions of individual accessories should assist you in deciding which ones are the best to add to your layout. Do some pricing and space estimations, and you will know which accessories and operating cars are appropriate for your situation.

So now you have it all — trains, lights, accessories, scenery — in one happy assemblage designed to bring delight to you, your family, and your friends. From experience, I know that you will have taken a lot of trouble to achieve your idea of the perfect Lionel layout. The next chapter in this book will shift the focus slightly. Previously, I have told you how to get your layout into the way it now awaits your command, ready to beckon the onlooker. Now it is time to tell you how to keep your Lionel layout that way! You should learn all you can about basic testing, repair, and maintenance so your layout will remain a source of pleasure. Pick up your toolbox, follow me to the garage or basement, and listen to me while I tell you about the maintenance operations you should understand. This, too, is part of the fun!

Chapter IX
REPAIR AND MAINTENANCE

"Fierce-throated beauty!
Roll through my chant with all thy lawless music,
thy swinging lamps at night,
Thy madly-whistled laughter, echoing, rumbling like
an earthquake, rousing all,
Law of thyself complete, thine own track firmly holding..."
—Walt Whitman, "To A Locomotive In Winter"

When I was first involved with the operation of Lionel trains about twelve years ago, I couldn't have told you the difference between a smoke pellet and an eccentric crank. (No, not a grouchy old man!) To me, my little 8303 Jersey Central Steam Locomotive was not subject to breakdowns. One day, the engine began its usual oval circuit around the dining room table, but I noticed that it needed more power than usual. Then it began to screech unmercifully, finally grinding to a dead stop! Something had gone wrong!

I hurriedly took the sick engine to a local repair shop, hoping that the shop would not have to replace the motor. About a week later, I got a phone call that the locomotive had been repaired and was ready. When I arrived at the shop, I scanned the repair bill and the list of work that had been done. All I saw was "Cleaning and Lubrication...1 hr. total...$23.75." That was nearly the value of the locomotive! The service technician explained that a one-hour charge was the minimum and that the locomotive simply needed oiling and grease on the gears! Of course, the engine ran perfectly, but I had learned a very expensive lesson: Do your own repairs to the greatest extent possible! Use good judgment about what you can or cannot do yourself, of course.

From that time on, I secured a good service manual and learned how to do my own maintenance and repairs. Before too long, I learned that the repair and maintenance of Lionel trains is not very complicated at all; the skills needed for these services are well within the learning ability of nearly everyone, even the least mechanically inclined among train operators. Now it is routine for me to rewire circuits, maintain my own motors, rebuild smoke units, and so forth. You, too, can become a pretty good repair expert. Needless to say, I never took another locomotive to that repair shop again! The only time I will take a piece of Lionel equipment to a repair shop (I've since found a good one because my Friday night hangout, the Toy Train Station, does fine repairs) occurs when a reversing switch needs rewiring or a vibrator

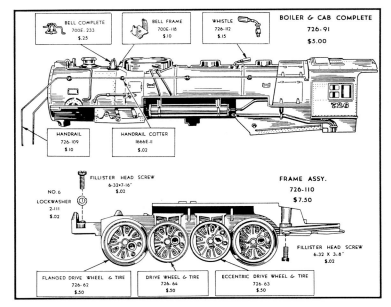

Lionel's schematic diagrams are famous for their completeness and accuracy.

mechanism becomes too tricky to adjust. I now do everything else myself. So can you!

Sometimes, in repairs, necessity will test your ingenuity. Once I was repairing and rebuilding a No. 60 Lionelville Trolley I had gotten inexpensively. It was cosmetically fine, but it needed a great deal of motor work. While I was rebuilding it, I had carried the motor (without thinking about the consequences) from my kitchen out to the garage workbench. Now, one of the parts is a miniscule ball bearing which fits into the brushplate. I dropped the motor onto the den carpet and lost the ball bearing! Can you imagine looking for a metal ball bearing in a gray carpet? No luck! I didn't think of using a magnet on a string. I didn't have a spare bearing at the time (I do now!), and I really wanted to test that motor. So I cut apart a small key chain and used one of the little metal balls from the chain as a replacement ball bearing! As a temporary testing expedient, it worked fine!

On another occasion, I had a big ZW Transformer which had seen better days. One of the handles had become so abused over the years that its plastic inner surfaces had been worn off. Thus, it would not bear against the control which brought the throttle back when the lever was pulled back, and the throttle would not turn off all the way due to the lack of tension of the plastic handle against the shaft. To fix this, I installed a small radiator hose clamp for automotive fuel lines and tightened it against the plastic around the shaft. It worked perfectly — even better than the other throttle which had not come loose! Admittedly, these are very unusual repairs, but they do point out that if you use your ingenuity, there's a way to fix almost anything in Lionel applications!

REASONS WHY YOU SHOULD DO YOUR OWN REPAIRS AND MAINTENANCE

Actually, there are three reasons why you should learn to do your own repair and maintenance work. I've already discussed the first reason indirectly — money. Repair work done by a professional can get expensive, just as it does at an auto repair shop. Lionel trains are no different. Believe it or not, Lionel supplied its service stations with repair literature as extensive as the manuals found in auto shops. The possession of these service manuals or a good repair and maintenance book will give you all the guidance you need before you begin a repair job. The money you save will not only pay for the books, but also become available for the purchase of more and better trains. Remember a principle we established back in the track work chapter: Time and labor are a substitute for money in this hobby.

The second reason for learning how to do your own repairs is to discover for yourself the fine craftsmanship and the inventiveness which have been the hallmarks of Lionel trains from the beginning. I never cease to wonder at just how well Lionel trains are made when I take apart my 675 or 2025 Locomotive for service. This model is a difficult locomotive to disassemble, but it runs superbly if it is maintained properly. I look at the intricate intermeshing of the gears, the delicate and complex rod assemblies, and the obvious craftsmanship of this locomotive with considerable awe. No wonder I have locomotives older than I am which still work perfectly! (I wish I could make that claim about myself!) It is even more wondrous that these engines were built not as fine machines, but as toys to be played with by children! When you see for yourself the workings of a spur-gear or worm-drive electric motor, a vibrator mechanism, or a solenoid mechanism, you will understand why Lionel trains have a deserved reputation for durability and long life. That's a pretty good lesson to observe!

The third reason why you should learn to repair your own trains is that these repairs are, in fact, part of the fun. Joshua Lionel Cowen encouraged young people to study the workings of his electric motors; in fact, one of the most popular items he sold in the 1920s was the "Bild-A-Loco" kits, which required assembly by the purchaser. It's no different today; you and your children can learn a great deal about the workings and principles of small electric motors and mechanisms through your repair efforts, not to mention the solid lessons in wiring and the use of tools. Repairs of Lionels are relatively easy and quite safe — a good deal easier and safer than working on the family car! There's nothing quite so rewarding as the successful meeting of a repair challenge. My own favorite repair is the conversion of a smoke unit in the older Lionel steamers from the toaster-wire element which uses the outmoded pills to the new diode-resistor unit which accepts the

far superior liquid smoke fluid. Later in this chapter, I'll tell you how to do this conversion. Every time I see a nice old steamer roaring down the track with billowing smoke puffs coming out of its stack, I feel considerable satisfaction.

BUILDING A TEST TRACK AND ASSEMBLING THE RIGHT TOOLS

If you're going to do your own repairs, don't go halfway; either get the right test facilities and tools or confine yourself to simple lubrication. This is just a matter of common sense. No repair shop of any kind can operate without the right tools and facilities. You, too, should have a mini-repair facility in your home where you can perform the two services needed for any repair or maintenance tasks — diagnosis and treatment. Fortunately, since you are dealing with a relatively small set of objects, you can repair your trains at a small desk just as easily as you can at a large garage or basement workbench.

The first part of your repair facility should be the construction of a test track. In the "old days," Lionel supplied its service stations with some elaborate test devices which had everything built into a large metal cabinet — light bulb test circuits, amp and voltage meters, transformer throttles, and so forth. Atop these tester cabinets was a length of track which could test any function of Lionel's equipment. These testers are very expensive now, and they do not come up for sale very often. However, you can build the rough equivalent of the Lionel testers for far less money.

For your test track, use a piece of pine board about three inches wide by one inch thick. Cut off about two and a half to three feet of this board — enough to place four sections of O Gauge track on its top surface. I specify O Gauge track because it will hold up better than the lighter O27 track, and the O Gauge remote track is better for testing purposes. One of the four O Gauge track sections should be a UCS remote track, complete with its two-button controller. This track will enable you to test Lionel's operating cars and truck uncoupling mechanisms. Another should be an insulated track section; this will allow the testing of track side signals under real operating conditions. Two rugged bumpers should be installed at either end of the test track sections; I'd suggest a pair of the die-cast tuscan 2283 models, which are readily available at a good price. Since they attach to the track with screws, they are not very likely to be knocked off the track by a locomotive.

Now, all you will have to do to complete your test track is to secure a small transformer with a direction and whistle control. For this purpose, I use an old prewar No. 1041 Transformer, which has 60 watts — enough power to test anything you put on the track. Many similar small transformers will also do well. In a pinch, you can secure a small transformer without whistle and direction controls and hook it to the test track through a 167C Controller, which will give you both functions. However, the 1041 is plentiful and available at a decent price. An American Flyer 100-watt 8B Model with a 167C Controller is also a relatively inexpensive and effective set-up for a test track. Finally, you should have several lengths of wire with large insulated alligator clips fastened to the ends. Use these to hook up power from the middle and outside track rails to lighted or animated accessories for their testing.

The tools you should assemble are for the most part just like any household tool set, except smaller. Screwdrivers, for ex-

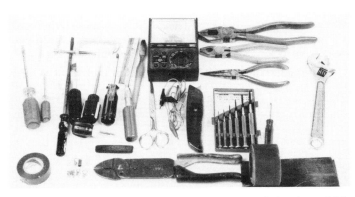

Some of the many tools, clamps, fasteners, tapes, and abrasives which you will find handy for your train work.

ample, are the most common tools you will use. I'd suggest that you get at least three of the smaller sizes of flat-bladed and Phillips-head screwdrivers and add to these a set of fine jeweler's screwdrivers. An angled screwdriver for tight corners would be useful, and I've found that a grip-type screwdriver is a very handy tool. With this screwdriver, you can place the blade in the screw's slot and expand the blade inside the slot so it will hold the screw while you put it in place. You'll find this screwdriver very handy for diesel locomotive body shell screws, the four screws which hold the old box tender shell to its base, and especially the slide-valve screws on some steam engines, which can be devilish to replace otherwise.

Next to screwdrivers, various kinds of pliers are frequently used tools. The standard pair of household pliers has some applications, but for Lionel trains there are several other types which should be used. A small pair of needle-nosed pliers is great for shaping track pins to rails, among many other chores. In fact, Lionel and other manufacturers have made a special pair of pliers with a notch at the ends made especially for reshaping track rails around their pins. Sometimes pliers also have the function of wire strippers and cutters. I make frequent use of a good pair of linesmen's pliers for that purpose, although there are many other types of wire cutters. Small nipper pliers can shape and cut materials very well. A special gripping instrument would be a medical hemostat; this is a special gripping tool which looks like a pair of scissors with a flat blade at the end. With these, you can hold two edges of materials together, perhaps for gluing or soldering purposes. The hemostat acts like a third hand.

There are many different types of abrasive materials which should form an integral part of your train tool chest. Among these are emery cloth (the "black sandpaper" you can get at any hardware store), grits paper (which I mentioned in the track cleaning section), emery boards for cleaning electrical points on whistle and E-unit relays, and the abrasive eraser material sometimes called a "bright boy." These materials can perform a wide variety of cleaning tasks for you.

You're going to be cutting and stripping a large quantity of wire, so wire stripping and crimping tools of many kinds should be in your toolbox. I've already mentioned linesmen's pliers, but there are other kinds of strippers and cutters, too. There is a really clever wire cutter and stripper on the market which can cut and strip as many as six wires simultaneously. This is a great aid to stripping wire on three-, four-, and five-wire Lionel accessories. A tension wheel on the device adjusts for any thickness of wire, and a moving metal edge inside it takes the insulation off the wire

as you squeeze a trigger mechanism, somewhat like a pair of grass snippers. To attach spade lugs to the ends of the wire, you would be wise to get an electrician's cutting and crimping tool. This tool crimps the lug to the bare end of the wire, keeping it in place securely. Most of these crimpers can also cut and strip wire as well.

Don't forget to secure or make up a variety of test leads and devices. You will need at least four or five wires with alligator clips on either end to make temporary connections for testing purposes. To make a crude but effective voltage tester, take the light socket out of an old toy street lamp post or set of Christmas tree lights and put a large-globe 14-volt lamp into it. Then attach alligator clips to the ends of the wire leads, and you have a voltage indicator. This is very handy for testing transformers, since if there is a "dead spot" in the transformer's secondary coil, you will find it because the light bulb will blink or increase its brightness erratically rather than steadily. When this light bulb tester is connected to transformer leads, it will also test the whistle and direction controls. The light bulb should go out when the direction control is used, and the extra DC voltage from the whistle controller will brighten the light bulb. For more sophisticated testing, an inexpensive voltmeter is handy for detecting voltage drops in sections of track. If you set the transformer's voltage at 14 volts, you should get uniform readings all along the track. If one track registers less voltage than the others, you've located a troublesome voltage drop. Another handy tool is a circuit tester, which can be used to detect whether a remote track is working when a button is pushed.

This is the best way to test your track voltage — a voltmeter. Here, I am sending about 15 volts into the track. If the voltage in the next track section is less, I know I have got a corroded center-rail pin on my hands at that point.

There are other handy tools to fill up that toolbox. A set of miniature wrenches has many different applications; you may need just such a tool to take a drive rod off a main wheel on a steam locomotive, for example. A soldering iron is very useful, of course; try to get the gun-type unit rather than the pencil-type unit, because the gun-type unit will heat up much faster, is easier to control, and has an easier tip to replace. However, a small pencil-type soldering iron can reach into tight places, as in the connections for an E-unit reversing switch and locomotive repairs. Resin-core solder is a must. Never use acid-core solder in toy train applications; it has a corrosive quality which can wreak havoc on

Lubricating points.

your tracks and equipment. A little jeweler's saw is very handy for cutting pieces of plastic and balsa wood, and no toy train enthusiast can do without an assortment of modeler's hobby knives such as those made by X-Acto. In these knives, saw and knife blades are available and can be interchanged among various handles.

Finally, one of the wisest acquisitions for the toy train modeler would be the Dremel Moto-Tool or its equivalent. This little wonder is a small electric drill and grinder with either rigid or flexible shafts and a staggering variety of attachments for many different uses. Several hobby supply houses offer a whole range of fine miniature tools, even motorized ones; while these can make repairs a lot more efficient, they are not absolutely necessary.

Another topic to consider is the acquisition of spare parts. Previously, I had said that you should never throw anything away, even the most rusted and bashed-up old junk piece you can find. The reason is parts. Believe it or not, several dealers I know specialize in this "junk," and they do quite well selling whole boxes of it to Lionel train enthusiasts. Pick up an inexpensive carton of junk parts and sort them out; you never know when something you've salvaged will come in handy! Over the years, I've managed to fill two carriers of plastic drawers with all kinds of odd parts, and they do come to the rescue many times. I have a large plastic bag full of parts just for my old 1121 Turnouts, all salvaged from junk! Several friends have brought me their 1121 Switches, and I've been able to restore missing parts, even replace whole solenoids!

LUBRICATION AND SURFACE CLEANING:

A POTPOURRI OF DOS AND DON'TS

As I had said in the opening to this chapter, I learned about lubrication somewhat expensively. Oiling and greasing your engines, rolling stock, and accessories is by far the most important maintenance chore you will perform, so it is essential that you learn to do it the right way. Many newcomers to the hobby make the mistake of over-lubrication. That just results in oil and grease fouling up the electrical contact points and much dirt on the tracks. A little lubrication goes a long, long way! Another nasty result of over-lubrication is the congealing of grease on moving parts, which can bring the strongest locomotive to a dead stop in extreme cases. I can't begin to tell you how many F-3 and steam turbine locomotives, which have worm drive motors, I've had to clean of congealed grease inside the worm drive gears. This is a dirty job which should be performed on all used examples of the turbine and F-3 engines. The same is true of the magnificent Berkshire

steamers and the large Hudsons. The new teflon-reinforced greases do not congeal in this way, but that doesn't mean you won't have to service older motors for this problem.

The right kinds of lubricants are just as important as their quantities. The best oil for Lionel trains is light machine oil dispensed from a needlepoint oiler — nothing else will do the job right! Sewing machine oil or clock oil are both excellent for Lionel trains and, according to Arthur Broshears (who will be talking about this in the next chapter), automatic transmission fluid is really efficient. You can get this light oil from many companies such as the Labelle firm, which makes an excellent line of plastic-compatible oils and greases especially for the toy train hobbyist. Labelle has marketed a kit with oil, grease, and application tools which is really handy for toy train operators. There are some lubricants which should never be used, among them heavier greases and such household oils as 3-in-1 Oil. These greases and oils will eventually leave a varnish which will gum up the works of your motors, and they also will discolor plastic surfaces.

There are some very good spray lubricants on the market, especially WD-40 Oil, but they should be used with caution. Since WD-40 is meant to be applied in larger quantities than would usually be used on toy trains, just the slightest squirt of the pressurized oil through its application tube should be enough to lubricate your moving parts. WD-40 is a good temporary lubricant, but regular oil will last longer.

To get rid of congealed grease and dirt before lubrication, there are several types of spray cleaners you should secure and use. I have mentioned my favorite solvent for many toy train uses, CRC 5-56 Compound. This solvent drives out rust and dirt and dissolves congealed grease and old oil deposits on motor surfaces. I've brought some really filthy motors back to life with this solvent and the careful use of Q-Tips! Among other cleaners available to you are television tuner cleaners, which are great for contact points on whistle relays and E-units, and spray pistol and rifle cleaners, which are excellent for metal surfaces. Radio Shack sells a fine cleaner/de-greaser (part no. 64-2322). I stress that none of these are lubricants; they are used to clean out motors, etc. before lubrication. I'd be very hesitant to use any of these to clean painted surfaces or plastic.

The best way to clean an old piece of plastic or painted rolling stock is to use a mild solution of dishwashing detergent and water together with an old, soft toothbrush. If your equipment is a metal prewar piece with flaking paint, I'd be hesitant to attempt to clean it, even with detergent and water. The cure of flaking paint is a job for a professional restorer; many good and experienced people who do this work advertise their services in the model railroading magazines.

A few final pieces of advice about cleaning: Many times, when you buy an old used piece of Lionel rolling stock, the metal trucks and wheels will have whitened with age. This is the result of a mildewing process on the metal surfaces. To get rid of this mildew, use a toothbrush to apply a little vegetable oil such as Crisco Oil, and the mildew will disappear like magic! Rust is another matter, and a far more difficult problem. You can at least get rid of some of the rust on metal surfaces by applying a product called Naval Jelly with a small paint brush, but the surface will never look exactly like new. Some train enthusiasts have purchased tumbling machines which do a great job of getting rid of rust and dirt, although the process is long, noisy, and laborious. This tumbling process works extremely well with rusted trucks and wheel sets, although of course these must be removed from the piece of rolling stock before the treatment.

Now, let us get to specifics about lubrication of motors and friction points in your rolling stock. First of all, remember that Lionel put out some excellent instruction sheets for its equipment showing the proper oiling points for each type of locomotive. A good repair and operating manual will have this information. In general, however, lubrication of the moving parts is easy if you use the right oils and greases and apply them sparingly.

First, let's look at the motor of a steam engine. Lionel's steam locomotives usually work with either of two types of motor: spur-drive or worm-drive. Of these, the spur-drive motor is by far the most common. The wheels are attached through the frame of the locomotive with porous bronze bearings which can hold a supply of oil. It's important to get a drop of oil into each of these bearings and work it into the surfaces. To do that, place your needlepoint oiler between the frame and the inside surface of each drive wheel and apply a drop (ONE drop!) of oil. After you treat each wheel, rotate the wheel manually to work the oil into the bearing. Repeat this process until all the drive wheels have been lubricated.

The next step is to get at the ends of the motor's armature shaft. Look at the brushplate where the two caps holding the brushes protrude from the plate. Right between these will be a metal shaft. This is one end of the armature; place a drop of oil onto the shaft at the point where it meets the brushplate and rotate the wheels to work the oil into this friction point. Now, go to the other side of the locomotive motor. The other end of the armature shaft usually is found protruding from a porous bronze bearing attached to the motor frame. Apply another drop of oil to this end of the armature and work it in by rotating the wheels.

Now you should apply your light grease to the locomotive's spur gears. Apply a thin film of grease to each of the gear surfaces, small and large. Rotate the gears so you work the lubricant into the gear surfaces. Be very, very careful about how much grease you apply; only a little is needed. If you overdo your grease work, your steam engine's wheels will throw excess grease all over your rails — not to mention the motor surfaces. Modern Teflon greases are best to use in this application, although — believe it or not — I still use an old tube of original Lionel lubricant from the late 1950s! It happens to be perfectly preserved, and after all, it was especially formulated for this use!

Next, let's look at the worm-drive motors, which are used in the F-3 diesels, the steam turbines, and the Berkshire steamers. Things get a little more complicated here. Oil the drive wheels as you would the spur drive motors, but the armature shaft here is a special problem. On Lionel's worm-drive motors, be careful to just use one drop of oil at the brushplate between the brush holders, and no more. Any excess oil will soon leak onto the commutator plates, where it will cause you great grief as it gums up the brushes and plates. The other end of the armature shaft on these motors contacts a worm gear. This gear has to get a supply of grease every so often. On the steam turbines and Berkshires, this procedure requires disassembly of the locomotive. You'll find a little metal plate covering the gear; simply lift off this cover, clean any old grease out of the worm gear, and apply new grease sparingly. On the F-3 diesels, there are two types of worm motors, horizontal in the older models and vertical in the newer models. You'll see a small hole in the horizontal models in the metal casing between the motor and the double gears. Place a drop of oil into this hole and a little grease on the exposed gears. On the newer

models, look down through the motor where the gear on the armature meets a worm drive gear at the base of the motor's attachment point to the frame. Clean this sump out if necessary (sometimes you'll have to take off the motor to do a thorough job of this) and apply new grease along the turned section of the armature shaft. That grease will work its way down onto the worm drive gear.

Most of the diesels produced since 1970 possess a motor which is integral with the drive wheels and trucks. This motor has nylon gears and is relatively easy to lubricate. After you've removed the plastic cab (more on that later on), turn the armature of the motor so you can see the end of the shaft going down into the gear works. Apply a little grease to the shaft of the armature where it contacts the drive gear. Proceed as usual with the other oiling and greasing points of the locomotive motor.

Incidentally, replacing the drive gears on their shafts is no easy job; it's best left to a professional if the gear is stripped, especially if it is an older brass gear. However, you can replace the nylon gears in a modern era diesel locomotive fairly easily. Many of these motors experience a problem with the nylon gears from the first five years of Fundimensions production. This is known as Cold Flow failure. The main nylon gear will strip very easily because the nylon surface is too soft where the gear is attached to its turning shaft. Recent engines do not have this problem. If you have been the victim of Cold Flow failure, secure a replacement main gear (easily available at a modest cost) and fasten it to the turning shaft with cyanoacrylate glue (such as Krazy Glue), which will prevent the problem from occurring again.

Many of the modern era motors in both steam and diesel form have rubber traction tires around the drive wheels. Unfortunately, these little tires can become glazed if they are exposed to grease or oil on the tracks. They also become brittle with age and crack, and they can stretch so they jump right out of the sockets in the drive wheels. This causes loss of traction and a phenomenon known as "axle hop." You'll know it when you see it; under load, the locomotive will shake like a belly dancer! You might even find the rubber drive belt tangled around the wheel or axle. To prevent this problem, replace the rubber tires with new ones, easily available at low cost. Pry the old tire loose from the drive wheel with a small screwdriver. Work the new tire onto the

Be sure to get one drop of oil on each end of the motor's armature shaft, as I'm doing here. This end is located between the brush wells. Never oil the brushes themselves! M. Feinstein photograph.

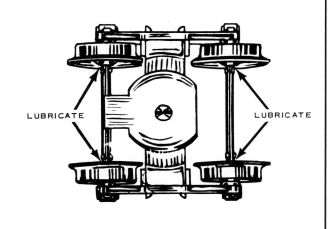

This instruction sheet shows lubrication points for the wheel sets. On modern equipment, lubrication usually isn't necessary.

wheel carefully; it's a job which requires some patience. Then, apply some rubber cement to the inside surface of the wheel and cement the traction tire to the wheel slot. This will prevent axle hop and keep the tire on the wheel, and since you've used rubber cement, you can pry the tire off the wheel when it is worn out. As a matter of practice, I replace all glazed traction tires whenever I purchase a diesel locomotive made after 1969. This rubber cement treatment works very well.

Since I don't usually run postwar rolling stock on my layout, I seldom oil the bearings of the freight and passenger cars. The rolling stock produced since 1970 features needlepoint bearings and Delrin plastic (or metal) trucks, and this arrangement is so friction-free that oiling is rarely required. Postwar rolling stock is another matter, since the wheels rotate on the axles instead of within bearings in the side frames. Clean the wheel sets with a small screwdriver blade scraped against the wheel surface where it meets the flange. Then, use a small drop of oil at each point where the wheel contacts the axle; rotate each wheel to work the oil into the axle hole. This will help the wheel sets of postwar freight and passenger cars rotate more freely, but because of their design and age they are no match for the easy-wheeling modern era freight and passenger cars, which I prefer to run due to less stress on my locomotives and the opportunity to run longer trains with the same power levels.

DISASSEMBLING YOUR LOCOMOTIVES FOR SERVICING

Perhaps I've put the proverbial cart before the horse, since often a thorough lubrication of a locomotive requires the temporary separation of the locomotive cab or boiler from its frame. However, now that we've reviewed basic cleaning and oiling instructions, it is wise to discuss locomotive disassembly. Most Lionel locomotives pose few problems for the toy train equivalent of the "weekend warrior." In the steam locomotive area, some older models must be taken apart with considerable care because you must detach the drive rods from the steam chests in order to get at the motor housing, reversing switch, and smoke unit. These

include the 675/2025/2035 2-6-2 models, the 1666/2026/2036 models and all their derivatives, and the 637/2037/2029 models. By far, the toughest of all these are the 675/2025/2035 models. Disassembly of these locomotives must be done with a great deal of patience and care. On the other hand, all of the Hudson, Berkshire, and steam turbine models are a snap to take apart. It's impossible to cover all the Lionel steam locomotives comprehensively in this area, so some general instructions here will do as long as you have a diagram of the locomotive from the instruction sheet or a service manual-repair guide.

First of all, place your locomotive on a large, soft piece of toweling to prevent any possibility of scratching the painted surfaces. In addition, prepare an area to place all the parts in some

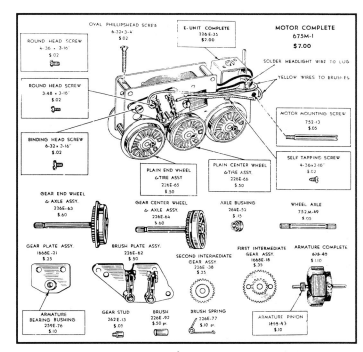

Schematic of motor unit for 675 Steam Locomotive.

semblance of order, so you can reverse the disassembly process when you put the locomotive back together. The more you organize your task before you touch a screw, the better. Keep a repair and operating manual handy; open it to the page where an "exploded" diagram of your locomotive appears. Not only will these diagrams give you all the part numbers you may need to replace a part, they will also show you how each of the parts fits with its mates. The presence of a good repair manual eliminates a great deal of guess work!

The main screws which hold the boiler to the frame on a Lionel steam engine are usually a large Phillips-head screw at the top of the boiler and another large slotted-head screw attached at the bottom through the steam chest piece. (Actually, these are bolts, but most people use the term "screws" for them.) Before you attack these, take off the front or the rear trucks of the locomotive — sometimes both. If the locomotive has a separate piece for the boiler front, detach this piece by unscrewing the small screw (if any) at the top which holds the boiler front to the boiler casting. After you take out the top screw, detach the bottom screw from the steam chest piece. On the Hudsons, Berkshires, and steam turbines, the boiler will now lift clear of the chassis. In addition, these three models do not have screws on their boiler tops; they just have three or four screws on the bottom. On the locomotives which need to have their drive rods disassembled, you have some further work to do. Use a gripper-type screwdriver to take out the screws, one on each side, which hold the slide valves into the steam chests. Before you take off the steam chest piece from these locomotives, detach the slide valve piece from the drive rod and put it in a safe place. In this way, you won't be surprised by a bouncing part on your floor! Now, take off the steam chest piece very carefully, making sure that the light bulb in its holder is detached from its holding socket, if that's possible. (Sometimes you can't do this, and you have to put up with a semi-detached steam chest piece.) Now, you should be able to lift your boiler off the chassis, as long as you've remembered to punch out the holding rod at the rear of the motor frame from its holes where it runs across the boiler to support the motor frame.

When you are through whatever service you are to perform (more on servicing the inside components later), most of the time all you will have to do is reverse your disassembly procedure to reassemble the steam locomotive. However, on the locomotives which require disassembly of the drive rods, there are a few precautions necessary to prevent running problems. First of all, when you place the boiler shell back on the frame, check to see that the rod which works the smoke unit piston is in its proper place and that the wire leading to the headlight is not fouled in the smoke mechanism or assembly. When you reattach a separate steam chest piece, rotate the driver wheels so the main drive rod on one side is in its rearmost position. Slide the end of the drive rod onto the slide valve piece and insert the slide valve, the drive rod, and the eccentric rod into the holes provided for them on the steam chest. Now, rotate the drive wheels so the drive rod on the other side is in its rearmost position and repeat the assembly process. Then tighten the whole assembly by installing the eccentric rod screws (if any) and the slide valve screws, using a gripper screwdriver so you won't go bananas by dropping the screws into the boiler itself.

One more note on these complex locomotives when you reassemble them: Sometimes the eccentric crank pieces on the center drive wheels will loosen and slip out of place. If the locomotive is reassembled when this has occurred, the drive wheels will not be properly quartered and the whole drive rod mechanism will jam when you first run the engine. I've seen these engines with bent rods because of this. To prevent this little catastrophe, make sure the eccentric crank pieces are quartered properly. These little pieces attach to the drive wheels by means of a small screw and two little prongs which fit into recesses on the wheel. When the assembly is properly done, the eccentric cranks will point in opposite directions so that when one rod is fully drawn out of the steam chest, the other one will be fully extended into the steam chest. If this is not the case, simply rotate one of the eccentric crank pieces so that the prongs fit into the wheel in the opposite holes from their starting points. Tighten these crank pieces securely to prevent any possibility of slipping out of the wheel sockets. The rod mechanisms of these locomotives are beautiful to watch when the engine is running, but are they ever a devil to keep in synchronization! Fortunately, basic lubrication and cleaning can be done without taking the boilers from the frames of these engines.

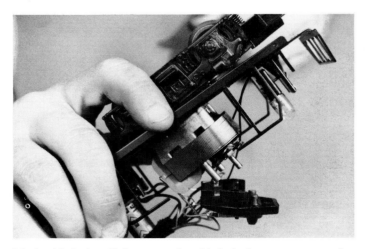

Maybe this looks a little strange, but this is the best way to reattach a brushplate to a motor so that the brushes stay in place. Turn the whole chassis upside down and push on the brushplate from below, with the brushes in their wells. M. Feinstein photograph.

With many Lionel steam locomotives, you can clean off the commutator plate without disassembling the engine. Just put some solvent on a cotton swab, place it against the copper plate segments, and spin the wheels a bit. M. Feinstein photograph.

Most of Lionel's diesels attach to their frames by means of two small screws, one at either end of the cab. On the F-3 diesels, the cabs attach by a screw at the pilot end and two spring clips at the other end of the cab (except for early models, which have three screws). On some models, particularly the GP series made from 1971 to about 1975, some delicate plastic side railings are imperiled unless they are disassembled before the cab comes off. That's an easy procedure; merely separate the wire piece from the small plastic uprights before you take off the cab. When you reassemble the cabs to the frames, beware of cracking the plastic cab by overtightening the attachment screws! The NW-2 switchers and the big Fairbanks-Morse diesels are particularly prone to this problem; I've seen many of these cabs with cracked screw holes. Actually, the best way to reassemble the screw to the cab shell once the shell is in place is to balance the screw atop your screwdriver (easy to do with the Phillips-head screws) and turn the locomotive itself on its nose to start the screw in its screw hole.

Two special precautions apply to specific models of the Lionel diesels. Some of the GP Series diesels have stamped-steel railings with curved edges which fit into recesses in the cab under the windows. These edges can scratch the bejabbers out of the attractive paint jobs on the cabs if you're not careful when you take off the cab shell. This can be prevented by carefully sliding two 3" x 5" index cards between the cab shell and the railings when you take off the cab. The cards will shield the cab from the railing edges. Use the cards again when you reinstall the plastic cab shell. Make sure no wiring is caught under the cab shell edges against the stamped-steel frame when you replace the screws.

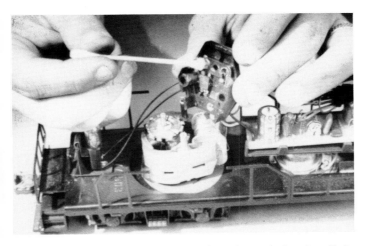

When you are cleaning up your motor, don't forget the brush wells in the brushplate — see the dirt on the cotton swab? Note the nice clean commutator plate on the armature. M. Feinstein photograph.

The other precaution applies to the F-3 diesel series. Once you have unscrewed the holding screw from the pilot piece, you'll have to deal with the two spring clips at the back of the cab. Very, very carefully and slowly, lift the front edge of the cab shell and move it from side to side, gradually working the clips at the back free of the frame. Exert too much force during this operation, and you'll crack the cab shell! Once you have the front of the cab free of the notch at the pilot where the cab shell slips down into the frame, you'll have a little more room to work the shell free. Be extremely careful during this operation — I've seen many an F-3 cab shell cracked at the rear!

SERVICING THE ELECTRIC MOTOR IN LOCOMOTIVES AND SOME ACCESSORIES

Now that we've discussed the basic lubrication and disassembly of the locomotives, it is time we got specific about the kind of services you should perform on the motor itself once you have your little beauty apart. Note that the instructions I give here will also work for many accessories which are powered by Lionel's big universal AC-DC motors, rugged pieces of equipment indeed! Even so, occasionally you are going to have to disassemble the motor itself for cleaning and brush replacement. Do this every once in a while, and you will keep your electric motors in a top-notch state of performance. Here's how to dismantle and service your electric motors.

First, you must remove the brushplate at the top of the motor. This is a Bakelite plastic, nylon or (on the steam engines) fiber piece which holds the motor brush wells and one end of the motor's armature. Two wire terminals are also found here; ordinarily, these are not your worry, unless you are going to replace the brushplate itself. In that case, you will simply unsolder the wire leads from the old brushplate and re-solder them to the new one. Two small screws usually hold the brushplate onto the motor frame. Remove these screws — but don't take the plate off its retaining pegs just yet! Turn the whole locomotive upside down before you work the brushplate loose. In this way, the carbon brushes will stay firmly put inside their brush wells, and they won't drop unexpectedly to the floor.

Now, remove the brushes from their wells and set them aside for cleaning later. You have now exposed the commutator plates atop the rotating armature. To clean these, place the end of a toothpick into the slots between the commutator plates and scrape out any accumulated dirt. These slots must be clean for proper electrical continuity. NEVER use anything metal on the slots or these plates; you could scratch or even detach the plates, ruining the armature in the process. Now, put some cleaning solvent on the end of a Q-tip and clean off the commutator plates until their copper finish shines. You might have to use a friction cleaner such as an electrical "eraser" cleaner to get all the dirt off. Also clean the areas around the motor frame, the inside surface of the brushplate, and especially the brush wells with your solvent. Dirt is your enemy; the more you remove, the better your motors will run!

On many Lionel engines, the armature can be removed from the motor assembly itself. Do this if it is at all possible, because this procedure will enable you to do a more thorough cleaning job. You should be able to remove the armature from most of the diesel locomotive motors, but not from the spur drive and worm drive steam locomotives. If you can get at the geared area on the lower armature, clean it off with solvent. Now look into the bottom of the motor. You should be able to spot the main drive gear down where it is connected to the drive wheel axles. This little area, which I often call the "sump" because it holds lubricant, should also be cleaned out, especially if it is packed with congealed or dirty grease. Once all these areas are cleaned (and in the process, your pile of dirty Q-tips will really accumulate!), use a little lubricant to re-lubricate the main drive gear. In addition, place a thin film of lubricant on the machined area of the lower armature rod where it is meant to engage the drive gear. When you replace the armature, make sure it engages the drive gear properly. You can do this by rotating the armature until it locks into the gear and turns the drive wheels.

Now, before re-assembling the motor, clean off the brushes, those little carbon rods you took from the brushplate. Do this with a clean cloth soaked in a little solvent. Bring the ends of the brushes to a shine by using an eraser-type cleaner. If the brushes are too worn or badly encrusted, they should be replaced with their proper equivalents. The brushes should be the same length, but I've been surprised on some locomotives I've taken apart because one brush is shorter than the other. This can result in the locomotive running faster in one direction than the other; another cause of this problem is that one of the little springs inside the brush holes is pressing the brush onto the commutator plate more firmly than is the other spring. Pull the end of each spring back carefully to restore proper tension if that is the case.

Ready for re-assembly? Here are a few suggestions to make the re-assembly of a motor less frustrating. First, make sure the armature is engaging its drive gear properly, as I've noted above. Turn the locomotive upside down so the brushplate must be moved upwards to be fastened to the motor housing. Insert the carbon brushes into their holders on the brushplate; the upside-down position of the locomotive will insure that they stay there in spite of the spring tension. Now, keeping the locomotive inverted, work the brushplate back onto its holders. Keeping the brushplate secure with your finger, you should then turn the locomotive right side up and install the holding screws for the brushplate; don't over-tighten them, or you'll run the danger of cracking the brushplate, especially the old Bakelite ones, which get very brittle with age.

Two final notes about brushplates are worth noting. First, many of the diesel motors have carbon brushes with little slots to accept the spring rods of the plate. Turn each brush gently with a small slotted screwdriver until the spring rod rests inside the brush slot. With the newer diesel locomotive motors, many people don't realize that the top hole for the armature end is adjustable to reduce "play" in the armature when it is powered and engages the drive gear. There's a projection atop the brushplate which has a miniscule hexagonal screw fitting inside. You can tighten or loosen this fitting with a small Allen wrench; check the up-and-down movement of the armature by running the locomotive on your test track with the cab shell off. The armature should move upwards just a little bit when this brushplate fitting is properly adjusted. If there is too much upward movement, the motor will put too much stress on the drive gear. On some of the diesel motors made in the mid-1970s, the main drive gear was made of a fragile fiber material instead of its usual nylon. Too much stress on this gear can strip it, and since the gear can't be removed from its driveshaft, the whole motor housing has to be replaced. This nasty fate happened to a Jersey Central GP-9 I own. There's nothing like replacing a whole motor to stress the importance of preventive maintenance!

The motors in the older postwar whistle tenders are often neglected with regard to maintenance. Sometimes, when you buy a good postwar steam locomotive with a whistle, the whistle motor in the tender has never been serviced — and that's a good thirty or forty years of neglect! As a result, the whistle will have a rattling sound, or you can hear the dry armature ends screaming for oil. Lionel's postwar whistle was a fine mechanism, and most whistle motors can be restored to fine operating condition.

To service the whistle motor, take the cab shell off the tender frame. This is usually fastened with a screw-slot arrangement at

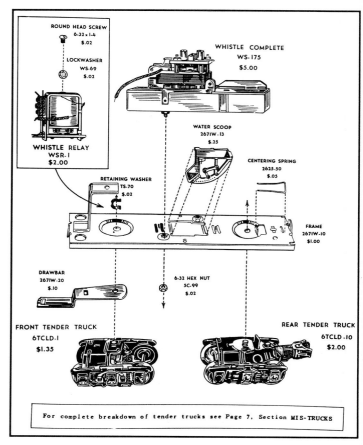

The cab removed from a postwar whistle tender.

front and rear (the 2046W model) or four small screws at the bottom (the 6466W model). After you've exposed the whistle motor, you must unsolder the wire connections to the brushplate in order to remove it for cleaning and lubrication. Then you must unscrew two large hex nuts which hold the brushplate in place. Follow the general directions given above to clean the motor, brushplate, and brushes. You won't be able to remove the armature because its lower end is fastened to a whistle impeller, a kind of miniature fan which blows air through the plastic or metal whistle chamber, producing the whistle sound. (The metal whistle chambers made in prewar years and in 1946-47 sound much better than the plastic ones, by the way.) When you are finished cleaning the motor, reinstall the brushes and brushplate; then resolder the wire connections.

Sometimes the fiber brushplate is badly worn where the armature end sticks through the plate. The enlarged hole at this point will allow the armature end to wobble as it spins, producing a harsh rattling sound. The only cure for this is the replacement of the brushplate; fortunately, replacement parts are available.

Before you replace the tender shell, you should perform two more operations. First, check the whistle relay for proper operation. Place the shell-less tender on your test track and operate the whistle. The little spring of the whistle relay should snap up and hold the contact points of the relay closed; then, when you release the button, the points should open once again. Sometimes the contact points get dirty, and they will then stick. Clean these little points by spraying solvent between them and then gently sanding them with a small emery board. You can adjust the tension of the spring by bending the ends of the copper spring up or down, but that's a delicate job which requires great care.

Finally, look over the plastic or metal whistle box to check it for leaks. The whistle chamber should be air-tight. If it isn't the whistle will "wheeze" when you blow it. Check for leaks by examining the seams of the whistle casing. If it needs re-sealing, modeling cement should do the job nicely for the plastic whistle housings and automotive gasket material will seal up the metal housings.

Some of the newer Lionel steam locomotives have a neat feature known as the "Sound Of Steam." This is a chugging sound produced by an electronic circuit and a loudspeaker inside the tender. It's not quite as good as American Flyer's old "choo-choo" sound, but it's very good as a rule. The sound is produced by the rapidly alternating opening and closing of two copper contact plates, one of which is attached to a push rod which moves in conjunction with the locomotive's drive wheels. A wire leads back from the locomotive, where it connects to a similar wire from the tender by means of a small plug. The opening and closing of the circuit produces a burst of static known to radio operators as "white noise." This noise may be a pain to radio people, but in a Lionel steam locomotive it produces a nice chugging steam sound when it comes from the loudspeaker in the tender. If you have the engine stopped and you get a loud hiss from the tender, don't worry — that's normal and quite realistic.

The older Sound of Steam locomotives can be adjusted to vary the intensity and frequency of the sound. This is also necessary when the copper contact points in the locomotive no longer meet or stay in the closed position. There is a hole in the bottom of the steam chest piece which allows a small Allen wrench to be inserted into a fitting which adjusts the position of one of the copper plates. You may have to take the boiler shell off the locomotive in some cases. The newer ones are a different story because they work off an eccentric roller mounted on the tender wheels. This off-center roller rotates with the axles and pushes one copper plate onto the other. In this case, the copper plate itself must be bent — with great care! As a rule, the units with Sound of Steam alone sound better than the ones with both the Sound of Steam and the electronic steam whistle, which is quite spectacular. You can't do much to adjust the whistle; its operation is all electronic. Lionel has had trouble with these electronic whistle circuits, even though in the last few years they seem to be more reliable. When that whistle is working properly, it is first-rate. It even has a falling "trill" to it when the whistle control is released, just like the real thing!

SERVICING THE REVERSING SWITCHES (E-UNITS)

Electrically speaking, Lionel's mechanical reversing switch, known as an "E-unit," is a solenoid-operated rotary sequence switch activated by a pawl and drum assembly. Interruption of the electric current causes the solenoid rod to snap back into its cylinder, pulling a latch-like device with it. This in turn catches onto the teeth of a rotating drum which has copper contact points contacting a four-pronged copper plate. The contacts on this plate vary the polarity of the circuit, which determines the direction of spin of the motor's armature. Of course, that also determines the forward, neutral, or reverse mode of the locomotive. Lionel's best E-units are of the three-position type. Depending upon the posi-

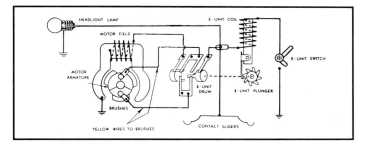

Three-position E-unit.

tion of the rotating drum, your locomotive will be going forward, staying in neutral with power on, or going in reverse. The sequence is forward-neutral-reverse-neutral-forward, etc.

Some less expensive locomotives have only a two-position E-unit which gives you no neutral position; the sequence is merely forward-reverse-forward, etc. As you can imagine, this type of reversing switch has serious limitations when you wish to operate a trackside accessory such as the Operating Milk Car, which needs power in the track to operate. Without a neutral position, the locomotive won't stand still for the operation. Even worse are some inexpensive Scout-type postwar locomotives which employ an insidious mechanism whereby the brushes themselves actually revolve in their brushplate. These can be identified by a little fiber lever atop the boiler. Unless these locomotives are operating

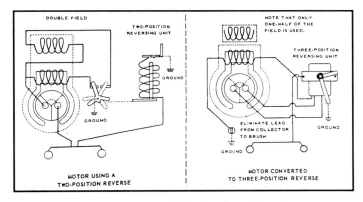

Two-position E-unit.

perfectly when you buy them, my advice is to avoid them like the plague! Many of these locomotives have had their whole motors replaced because the reversing mechanism is so difficult to repair.

On almost all the Lionel locomotives, there is a lever which will allow you to lock out the reversing switch so the locomotive will only go forward or reverse or stay in neutral. This can be important when you are using an accessory with a train-stopping feature such as the 132 Freight Station, the 253 Block Signal, or the 313 Bascule Bridge. It can also be important when you are using relays to run more than one train on the same track, since each train will be stopped before it gets too close to the other one.

The new all-electronic reversing switch, a real marvel produced in the last five years, also has a little cut-out switch which performs the same function as the lever. These electronic reversing units are found on the new can-motor drive locomotives; they have a device known as the "power-up" feature. This means that the locomotive will always start in forward motion when you first apply power to the engine, no matter what direction it was in when you last applied power to it. As a matter of habit, when I shut down the power to the regular mechanical E-units, I make sure that the locomotive is in the neutral position so that the next direction will be forward. You will have to train yourself to do that, of course, but the power-up feature relieves you of the possibility that your engine will fly off into reverse unexpectedly.

Lionel's mechanical E-unit has a fascinating history behind it. In the late 1920s, Lionel introduced a two-position reversing switch known as a "pendulum" unit. Although this was Lionel's first remote reversing switch, it was nowhere near as good as the one Ives introduced around the same time, which was almost identical to the modern mechanical three-position E-unit. Joshua Lionel Cowen wanted possession of this reversing switch very badly, according to some train scholars. Since he couldn't get around Ives' patents for their reversing switch, he took advantage of the severe financial difficulties Ives faced in the first years of the Great Depression (and before) and eventually, in partnership with American Flyer, bought the whole Ives Corporation! That's how Lionel managed to acquire the three-position reversing switch although, curiously, the firm didn't introduce it right away. The possession of the Ives reversing switch conferred great operating advantages upon Lionel trains, although it certainly wasn't the sole reason for Lionel's buy-out of Ives. American Flyer was also in on this deal, so it was able to introduce its own version of the three-position sequence reversing switch for its own trains with its own patents. The solenoid-operated reversing switch has been a faithful performer in Lionel trains ever since. Its greatest legacy has been the familiar E-unit "buzz," perhaps the most familiar noise of all to Lionel train operators. The new electronic reversing switch is, of course, completely silent. I actually find the silence a little uncomfortable!

With all that as background, let us examine the mechanical E-unit for its strengths and weaknesses, and perhaps some servicing possibilities. Unfortunately, the E-unit is somewhat difficult to service, though it's not impossible. The weak points usually are a swollen rotating drum which sticks inside its rotating holes and/or burned or corroded copper fingers on the plate which contacts the copper on the drum. In addition, the drum's plastic side projection can be broken. Of course, the solenoid itself is a very reliable operating mechanism, and very little goes wrong with it.

The servicing of the E-unit can take place without its removal from the locomotive, but this is usually a difficult process because of the tight access. It's usually better to remove the E-unit from the locomotive by unsoldering its wire contacts and removing the screw which holds it to the chassis. Once you have gained access to the E-unit, examine the rotating drum and the contact fingers very carefully. Spray some solvent (or graphite lubricant) into the solenoid chamber to keep it operating smoothly; this should be all the solenoid needs. In addition, clean off the contact surfaces of the fingers and rotating drum with solvent on the end of a Q-tip. If the drum fails to rotate smoothly within its pivot holes, it will probably need replacing. Examine where the plastic meets the copper. If there is a gap between the plastic and the copper sections of the drum, the plastic on the drum has swollen from excess heat. Very carefully, pry the sides of the E-unit loose by using a pair of needle-nose pliers placed inside the metal framework. Take the old drum out and insert its replacement,

being careful to align it properly with the takeup pawl attached to the solenoid. Then press the frame sides back into place.

Repair or replacement of the fiber plate with the contact fingers is very tricky; you must exercise extreme patience. First, pry the plate loose from its holding slots on the E-unit framework. Then unsolder the one or three wire connections from the plate and re-solder the wires to a new plate and finger assembly. Be careful to solder the wires in the same sequence! Then replace the plate so that the new copper fingers contact the rotating drum solidly and press in the framework sides of the E-unit. This is not an easy repair; it may take a miniature soldering gun to perform properly, and it certainly calls for some skill. Many operators like to leave this job to a trained Lionel technician. I've done a few repairs on E-units, but just as many times I've had this job done by a pro.

Often, the mechanical E-units will buzz very loudly — an annoyance at times. There really isn't much you can do to cure this problem except to make sure that the screw which holds the E-unit onto the chassis is securely tightened and that the metal framework of the E-unit is also assembled tightly. Due to manufacturing tolerances, some of these E-units are noisy from birth, and you'll just have to put up with the annoyance or replace the entire E-unit. On the other hand, I have an old 224E made in 1938 with an E-unit which is absolutely silent! E-unit buzz is mostly a matter of luck; the chief offenders seem to be the modern series of GP-7, GP-9, and GP-20 diesels produced since 1970. But it's such a nice, familiar sound...!

Actually, some of my railroading colleagues have come up with ways to reduce or eliminate the buzzing sound of the Lionel E-unit. For that information, see the articles by Arthur Broshears and Richard Sigurdson in the next chapter.

SERVICING THE SMOKE UNITS

When Lionel first introduced a smoke feature for its steam locomotives in 1946, it didn't have much relationship to the more modern smoke units of just one year later and the smoke units produced today. That first smoke unit in the 671 Steam Turbine and the 726 Berkshire Locomotives used a special light bulb mounted within a metal chamber to produce the heat necessary to vaporize the smoke pellets. The light bulb had a depression in it to hold the smoke pellet. If you've ever seen one of these original 1946 locomotives run, it's quite a sight. (Many of these locomotives were converted in the next year.) The smoke has a glow to it from the light escaping from the stack; it looks like fire coming out of the stack! (American Flyer's locomotives, which always smoked better than Lionel's, added this "stack-glow" feature later on.) If you are fortunate enough to possess one of these original locomotives, for heaven's sakes, don't convert it to a newer method! Replacement lamps are actually available, and the lamps will work with one or two drops of the new liquid smoke instead of the obsolete smoke pellets.

By 1947 Lionel had changed its smoke unit to the familiar version which uses a length of thin nichrome wire wrapped around a small ceramic or mica plate inside the smoke chamber. Heat is caused by the resistance of this wire to the electric current passing through it; this vaporizes the smoke pellet (or liquid), and the smoke is pumped out of the chamber by means of a plunger and push rod synchronized with the drive wheels. This was a very reliable smoke unit which continued essentially unchanged until the end of postwar production in 1969. Every once in a while,

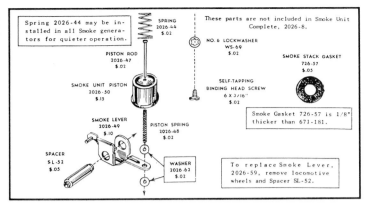

Schematic of the drive rod and plunger from the 2026 Smoke Unit.

the nichrome wire would burn and eventually break, cutting the heat circuit and disabling the smoke unit. Many older steam locomotives are found today with the smoke units in this condition. Yes, they can be fixed! More importantly, they can be converted to the newer heat resistance diode in current use on modern Lionel steamers.

In the mid-1950s, Lionel introduced another, less expensive all-plastic smoke unit which used a new liquid smoke. This unit worked well, but it was prone to damage from overheating, and some units actually used the locomotive headlight as part of the smoke circuit. This means that the wrong lamp would burn out the smoke unit or reduce its smoke output drastically.

Lionel's newest smoke units differ from the old ones primarily by their use of a plastic cap instead of a metal one and a heat-resistant diode instead of the old "toaster-wire" arrangement. Since the newer steamers run more efficiently on less voltage, the newer smoke units do not smoke as well as the older ones. There usually isn't enough voltage going through the newer steam locomotives under normal operating conditions to produce the copious smoke of the older units. You could put more heavy cars in the train and thus increase the operating voltage of the newer steamers, but their motors are under strain at too high a voltage.

If the smoke unit on your postwar steamer doesn't operate, there could be several reasons. For one thing, the nichrome toaster wire could be burned out. For another, the plunger might be stuck, or the little air hole might be plugged up with smoke pellet "gunk," one of the chief drawbacks of the old smoke pellets. Let us assume, for the sake of completeness, that you have decided to rebuild the smoke unit on your postwar steamer. Further, let us also decide to replace the nichrome wire with the new liquid smoke diode. (You can use liquid smoke with the nichrome wire units as long as you just add three or four drops of smoke fluid at a time. Never flood the smoke chamber! If you add too much smoke fluid, the quantity will be too much for the unit to vaporize.) The following procedures should be followed when you service the Lionel smoke units, with some minor variations for the modern era locomotives:

The first chore you'll have to perform is removing the metal cap from the top of the smoke unit once you take the boiler casting off the chassis. Many times, this will be quite difficult. In the first place, Lionel glued these caps to the smoke units with electrical cement. Moreover, if too many smoke pellets had been used, the residual powder from the pellets will have formed a hard shell of debris which would add to the fusion of the cap to the metal smoke

unit frame. To get a stubborn metal cap off, scrape around the edge where the cap meets the frame with an X-Acto knife or some such tool. Remove all the cement and gunk you can from the seam. Then, insert the blade of a small screwdriver into the hole at the top and pry the cap off the frame. Be careful not to insert the metal end of the screwdriver too far into the hole, or you'll make a mess of the nichrome wire plate and the fiber material which fills up the chamber. You may have to repeat the process for a while, but the cap will eventually pop loose.

Now, if you intend to re-use the nichrome wire plate, clean out the inside surface of the cap and the walls of the chamber of as much accumulated smoke pellet residue as you can. There may be quite a bit of this stuff! You'll see a little projection with a hole which runs down into the lower end of the chamber. This hole must be clear of all residue, since the air coming through it from the plunger drives the smoke out of the stack. Insert a piece of wire down this hole and clean it out. Now, replace the metal cap into the frame by pressing it down into the opening. If you're going to replace the nichrome wire with the new diode unit, read on a little further before you take this step; you have some more work ahead of you.

Now you should pay some attention to the lower end of the smoke unit. Take off the screw which holds the unit to the chassis. Lift the smoke unit off the plunger rod; in some cases, the plunger rod is attached to the plunger and it will also come off. Try to extract the plunger from its socket. If it comes out easily, clean out the plunger socket of any accumulated residue and then reassemble the unit. However, sometimes the plunger will actually be glued to its socket because of excess smoke pellet residue. Scrape the residue off where the plunger meets its socket and gently pry loose the plunger until it comes out. Then clean the unit as I've described above and reassemble it.

If you're going to replace the nichrome wire with the new Lionel resistance diode, you must get the right part from your Lionel dealer. The diode comes with a plastic cap; it is inserted into a little slot built into the plastic cap, and two bare wires coming from the diode project from small holes in the cap itself. One of these wires must be led back to the power source on a small tab mounted on the E-unit, and the other one must be used as a ground. Some people prefer to discard the plastic cap and re-use the old metal cap, but that's a lot more trouble from a wiring standpoint because the bare wire leading back to the power tab has to be insulated from the metal cap. I see no harm in using the plastic cap because you won't be sending enough heat into the chamber to melt it or wreak any other kind of havoc. I've had no trouble with the plastic caps.

First, unsolder the wire from the tab on the E-unit and put aside the old nichrome wire plate and the metal cap. Solder a new length of wire from the metal tab so that the other end can be spliced to the bare wire coming from the diode inside the new plastic cap. I prefer to insulate this bare wire with a little tape or wire insulation, just in case it might touch the metal boiler casting and cause a short circuit. A butt-end splice can be crimped onto the diode wire and the power lead to make the connection; be sure it too is insulated with some friction tape. Once this is done, cut the other bare wire leading from the diode so that about one inch of it remains. Bend this wire so that its end follows the lower curve of the plastic cap where it will be inserted into the metal frame. Make sure that the place on the frame where this wire will make its contact is clean so you will get a good grounding connection. Now, insert the plastic cap into the frame, keeping the ground wire firmly wedged between the plastic cap and the metal frame of the smoke unit. The plastic cap will bend a little bit so you can wedge it into the opening along with the wire.

Replace the round cloth washer which was once atop the metal cap with a new one and reassemble the locomotive chassis to its boiler shell. Make sure that the smoke unit's cap hole projects into the smokestack and that the wire lead to the headlight does not become jammed between the smoke unit and the boiler. In addition, check to make sure that the plunger and its rod are in place and operating correctly before you reassemble the engine. Test the plunger motion by rotating the drive wheels and observing the plunger moving in and out of its socket at the lower end of the smoke unit. Once you have placed a few drops (not too much!) of smoke fluid inside the smokestack and you run the engine, it should smoke quite well if you've done the work properly.

There are several good brands of smoke fluid on the market today, among them Lionel's own and some smoke in various scents made by the Lehigh Valley Train Company. Of these, I prefer a product known as Supersmoke; it has the best volatility and performance of any smoke fluid I know. Just make sure that you only add three or four drops to the smoke chamber at any one time. This fluid will not clog up the smoke units, as the old pellets once did. It also smells a heck of a lot better!

SERVICING SOLENOIDS AND VIBRATOR MECHANISMS

Many of Lionel's accessories operate by means of solenoid devices or vibrator mechanisms. As with any of Lionel's equipment, these will need some attention from time to time. You will, however, find both of these mechanisms to be very reliable performers which won't need a great deal of work, especially the solenoids, which are extremely simple and rugged mechanisms. About all these devices need is an occasional spray of solvent inside the hole where the rod is moved by the twin magnetic coils. This will keep the rod moving smoothly. Try not to keep the solenoid in operation for any extended length of time, since the heat build-up in a solenoid can warp the coil housings and ultimately destroy the solenoid. This danger most frequently occurs with Lionel's non-derailing O27 turnouts such as the 1122E and

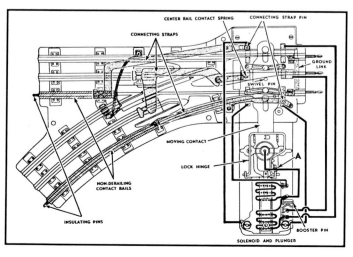

Schematic of 022 solenoid mechanism.

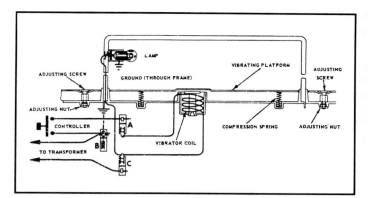

Schematic of vibrator mechanism, 356 Freight Station.

5021-22 models. If you let a train stand too long on the turnout with the track power on, you could do damage to the solenoid. The O Gauge 022 Switches do not have this problem, especially if they are operated from a constant voltage source.

The vibrator mechanisms are a little trickier, but not much more so. When electricity is sent through a magnetic coil, the coil vibrates across an air gap which transfers the vibrating motion to a wide range of surfaces, enabling little figures of all kinds to move about. Sometimes the vibrating motion is transferred into rotary motion by means of a drive string and wheel attached to a tension spring.

To adjust a vibrator mechanism, usually all you have to do is bend the bracket to which the coil is attached back from or towards its metal plate until you have achieved the desired strength of vibration. In some instances, you will reset adjustment screws instead of bending the bracket; the individual entries in a repair and maintenance manual will help you in this regard. If the vibrator is attached to a drive string and wheel, the adjustment job is a little trickier. Most of the time the vibration in these devices lessens with age because the drive string stretches over time. To restore proper tension, simply pull the string through its fastening grommet to stretch the tension spring a little more. Then crimp the adjustment grommet securely closed to hold that tension. Be careful not to over-tighten this mechanism!

SERVICING LIONEL'S REMOTE-CONTROL TURNOUTS

I've already spoken at some length about Lionel's turnouts in the track work chapter, but a few maintenance tips about them will not be out of place here. The main service you can perform for Lionel's turnouts is to make sure that the operating mechanisms and the frog rails move freely. On the old 1121 O27 Turnouts, this is a relatively easy task because the solenoid drives the frog rail directly. Do not fasten them to the layout too tightly, or the moving rails will jam. If the frog rail binds or kinks, check for a bent center rail which has been forced down onto the moving plastic piece. Gently pry up the rail until the motion of the turning plastic piece is free. Inside the mechanism, make sure that the bail wire locks the mechanism securely. This U-shaped wire catches on metal projections which keep the turning rails in place under the pressure of the train. If the bail wire doesn't lock, remove it and bend it outward slightly until it will clear the metal tabs when it is placed back into the mechanism. Clean out the solenoid with solvent, of course, and also clean the moving metal parts. A thin film of lubricant on the moving metal surfaces is usually a good idea.

The 1122E O27 Turnouts are a little more complicated, since these change the position of the rails through a tooth-and-cog gear mechanism. This mechanism must move freely. Apply a thin film of lubricant on the metal tooth rack and turn the signal lamp holder to check for proper operation. If the signal lamp bracket is bent, the plastic signal hood will bind against the cover, impeding the operation of the switch. Make sure this bracket is absolutely horizontal. As with the 1121 models, make sure all the moving gears and parts are clean and lubricated for smooth operation.

The fine O Gauge 022 Turnouts are really rugged and reliable as a rule, and so are their modern successors, which (unlike the flimsy O27 Gauge remakes) are built exactly like their predecessors. Basic lubrication is the best rule for these turnouts, as in the O27 turnouts, so follow the same general instructions. The motor units of these turnouts can be moved to the other side of the rails for use in ladder-track sidings. Simply detach the mounting screws from the base, turn the motor around, and re-attach the screws, making sure that the turnout's drive rod is securely connected to the moving rails. In the next chapter, Edward Stencler will have a few words on the wide-radius O72 O Gauge turnouts; his instructions will apply to the 022 models as well.

To summarize this chapter, I quote some excerpts from an instruction sheet called "First Aid For Your Trains," issued by Randy's Hobby Shop of Mount Pleasant, South Carolina. The information comes from a highly skilled repairman and good train friend, I. D. Smith. It's good advice!

1. Do not use steel wool on tracks. For S Gauge and larger track, use No. 600 non-magnetic emery paper. For HO or smaller track, use track "eraser" or very fine emery paper such as "Flex-i-grit."

2. Avoid storing your trains in attics or garages. Hot summer weather causes oil and lubricants to dry out and gum up; wire insulation dries out and cracks. High-humidity storage areas should be avoided to reduce rusting.

3. When you are storing trains, pack them with individual protection. Place heavy items on the bottom of boxes and remove any batteries. Leave couplers open to relax the coupler springs. Never wrap cars in newspaper because newsprint can damage finishes. Storage in plastic bags <u>made specifically for the purpose</u> reduces rusting.

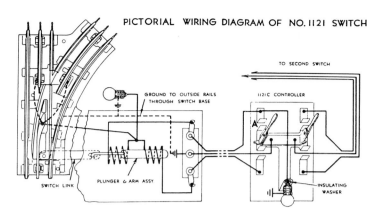

Schematic of 1121 Switch mechanism.

4. If you run your trains on track laid on a rug, sweep the rug to reduce the possibility of pet hair and rug fibers entangling the gears and wheels.

5. Avoid catastrophic train wrecks. The part you need may not be available.

6. Remember that the most costly repairs are performed by people who:

(a) do not possess the right tools;

(b) do not know how to disassemble or reassemble a unit correctly, resulting in breakage or damage of parts;

(c) reattach loose wires where they think the wires go; and

(d) perform makeshift repairs of parts which cause other damage.

One axiom of model railroading in general and Lionel in particular is that no one model railroader has all the information you will need if you are to build the ideal Lionel railroad. That is why I've asked some of the best and most experienced model railroaders in captivity to share some of their operating tips and special projects with you through this book. I am really grateful for their generosity, a trait I've found in model railroaders more frequently than with any other segment of society. Sometimes these people may contradict something I've said through an honest difference of opinion. More often (I hope!), they will add their own special expertise to your appreciation of Lionel trains. It is time you listened to some of the many voices of Lionel model railroaders. Before too long, you might be adding your own voice to them!

CHAPTER X

SPECIAL AND ADVANCED PROJECTS

The following series of articles represents the thinking and practice of some of the most experienced people in Lionel railroading. Although I do not personally know all of these people, I am familiar with their work and can recommend them to you. For the most part, they represent areas of Lionel railroading for which I lack experience. Whether you are a novice or seasoned veteran, these articles will add a wealth of knowledge to your abilities.

MAINTENANCE AND REPAIR OF FUNDIMENSIONS TRAINS

By Arthur L. Broshears

This first article is the work of a long-time practitioner of the art of Lionel. Arthur Broshears is the proprietor of the Loveland-Little Miami Train Shop in Loveland, Ohio. He is a former officer of the Lionel Collectors' Club of America as well. Mr. Broshears will share with you his vast experience in Lionel repair and maintenance in many areas.

1. Lubricating Your Trains and Cleaning Your Track: To me, the most important aspect of Lionel train maintenance is lubrication. If your trains are under-lubricated, they will encounter rapid wear. If they are over-lubricated, the track will accumulate dirt and "goo" (dirt and oil combined) more rapidly, and slippage of locomotive traction wheels could also result.

I start my lubrication chores with gear teeth lubrication. I use a cotton swab such as a Q-tip with one swab cut off, using the remaining swab end as a grip, and Black & Decker heavy duty grease (Catalogue No. 60514). This grease is formulated to cling to either metal or plastic gears; therefore, it can be used sparingly.

With my swab dipped into the grease, I turn the engine upside down and apply small amounts on each wheel gear. Then I rotate the wheels to distribute the grease evenly on contacting gears. I then apply a liquid lubricant to all gear pivots (axles).

For wheels and any moving parts which need lubricant, I use automotive automatic transmission fluid. This, of course, is readily available in any auto supply store relatively inexpensively. I once had an experience with a layout in my store which I ran almost continuously for eight hours a day. Before I began the use of automatic transmission fluid as a lubricant, I would have to lubricate the wheels and other parts every day. I decided that I needed a lubricant which would not only resist heat, but also adhere without dripping off. I found that automatic transmission fluid worked better than any lubricant I had previously tried. It is important to use a small amount at each point of movement to prevent over-oiling. By experimenting, I found that by using this lubricant I only had to re-lubricate my rolling stock and locomotives after about 84 hours of running! In other words, when I ran my store layout 12 hours a day, seven days a week during the holiday season, I only had to lubricate the trains once a week! I now use these lubricants — the Black and Decker grease and the

automatic transmission fluid — whenever I service my customers' engines and cars.

When track gets a little dirty, the first impulse many people have is to grab for the steel wool pad. THIS IS A NO-NO! The steel strands can pull loose and cause a short circuit. Worse, they can become attracted to Lionel's Magnetraction motors and ruin them. The wonderful world of science has brought forth a non-metallic cleaning pad known as "Scotch-Brite," the 3M Company's trade name for the product. This pad is absolutely perfect for polishing track and, of course, is readily available in your food store's cleaning aisle. With this pad, I use rubbing alcohol to clean any accumulated dirt and goo before polishing. Many times, polishing the track will not be necessary if dirt is removed on a regular basis.

2. Installing Wheels Onto the Axles of Locomotives: Some people would like to make repairs to driving wheels on steam locomotives and diesels, but they do not have a wheel press, wheel puller, or other necessary tools. However, removing and reinstalling these wheels can be performed easily without these expensive tools.

Removing the locomotive's drive wheels is quite a simple process. First, remove all the drive rods if the locomotive is a steamer. Then lay the motor assembly across your knees. With a drift (punch) and a claw hammer (actually, a ball peen hammer is better), center the punch on the axle and, with a firm blow, hit the drift. Do not strike it too hard! Be sure the wheel and axle assembly can fall between your knees, and continue hitting the drift until the wheel is free. Caution: Do not "tap" the drift, as this will swedge (enlarge) the end of the axle. If that happens, the axle end cannot go through the drive wheel without damaging its insertion hole. This procedure can be used to remove any wheel that is pressed onto an axle, whether it is a locomotive, a pilot, or trailing truck, etc.

Except for Lionel's small motorized units such as the No. 41 U. S. Army Switcher, the reinstallation of wheels is very simple on the diesel locomotives. However, the procedure is more complicated with the steam locomotives until you learn the installation process. In the absence of a wheel pressing tool, the only tool you will need to install wheels is a bench vise with at least a 3-1/2" jaw opening. On diesels which do not have side rods, simply place the free wheel on the end of the axle and place the assembly in the vise for tightening.

To avoid tightening the wheel onto the axle too tightly, fold a shipping tag or matchbook cover three times and tap the folds flat with a hammer. As you tighten the vise to press the wheel onto the axle, gauge the distance between the wheel and its boss (frame) by slipping the folded tag or cover between them. When the paper gauge slips between the wheel and its frame with light resistance, do not press the wheel any more, as this distance will give you the proper clearance needed for free rolling of the wheel set.

After you remove the assembly from the vise, spin the wheels to check for "wobble." If the assembly was placed in the vise squarely, the wheel set will run true. If the wheel is off-center, tap the edge of the wheel very lightly at its furthest point from the boss or body of the chassis. Repeat this process until the wheel set runs true.

The reinstallation of wheels onto steam locomotives and motorized units is a little more difficult because you must "quarter" the wheels for proper rod action. If you look at the drive rods of a steam locomotive, you will notice that when one drive rod end is at a point of deepest insertion into the steam chest piece, the other rod will be at a halfway point of retraction from the steam chest. This means that the wheels on one side of the engine are 1/4 turn (90°) offset from those on the other side. If the rods are not operating in this way, they will jam the wheels. The realignment of the drive wheels to proper rod positioning is called quartering. There is no simple way to explain this operation, so my explanation may seem somewhat crude. However, we do not have a wheel press with quartered dies.

Until I obtained a wheel press, I used the following procedure for many years to quarter the wheels of steam locomotives. I took a 1/2" thick by three inch wide board and cut it to a six-inch length. Then, using a saber saw, I cut a channel into the center of the board about 1/4" wide and four inches long. Using the first board as a pattern, I cut a second board identical to it. After all my cuts were made, I trimmed both boards to a total of two inches wide.

To align the drive wheels properly, I would install the locomotive's drive rods on one side of the locomotive, center-lining them with the axles (two, three, or four as the case might be). Then I would place the first piece of wood along the drive rods so they would rest in the cut-out slot. On the side where the wheels were to be reinstalled, I would place the wheels so they were in opposing positions to the wheels in the slot, aligning them by reinstalling the main drive rod. I would then place the second block of wood so that the drive rod would be inside the slot. Now that the wheels were positioned properly, I would pick up the whole motor and wheel assembly, still inside the wooden blocks, and press the wheels onto the axles with a vise, making sure that I had my matchbook shim in place so as not to put too much pressure on the wheel sets. As I had said, this is a crude method, but when I needed to do a job and I didn't have a wheel press, this substitute "jig" did the job.

3. Cleaning Lionel Rolling Stock and Accessories: Great care must be taken when using cleaning aids to clean the paint and plastic surfaces of Lionel equipment. You want cleaners which will clean effectively yet remain harmless to the paint, metal, and plastic. After trying many cleaners, I have found that the following method works better than anything I have tried. For about five years now, I have been using just two compounds for all my cleaning: Dawn dishwashing liquid and ArmorAll automotive cleaner.

First, I remove the body from the car or locomotive. Then, under hot water (as hot as my hands can bear), I wet down the body, apply liberal amounts of dishwashing liquid with a small, soft paint brush, and set it aside. I then take the chassis, with trucks attached, and brush the detergent in over the entire chassis, setting it aside. I then go back to the cab or body and, under hot water, I scrub its surface with the paint brush while rinsing it with hot water. Be careful with scrubbing on rubber-stamped lettering; simply pat those letters with a paper towel. As soon as all of the soap has been rinsed off, I place the cab or body on a heat register to dry. I then do the chassis the same way. Once the pieces are placed on the heat register, the forced warm air will dry the cab and chassis spot free and the chassis will not rust. (If you don't have forced warm air heat in your home, you can achieve the same results with an electric hair dryer.)

After this operation has been completed, I brush on Armor-All and let the pieces set for at least three hours. After this, I use a large, soft-bristled four-inch paint brush and brush the pieces completely until all the ArmorAll is removed. This process will make the engine, car, or accessory look like new. If the item once had a nice luster when it was new, simply use a soft cloth to polish the surfaces until they shine. The advantage of ArmorAll is that whether the item has a matte or gloss finish, the trains will be easier to keep dust-free. An occasional brushing with a feather or lamb's wool duster is all you will need to do.

I then polish the wheels of my locomotives and rolling stock. This operation requires taking the wheels off the truck frames and inserting them into a fine wire brush mounted on a bench grinder. If you place the wheel or rail surface against the wire brush, dirt will come off easily and the wheel will look like new.

Finally, some plastic trucks will turn white after they have become wet or damp; if they are, brush ArmorAll onto them and let them set for at least an hour. Then, using a paint brush, buff them well. If this procedure does not remove all the mildew, use a glue brush and apply No. 1 kerosene. Then dry the trucks and apply the ArmorAll again.

4. Miscellaneous Maintenance Tips: I have frequently found that the motor brushes on MPC equipment are not as good as the exact replacements for postwar electric motors. If you use the postwar brushes in MPC motors (Part No. 622-121), the motor seems to have more power and less arcing. The postwar brush is a little larger in diameter, and its slightly fuller length bridges the

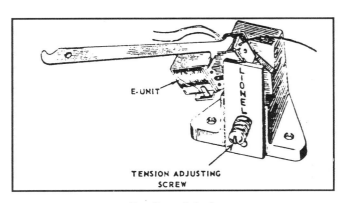

E-unit repair tool.

commutator segments a little better. The less arcing (sparking), the more power from the motor.

MPC's three-position E-units make a great deal of noise and rattle. I have found that most of this noise can be eliminated by putting more tension on the copper drum contacts and tightening the metal shield on the bottom of the E-unit. This shield is very easy to tighten by crimping the two tabs which secure it to the fiberboard.

One problem with the recent production of the Berkshire steam locomotives has been stripping of the brass gears in the motor. Through experimenting, I have found that the worm on the motor armature is not meshing deeply enough with the brass drive gear. Thus, when the locomotive has a moderate to heavy load, the end of the worm will lift very slightly and cause extreme pressure on the top of the gear. This, in turn, wears the gear out very rapidly, causing premature failure.

I have found that the best way to solve this problem is to remove the motor from its mount and place a small piece of shipping tag cardboard over each guide pin. Make sure that the hole for the guide pin is cut from the cardboard before you place the tag over it. Then, reinstall the motor and tighten it securely. This procedure changes the angle of the worm to the drive gear very slightly — enough to let it ride a little deeper in the drive gear, improving its life by about 75 percent.

A SHORT COURSE ON ELECTRICITY
By Carl Weaver

Carl Weaver is the author of a terrific Greenberg book which details operations for Marklin HO trains. His assistance has been very valuable to the writing of this book; he has made numerous additions and suggestions which have enriched the platform and wiring chapters substantially. For further information about his book, refer to the annotated bibliography.

You don't have to know anything about electricity to run your trains, but you sure need to know some basics before you can wire them and keep them running safely. A little knowledge can save you from having to call on a friend every time something goes wrong or a change in the wiring has to be made.

Two concepts are all you need to get started. The first concept is that electricity makes a loop. It leaves the transformer, travels by one wire to the item you want to operate, then travels back to the transformer by a ground. The ground can be a second wire or one of the outside rails of Lionel's three-rail track. In any case, you must complete the loop, or circuit, before the light will light, the accessory will operate, or the locomotive will run.

The transformer is like a pump. It pushes the electricity out of one of its terminals, around the wire loop into the center rail of the track, into the locomotive through the engine's roller or slider pickup, out of the locomotive motor through the outside rails, and back into the pump through the other terminal. In the case of a lamp, electricity leaves the transformer terminal, travels by wire to the center contact on the bottom of the light bulb, through the filament to the screw or bayonet base, and back to the other terminal of the transformer through a second wire.

The second concept you should understand is that electricity flowing through a wire is like water flowing through a pipe. Electricity flowing through anything metal is called current. If the wire you are using is too light in weight, current flow will be restricted; it will react just like water does when it flows through a small diameter hose instead of a larger pipe. Therefore, you should make sure that the wire you use to send electricity to the track or accessory has a large enough diameter to carry the current flow needed to operate the item. Some telephone wire is 24-gauge; this is usually too small. Wire with a gauge of 22 or 20 is better and 18-gauge wire is the best for most applications. (Wire is measured by its gauge or size; the smaller the number, the thicker the wire — and the more current it can carry.) Multiple-strand wire is more flexible than solid wire and is less likely to break from constant use. On the other hand, solid wire is easier to use when you attach wire to the Fahnstock clips of some Lionel accessories and track lockons.

Current traveling around a loop can be interrupted by a switch. When you move the switch to the off position, a space is created in the loop and the current is prevented from flowing. When the metal path around the loop is not complete, the electricity stops flowing even though the transformer (pump) is still trying to push it. This electric "pressure" is measured in volts. Sometimes the electricity stops because the loop is broken by dirt on the sliders or rollers or the wheels, and the electricity cannot get to the motor. A broken wire, a loose terminal on your transformer, or a broken solder joint can also prevent the electricity from flowing.

With many Lionel accessories, the entire current loop is there except for a button, slider, or lever-type device which interrupts the current until you want it to work for you. When you operate the lever, slider, or button, you make the circuit complete by a momentary contact and the device operates. When you release the switch or button, the current flow is interrupted again.

When you want your train to operate fast or slow, you turn the rheostat knob on your transformer, which is a faucet-like valve for electricity. A rheostat adjusts resistance to the current flow. The more you turn it on, the less resistance there is and the more current can flow, making the train travel faster. When you turn the rheostat the other way towards the off position, you create more resistance and the train travels slower.

A short circuit is something you don't want on your layout because it interrupts the current flow. A short circuit is like a hole in the wall of a water pipe where all the water runs out. In the case of electricity, the current takes a short cut back to the power source instead of traveling around its intended loop. When a short circuit occurs, locomotives will not run, lights will dim or go out, and the transformer will shut down automatically after a few moments to prevent its destruction (at least on most Lionel models).

Elimination of short circuits is absolutely essential to the safe and efficient operation of your train layout. Four common causes of short circuits include derailed locomotives or rolling stock, screws or other metal parts falling on the track and contacting the center and outside rails, bare wire ends touching each other, and stranded wire under screw terminals with the strands spreading out to an adjacent terminal.

What can you do with this new knowledge? For one thing, it should be easier for you to understand Lionel's wiring instructions, and you may even want to tackle some wiring on your own without instructions. However, the most important thing you can do with a basic understanding of current flow is to troubleshoot electrical problems as they occur. The whole key to understanding electrical problems lies in understanding what electricity is supposed to do.

A SHORT COURSE ON SOLDERING

By Carl Weaver

It is important to know how to solder correctly so you will obtain good electrical connections without damaging anything nearby — including yourself! There are thirteen rules to good soldering practice, as follows:

RULE 1: Always use a low-wattage soldering iron. The best type for model railroading use is generally in the 15 to 30 watt range, but not more than 40 watts. The soldering iron I use is Radio Shack's Model 64- 2055, which has a switch enabling me to use 15 watts for locomotive repair and 30 watts for layout soldering.

RULE 2: Always use small diameter resin core solder. Resin is the flux which will prepare the surfaces to be joined and help the solder to adhere. Solder is hollow, like spaghetti, and the flux is in the middle. Acid core solder will eventually cause corrosion. In wire connections, sometimes the corrosion is hidden in the joint and it cannot be seen readily. Problems thus become very difficult to find. Therefore, always use resin core solder. DO not use previously melted solder because there is no flux and the parts to be joined may come apart later. Avoid using large diameter solder, which requires a great deal of heat to melt and leaves too much solder on the joint. I use resin core solder of .032 diameter for everything.

RULE 3: Make sure that the soldering iron is hot before you begin. Give your iron adequate time to heat up. Before doing your job, test the iron with fresh solder. One way to make sure you do not ruin surrounding components when you solder is to have the tip of the iron hot so the solder will melt quickly.

RULE 4: Tin the tip of a brand new soldering iron with fresh solder. Melt a little solder onto the hot tip of a new soldering iron, according to the manufacturer's instructions.

RULE 5: Clean the parts to be joined. Solder will not adhere to grease, oil, paint, or insulation. Remove any of these things with sandpaper or solvent. Copper or brass should be shiny before it is soldered. Track rails should be sanded and cleaned of all rust and corrosion.

RULE 6: Melt the solder on the heated parts, NOT on the tip of the iron. The point is the hottest part of the tip. Carefully heat the parts to be joined while you hold the solder against them. Do not apply too much solder. Allow the solder to flow between the joined parts before you remove the iron. Hold the joint very still while the solder cools; you will see the solder change from shiny to dull as it cools and hardens.

RULE 7: Clean the tip of the soldering iron often. While the iron is hot, use a damp sponge to wipe off any collected debris.

RULE 8: After several uses, clean the tip with a fine, flat file when it is cold and then re-tin the tip with fresh solder.

RULE 9: When you solder underneath your layout, wear eye protection! A pair of safety glasses or goggles will provide inexpensive protection. Just to be on the safe side, you should consider gloves and long-sleeved garments as well. Think safety first!

RULE 10: BE CAREFUL! A hot soldering iron can cause painful burns very quickly!

RULE 11: Place the tip on a wire rack if you have more soldering to do. A hot soldering iron can start a fire! Most soldering irons come with a wire rack. If yours did not, make such a rack!

RULE 12: Be sure that the power cord for the soldering iron is not where you can trip over it.

RULE 13: Unplug the iron when you are finished, and let the iron cool on a wire rack.

SOME GENERAL COMMENTS ABOUT SOLDERING

One of the most important times to follow the above rules for soldering is during locomotive repair. Some of the parts on Lionel locomotives are fiber or plastic. Since one of the more frequent Lionel locomotive repairs is to re-wire the leads from the headlights and power trucks to their tabs on the reversing unit, you must be quick and accurate so you do not melt the insulation on the other wires or damage vulnerable components. Your iron has to be hot and the solder fresh. Make sure that you use a low wattage setting or a low wattage iron. Many model railroaders have several types of soldering irons, each for a specific application. So should you!

Soldering two wires together is simple. Be sure to twist the wires together before you solder them. Let the melted solder flow between the wire strands before you remove the tip of the iron.

A heat sink is a type of clamp which is useful for reducing the risk of damaging components connected to a solder joint. For example, if you have to solder a wire to one leg of a light-emitting diode, a heat sink clamp should be placed between the solder point and the diode. The clamp then absorbs the excess heat, rather than allowing the heat to damage the diode.

Nearly everyone is aware of the use of electrical tape to insulate a bare-wire joint. However, not everyone is aware of heat-shrink tubular insulation. This is a soft black plastic tubing which comes in varying diameters and lengths. You can purchase this tubing at most electrical supply stores. Simply slip the tubing over the wire before it is joined. Once the wire is soldered, move the tubing over the joint and heat it with a match or lighter. Hold the flame onto the tubing just for an instant — enough for it to shrink, but not enough for it to burn.

SOME USEFUL SUPPLIES FOR SOLDERING.

1. Small needle-nose pliers with very thin points for fine work.

2. A small diagonal cutter for cutting wire.

3. A wire stripper; a simple one such as General's Model No. 68 is good.

4. Heat sink clamps to protect components near a soldering area.

5. Heat-shrink tubing or thin insulating electrical tape.

6. A small, flat fine file for renewing soldering tips.

7. A small sponge for cleaning soldering tips of debris.

8. Fine pointed tweezers for handling small work.

9. Eye protection!

10. "Helping Hands," Radio Shack's Model 64-2093. This is a device with six ball joints and two alligator clips which adjusts to hold small items which you are soldering.

A BUZZ ELIMINATOR FOR E-UNITS

By Richard C. Sigurdson

*Richard Sigurdson has enriched the **Greenberg Guides to Lionel Trains** for many years with his comments on Lionel's locomotives and motorized units. In this article, he shows you how to eliminate the sometimes annoying buzz noise from Lionel's mechanical sequence reversing switches. Compare this method with the one proposed by Mr. Broshears, above, and apply whichever one works best. This method is a more permanent solution to the problem.*

The buzz of Lionel's E-unit is a venerable part of tinplate railroading, but it can be annoying. The buzz is caused by the E-unit's plunger vibrating within its coil. The body of the locomotive resonates with the vibration.

One solution is to replace the E-unit with a solid state device, as Lionel itself has done on many of its recent locomotives. This solution will produce a silent and more reliable reversing switch, but it involves a great deal of rewiring. An easier solution is to power the E-unit with direct current instead of alternating current. This can be accomplished with just three electronic components.

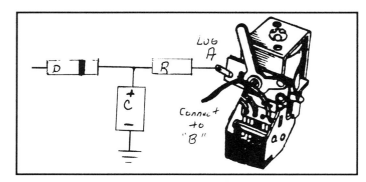

C = 1000mg - 16V electrolystic Cap (Radio Shack #272-958)
R = 3-5r 5w resistor (various numbers)
D = Silicone Diode - rated 2 amp minimum connect smaller diodes in parallel to increase current rating (Radio Shack #276-1653 or #776-1661).

Direct current is derived from a half-wave rectifier (D) which is filtered by a capacitor (C). The resistor (R) is a three to five ohm 5-watt resistor. Its purpose is to limit the voltage reaching the E-unit. The unit takes less voltage to activate using DC. After a period of continuous operation, the coil tends to run warm. If the engine is to be used in one direction only for an extended period, the operator should take the E-unit out of the circuit by using the E-unit lever.

Begin the installation of the electronics by unsoldering the three insulated wires (four if there are two lamps) from lug A on the E-unit; see Figure 3. Don't unsolder the coated wire from the coil. These wires can be soldered together. Following the diagrams, connect the components to the places indicated. Observe

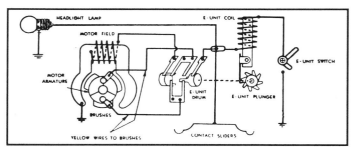

A typical E-unit installation in a Lionel locomotive.

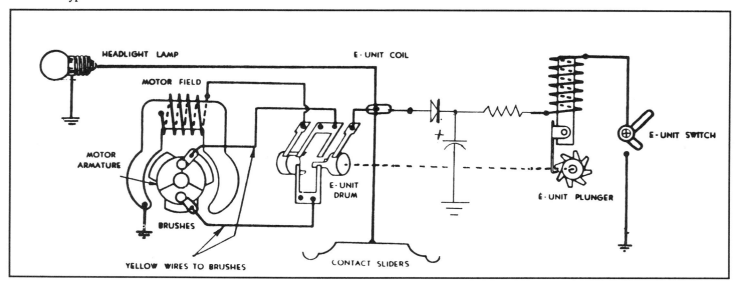

E-unit wiring after modification.

the polarity of the capacitor. The diode should have a band at one end which indicates the cathode. The leads can be kept short. The resistor should be kept in the open, away from any material that can be damaged by heat.

The parts for this installation can be purchased at any electronics supply house; here, Radio Shack part numbers are shown. This circuit can be used on all locomotives with mechanical three-position E-units. The horn or whistle may blow constantly due to the DC produced, causing the relay to pull in and trigger it.

Therefore, the best opportunity for use of this circuit would come on locomotives which do not have whistles or horns.

PARTS LIST

Capacitor: 1000 mfd. 16-volt electrolytic, Part No. 272-958

Diode: 3-amp, 50 piv. silicone, Part No. 276-1141

Resistor: 3-5 ohm, 5-watt; part no. varies.

TRICK WIRING BLOWS WHISTLE!
(Excerpted from Lionel's 1937 magazine entitled *Model Builder*.)

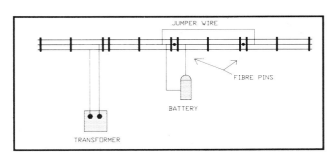

Diagram 1.

*This article first appeared in the March-April 1937 issue of Lionel's own magazine, **Model Builder**. It was reprinted in late 1987 by the Toy Train Operating Society. We reprint it here with the kind permission of Lionel Trains, Inc. Please note that some sections of the text have been modified to reflect more modern practices.*

Many model engineers possessing engines or streamline trains equipped with a whistle or horn have enjoyed pressing those red buttons on the whistle controller or working the transformer lever every time they wanted the whistle to blow. When there are switches to attend to and signals to flash, however, it is sometimes difficult to have a free hand with which to blow the whistle at the proper times; for instance, as the train approaches a crossing or a station. Fellows with many duties to attend to on their systems have wondered how they could make the whistle blow automatically — and here is the simple trick in detail.

All you need is one "D"-sized flashlight battery, a few fiber pins with which to insulate sections of the third rail, a little wire, and a battery bracket available from any electronic parts store. Figure 4 shows a portion of track — any part of your layout with the transformer connected in the usual manner. If you want to continue to make use of your whistle controller, leave it wired in the usual manner. Select the spot at which you want the whistle to blow and insulate the third rail there for a length of one track section. The third rail is insulated by inserting fiber pins in each end, as shown in the drawing.

Note: At this point, the original article instructed the reader to solder two wires to the battery. WE STRONGLY DISCOURAGE THIS PRACTICE! Today's nickel-cadmium and alkaline batteries may explode when subjected to such heat, and even the carbon-zinc batteries do not easily lend themselves to this practice. Purchase a battery bracket from an electronics supply store and solder the wires to each end of the bracket instead.

Attach one wire (either one) to the insulated section of the third rail and the other to the third rail on the opposite side of the fiber pin. Next, connect a jumper wire as shown in the diagram.

Start your train, and each time it passes over this insulated section of track it should give one blast of the whistle. The secret is simply that the little flashlight battery functions electrically just as your whistle controller does when you press the red button — provided you connect it exactly as indicated.

If one "toot" is not enough and you want two whistle blasts, look at Diagram 2 and see how it can be done simply by using two sections of insulated sections of track separated by one section connected to the remainder of your system by jumper wires.

A very long "toot" can be obtained by making the insulated third rail (marked "W" in the sketches) two track sections in length.

Try this simple stunt and see if your friends can figure out how your train whistles automatically every time it passes a certain spot!

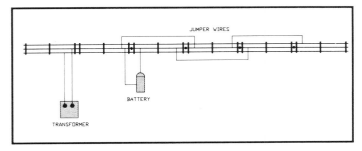

Diagram 2.

ENHANCED COUPLER OPERATION ON MPC CARS
By John Kouba

*Mr. Kouba is the author of an article on the 1986 Santa Fe Service Station Set in the latest edition of **Greenberg's Guide to Lionel Trains, 1970-1988**. In the following two articles, he explains two vital repair*

operations with considerable style and humor. All of us have felt as he does when Lionel equipment frustrates proper operations!

Nothing is more frustrating than to have a coupler open unexpectedly in one of your long-haul 30-car operations. Worse, such an event usually occurs when you have friends visiting your layout. Just as your engine reaches the top of a four-percent grade, a coupler opens and suddenly Lionel's fast-angle wheel design goes into effect as your engine takes off in one direction and your string of cars goes off in the opposite direction — at nerve-shattering speeds!

Fortunately, there is a VERY simple cure which takes less time than it does to read this article. I discovered the cure out of sheer necessity. At a local train meet, I recently purchased a unit train of Atlas ore cars fitted with K-Line trucks and couplers, which are essentially identical to Lionel's equipment. As is said, "the price was right;" the cars are lettered and painted in custom graphics and they are brand new, acquired directly from the distributor at a price I couldn't refuse.

So far, so good. However, when I got the cars home and made them into a great-looking unit train behind my mint-condition 671 S-2 Turbine Lcomotive, I soon discovered that I had a "small" problem! No sooner had my train pulled out for the long haul, when my steamer was headed one way and my ore cars were left standing there. As soon as I backed up the engine, recoupled it to the train, and started again, the cars separated again — somewhere else in the string! In an hour, I had discovered that no two cars would stay coupled together for any length of time or distance. My first thought was to stop payment on the check and make arrangements to ship all the cars back to the distributor.

A defective truck in hand, I decided over a cup of coffee that it was more sensible to cure the problem and get back to running my trains. Besides, it could happen again — and sooner or later, somebody had to come up with a solution, so why shouldn't I try? I had nothing to lose!

As most Lionel operators know, the MPC modern truck design has a new assembly for the coupler system. Made of Delrin, a duPont slick-surfaced plastic, the design eliminates the problem hair spring used in postwar couplers, and because of its properties, the modern trucks offer very little resistance when an operator is coupling or uncoupling cars. When it works, it works well. Fortunately, it works well 99 percent of the time. The remaining one percent happen to be the cars I had just bought and the occasional modern era car we buy. (Have you ever noticed that the car with the defective truck is always the one you've sought for years?) Your first solution is either to replace the whole truck — expensive and a waste of effort — or to find a dealer who stocks just the coupler armatures, which is the equivalent of buying a pound of chicken lips!

Once again, necessity (and frustration) breeds success — in my case, after three pots of very strong coffee and many failed attempts. For this project, you'll need the following tools and materials: X-Acto knife, jeweler's screwdrivers, pin vise (or Dremel Moto-Tool), hobby drill bits, and — last but definitely not

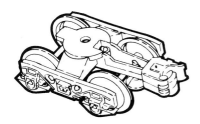

Operating coupler truck.

least — self-tapping 3/8" to 1/2" long tiny wood screws. I bought a box of these screws at a hobby shop with the nondescript label "PK-11 Track Screws" for 59 cents.

First, remove the wheel under the coupler by gently prying one end out with either a small flat-bladed screwdriver or a strong thumbnail. Now, take a flat-bladed jeweler's screwdriver and place it between the coupler shank and the armature plate and GENTLY pry up the armature — it will unsnap itself from the shank. By comparing my defective armature with one which I knew to work properly, I soon discovered that I had two problems. The armature spring had a V cut into it. On a working armature, the cut goes halfway through. This is what provides the tension on the latch pin which keeps the knuckle closed. The defective one was cut only a quarter of the way — not enough tension was generated on the latch pin to keep the coupler closed. The slightest vibration caused the pin to move slightly and — Bingo! — the coupler would open all by itself!

The second problem (as if one wasn't enough!) was the latch pin itself; it was a gnat's hair too short. In the closed position, the latch pin just barely held the coupler closed. However, if an upward force were applied to the bottom of the armature plate, then — Voila! The hinge pin would ride up higher against the coupler and keep it where it belongs — closed until ordered to do otherwise!

Here's how to solve both problems. On the bottom of the coupler shank, remove the raised ring with your X-Acto knife. This will reduce the space between the armature and the coupler shank as well as increase the upward length of the latch pin. Replace the armature plate. Directly in front of the raised ridge, drill a pilot hole through both the armature and the coupler shank. Insert the screw and tighten it. By careful adjustment of the screw, you can vary the tension applied to the armature. If the screw is tightened too much, the coupler will not operate. However, I find that drawing the screw up snug and backing it out half a turn works perfectly. When the armature is set to your satisfaction, snap the wheel set back into place. If further adjustments are necessary, you'll have plenty of clearance for the screwdriver to make corrections. The beauty of this solution is that it's permanent and only visible when the car is upside down. Now your cars will operate when you want them to — not when they decide to!

IMPROVED LIGHTING FOR ALUMINUM PASSENGER CARS

By John Kouba

The new Lionel and Williams heavyweight passenger cars are considered by collectors and operators alike as the state of the art in tinplate styling and operation. Both companies have produced (and continue to produce) colors and graphics never before seen in tinplate design. A major feature of these aluminum beau-

ties is the twin lighting in each car. With both companies, the light socket is an integral part of the truck design.

Unfortunately, these cars suffer from a design flaw inherent in the arrangement of the roller pickup of each truck. The only time all the lights are on, at best, occurs when the train is standing still. As soon as the train is under way, the lights start to flicker and blink — not exactly prototypical! The culprit is the spring attached to the roller assembly; it's too light to provide enough downward pressure on the rollers in order to maintain contact with the center rail. At first I tried using a jumper wire between both of the center rail contacts on each car. This only provided marginal improvement in operation. There HAD to be a better way!

Well, there IS a better way — and it only takes three minutes or so to fix each car! Cost? Believe it or not, about 99 cents — and that's for THREE cars at a time! First, go to your local Radio Shack electronics parts store and purchase a package or two of Vinyl Grommets (Radio Shack's Part No. 64- 3025). This is an assortment of 42 grommets, seven each of six different sizes. That was the hard part — now, let's fix those cars!

First, remove the truck assembly from the body of the car. Now, select a grommet SLIGHTLY SMALLER than the post which is attached to the center roller. We want a snug fit, but not one that is too tight for the roller to have some "give" to it. Slip a small-bladed screwdriver underneath the bottom of the post to support it while you GENTLY push the grommet over the head of the post. If you've installed the grommet correctly, it is now between the spring and the post-head. If the spring is hung up inside the grommet, use an X-Acto knife to pull the spring down GENTLY from the grommet until it clears the grommet. Go slowly! You don't have too much room here, and you don't want to wreck the spring itself!

If you've done everything right, you've now increased the tension on the center roller considerably. Put the truck back onto the car and do the other truck the same way. Once you've done the first car, the others will go very rapidly. Nothing encourages proficiency like repetition of a task!

OK — so now you've installed all your grommets. What's next? Well, all that tension has a tradeoff — increased resistance to the free-rolling capability of the cars. Solution: Reach for your handy tube of powdered graphite with a needlepoint applicator. With the car on its side, place the applicator tip in between the roller and the shaft riding through it. VERY GENTLY, tap a VERY small amount of graphite into the area. Continue to hold the car on its side and slowly turn the roller so that the graphite works its way down into the roller between it and its shaft. Now, do the other roller the same way. Then turn the car around and repeat the procedure on the other side of both rollers. While you have

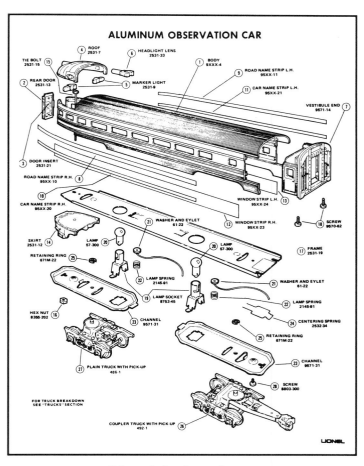

Schematic for observation car.

the car in this position, clean off any caked-on grease and dirt on the wheels and put a SMALL drop of LaBelle No. 102 Gear Oil on each axle and the needlepoint bearing of each wheel. The gear oil is specially formulated to stay where you put it; it won't run off and foul up the track or your nice clean wheel treads!

Now, put your cars back on the tracks, turn off the room lights, and bask in the glory of those interior passenger car lights as your main-liner express comes highballing through the "night!"

MAINTAINING AND OPERATING LIONEL'S O72 WIDE RADIUS SWITCHES
By Edward W. Stencler

Ed Stencler is a veteran Lionel railroader with a huge attic layout. He likes to run his trains at relatively high speeds, and for him the Lionel wide radius O72 Switches are "the only game in town." Although Ed has managed to secure many good examples of the prewar No. 711 switches, his instructions also apply to the newly reissued Lionel O72 switches, which carry the numbers 5165 and 5166. Ed is also one of the "Friday Night Irregulars" at the Toy Train Station in Feasterville, Pennsylvania.

If you're going to run your Lionel trains on a big basement or attic layout, you'll certainly want to show them to their best advantage. The largest and best of Lionel's trains look their best when they are used on wide radius track with a 72-inch diameter.

In fact, the newly-reissued Hiawatha Set can only be run on special wide radius track, at least in a practical sense. That means, of course, the presence of O72 wide radius turnouts if you are to have the usual panoply of Lionel track — yards, intersecting loops, and the like. For many years this meant diligent searches for the old prewar Wide Radius No. 711 O Gauge Switches, for which operators like me would pay any reasonable price regardless of condition. Then, last year, Lionel Trains, Inc. reissued these wide radius beauties, making it possible for Lionel operators to enjoy them again. Now, your Fairbanks-Morse diesels, your F-3 ABA diesel sets, and above all, your full scale Hudsons with their Standard O freight cars and full-sized aluminum passenger cars can all be enjoyed to best advantage at high operating speeds.

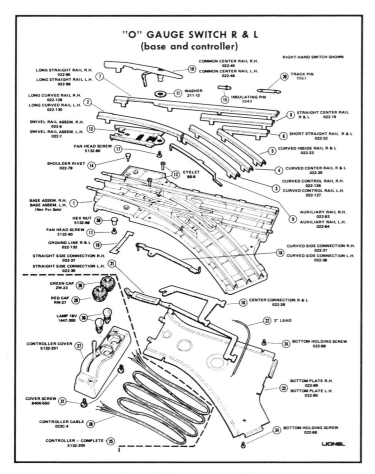

Schematic for O Gauge Switch.

The new 5165 (right-hand) and 5166 (left-hand) O72 Turnouts are made just like the originals except for the injection-molded plastic mechanism case; the 711's was metal. The reliable operating characteristics of the regular radius 022 models have carried over to these turnouts as well. The only real difference is in the controllers. The 711 prewar models had a metal case controller with a stout rubber-encased three-wire cord of rather impressive durability. The new turnouts have been issued with a plastic case controller with standard three-strand flat wire; this is identical to regular O Gauge production.

Since most operators of large layouts run their turnouts on fixed voltage, the connecting strip pin which accepts the constant-voltage plug must be kept absolutely clean. This strip pin may be the most important mechanism of the wide radius turnout. You may find it necessary to hook the fixed-voltage circuit to a strong source of fixed voltage, perhaps as much as 18 volts. The reason for this is that the wide radius turnouts need more voltage to operate in a "snappy" fashion, and this is especially true if your layout features a reversing loop which uses the non-derailing mechanism of the turnout. The faster the turnout operates, the faster you can run your trains without fear of derailment.

There are many advantages to using the O72 wide radius switches made by Lionel. First of all, in the Lionel model the operating mechanism is extremely reliable. The motor mechanism of these turnouts can be reversed for ladder tracks, as can the regular radius 022 models. It is not generally appreciated that the motor mechanism on the 022 models is fully interchangeable with the mechanism of the wide radius models. This means that if you find a base with good track and a healthy operating rail, you can fit a spare 022 motor to it and have a wide radius turnout. The old metal prewar controller boxes are preferable to the newer models, but any 022 Controller can operate these turnouts.

Another advantage to these turnouts is high speed operation without fear of derailment. As a rule, you can operate your trains over the curved section of a wide radius turnout half again as fast as you could with a regular 022 model. In addition, the narrow aspect of the turnout means that you can position interchange tracks and yard tracks more closely to your main lines, just as the real railroads do. If you are very fortunate, you may find some of the old wide radius 731 Turnouts with solid "T" rails; these are a great match for the new Gargraves track which takes graceful curves so well.

Other manufacturers make wide radius O Gauge turnouts in Lionel's price range, but from my experience they do not perform nearly as well. The only exception to this would be the wide radius slip switches available from Right-Of-Way Industries, which can be made to match Lionel's turnouts very well. If you have a great deal of room on your layout, try operating with Lionel's O72 wide radius turnouts. Many layout plans have been developed to take full advantage of these turnouts, and they can be adapted for many uses on the large layout. You won't fully appreciate their usefulness until you watch your Rock Island Northern or New York Central steamers fly at full speed right through the turnout onto another track without incident!

MAKE YOUR TROLLEYS RUN THEMSELVES

By Tom Rollo

Tom Rollo has made substantial contributations to previous Greenberg books. A Milwaukee resident and Wisconsin Bell Telephone employee, Mr. Rollo specializes in postwar Lionels and antique telephones. He is working with Chris Rohlfing and the author on a comprehensive guide to Lionel accessories, publication of which is scheduled for early 1990.

This is the fourth article I've written for Greenberg Publishing Company, Inc. and by now readers have probably guessed I am a Lionel collector. Well, you're right, but that is not the whole story. Since my childhood I have had an undying love for traction

— that is, streetcars, interurbans, subways, and elevateds. In modern day Madison Avenue parlance, this is known as light rail.

The light rail concept is purely American in its origins, resulting from inventions of Thomas Edison (the dynamotor) and Frank Julian Sprague (the controller and Multiple Unit Control). Sprague's contribution was really what started it all. His improvements to Edison's motor, together with a revolutionary method of mounting the motor in car trucks to absorb shock, made the use of the electric motor practical for powering a rail vehicle. Sprague's controller and the use of specially designed grid resistors permitted acceleration to take place in steps, much like Lionel's pre-Trainmaster transformers. The Sprague controller, however, did not control the motors directly. The controller operated a group of relays that applied power to the motors. With the use of jumper cables between cars, one controller could operate relay sets in a group of cars coupled together into a train. This is Sprague's Multiple Unit Control — the perfect finishing touch. These inventions and refinements ultimately retired the mules, horses, and steam locomotives from urban mass transit.

Sprague's first successful test, a demonstration for financial backers, took place on 200 feet of track laid in an alley just two blocks from where Lionel would ultimately locate its headquarters. At this point the trolley pole had yet to be invented, so the electric current to operate the car was distributed through a third rail located midway between the two running rails. To top it off (or bottom it off, if you prefer), the current collector mounted on the underside of the demonstration flatcar was a roller! Two years later, the first commercially successful electric streetcar system started in Richmond, Virginia. The boom was on! For the next twenty-five years the development of electric traction in all forms took place with such dynamics that it makes the hula hoop and the personal computer pale by comparison. That was the problem. Development took place so rapidly, and in some parts of the country so indiscriminately, that some small city systems were financially doomed from the start. For those that were able to make it through World War I, problems of deteriorating equipment and trackage, rising wages, and growing competition from a new-fangled notion called the automobile would bring the surviving systems to their knees. Enter Mr. Birney!

Charles O. Birney designed a very simple, steel-sided, single-truck streetcar (later double-truck versions were built) that was the savior of the small town system. The following is quoted from *The Time of The Trolley* by William D. Middleton, copyright 1967 by Kalmbach Publishing Company, Milwaukee, Wisconsin:

"The new streetcar was designed by Charles O. Birney, the engineer in charge of car design for Stone and Webster Corporation, operator of a number of street railway operations in Texas, Washington, and elsewhere in the United States. Birney's concept called for a small, extremely lightweight car that could be worked at low cost with a one-man crew. Because of the low operating cost, Birney argued, more frequent service could be given with a resultant increase in traffic.

"The 'Safety Car,' as it was called, was a single truck car averaging about 28 feet in length and seating approximately 32 passengers. Although the first experimental model, constructed by the American Car Company in 1915, weighed only about 5 tons, the standard production models were somewhat heavier, weighing anywhere from 7 to 9 tons. Even at that, Safety Cars weighed only about half as much per seat as most of the heavier equipment they replaced. One of the cars novel features was its "dead man control," which automatically brought the car to a halt if the operator released the controller or a special foot pedal without first setting the brakes.

"The first Birney cars, as they became generally known, were placed in service in 1916, and by 1920 over 4000 of them had been built. Ultimately, more than 6000 were in service throughout the United States as well as in a number of foreign countries. Their initial success was almost phenomenal.

"...A larger, double truck version of the Birney developed during the 1920s proved quite popular, and was turned out in quantity for a number of systems."

One Birney model actually was assigned the number 60 in service on The Milwaukee Electric Railway and Light Company's (TMER & L) Racine, Wisconsin city system. It differed from Lionel's only in the presence of two trolley poles, the trolley pole stand on the roof, and four pairs of roof ventilators instead of Lionel's three. Two trolleys were optional, depending on the individual system's operating environment. Lionel's model followed the more basic Birney with one "walk around" trolley pole. At the end of the line the motorman detached the trolley retriever from its bracket at one end of the car, pulled the trolley off the wire, and walked alongside the car, swinging the trolley out in a semi-circle. At the opposite end of the car, the trolley was placed back on the wire and the trolley retriever placed in the circular bracket at that end. This is the same effect that results from the Lionel trolley striking a bumper at the end of the track. Obviously Lionel could not duplicate the trolley rope and retriever. Notice in the illustration that the trolley pole is depressed to a relatively low angle. The Birney in this location probably could have done without the stand, since the trolley wire height is relatively low. The city of Racine was served by two interurbans. One of them used the city streets for entry into the downtown area. On those streets where the interurban and the streetcars operated on the same trackage, the trolley wire was much higher. Despite its big spring bumpers, Lionel's model was very accurate in appearance and operation.

The last small town Birneys in regular revenue operation were those of the Fort Collins Municipal Railway, Fort Collins, Colorado. Purchased during the "Birney Boom" of the early 1920s, the Fort Collins system remained in operation until 1951. The city never got rid of all of its Birney cars, however, keeping several on static display. Today, the Fort Collins Birneys are running once again on the Mountain Avenue line as a tourist attraction. After almost thirty years in regular service the cars have been returned to service for more — much longer than rubber-tired substitutes would ever last!

A LIONEL SMALL TOWN SYSTEM

The Fort Collins Municipal Railway was typical of just about every small town system in the United States. All streetcar lines were operated with single track. There were exceptions in downtown areas where lines met and a very short stretch of double track was operated to allow cars to pass one another. Long lines may have been equipped with a passing track somewhere along the route. Still, some lines were one big long loop. A trolley operated in only one direction around the loop, taking a pass through the downtown area. Sheboygan and Oshkosh, Wisconsin each had lines that operated in this way. There were others so small that the streetcar system consisted of one stretch of single track with no passing track at all. The Wahpeton-Breckenridge Street Railway had only two single-truck trolleys (that looked more like Lionel's early 200 Trolley) and 1.144 miles of track. To complicate matters, the two cities are in North Dakota and Minnesota respectively. This meant that regulation was controlled by the Interstate Commerce Commission. Fare accounting had to be maintained with the same detail as the passenger revenue of the Great Northern Railway and the Northern Pacific that served the two cities. There was no passing track, so only one little trolley was operated each day and each of the trolleys (numbered 1 and 2) were used alternately. This seems to the most logical prototype for your Lionelville operation. There is one difference, however; yours is much busier, and two trolleys must operate together on the same

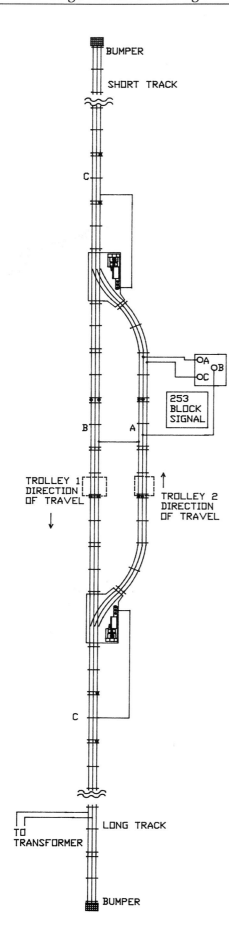

track without colliding with each other. Since you are busy running your division of the Lionel Lines, you have no time to be a "juice jockey." Your Lionelville Street Railway Company must be automated!

Yours is by no means an interstate operation, so there is no need to be concerned with the bureaucratic red tape of Federal regulation. One streetcar line with a passing track is all that is required. I suggest using O27 track, as its lower, lightweight profile is more suitable to streetcar operations. Any amount of straight and curved track can be used. You will need two bumpers of the more durable type such as the 260 Bumper that can be fastened to the track, and one pair of automatic turnouts such as 1122, 1122E, or 5123. Don't attempt to use the earlier 1121 version for this application unless you are willing to create your own non-derailing feature. The non-derailing feature found on the 1122 models first made in 1952, or any version thereafter, is important to this operation. You may use one right and one left turnout or two right amd two left turnouts, whatever is appropriate for your layout. In addition you will need one Lionel accessory equipped with a train stopper thermostat. This may be the 253 Block Signal, 115 or 132 Stations, or even Lionel Trains, Inc. re-run of the 115 Station (the 6-1115). If you choose to use one of the stations, it is not necessary to locate the station near the streetcar line. The station could be located in its more appropriate location next to the main line. All you are interested in is the train stopper, which can be wired to the streetcar line even though the station is somewhere else on the layout. The illustration below shows the use of the 253 Block Signal. Next, you will need to make four sections of insulated track. Roland has described how to make insulated track elsewhere in this edition. As a side note, this arrangement can be used for any of Lionel's "bump-reverse" units. You may want to use more sections of insulated track if you want to showcase Lionel's 50 Gang Cars. For the plodding little trolleys, however, four sections is plenty. Twelve insulating track pins will also be required. This may seem like a lot, but it isn't. As we move along, it will all come together.

Make four sections of insulated track in the usual way. Two of the insulated sections placed in the siding should be joined together. Insulating pins should be installed at the ends of the outside insulated rail you have made and in the ends of the center rail. This is shown as "A" in the illustration. Depending on your own needs, you may want to make this insulated section of track one or two sections longer. For trolley operation, two sections are adequate. Next, install four insulating pins in the ends of both outside rails of two sections of track adjacent to the siding. This is "B" in the illustration. These are regular sections of track. Since you are installing insulating pins in both outside rails, the cross-ties are also dead and insulating the rail from the tie is not necessary. The two remaining sections of insulated track are beyond the siding at least one section away from each turnout, "C" in the illustration.

The electrical connections are as follows: Connect the insulated outside rail in the siding to either of the insulated outside rails in the adjacent track. Next, connect the insulated rail in the right side beyond the siding to the post on the 1122 Turnout in the middle. This causes the turnout to change position after the trolley has passed the turnout. Connect the insulated outside rail in the left side beyond the siding to the farthest terminal from the motor housing on the remaining 1122 Turnout. You may install the 1122C Controller if you want to; however, for the automatic operation of the trolleys it is not necessary. Next, connect the accessory with the train stopper following the instructions for that accessory. The 253 Block Signal is illustrated here. Be careful not to make any other connections to any of the insulated track already discussed. Lastly, connect the transformer to the track as usual. I recommend using any of Lionel's pre-Trainmaster transformers, Type "B" or larger. The reason is that for proper operation a constant voltage is necessary. The step switch on these models is better for this purpose than newer models. These transformers can usually be found at swap meets or at retailers of used trains at very reasonable prices. For proper operation it is important that the length of straight track beyond the passing siding to the left be shorter than the one to the right. This is necessary to insure that the trolley controlled by the train stopper starts last and arrives back at the passing siding first. Install the bumpers at the ends of the track, just as you would do for any siding on the high iron.

Place two trolleys on the track, one is placed on the siding at the insulated track in front of the signal. Place the other one on the adjacent track over the two sections with the insulated outside rails. Set the train stopper control to the "fast" position. Make sure the trolley on the straightaway labeled "1" is set to move to the right (East). The trolley on the siding should be set to move in the opposite direction. Now apply power to the track. The trolley labeled "1" in the illustration will start first. As it travels onto the turnout, the non-derailing feature snaps the turnout to the straight position. After trolley "1" has passed over the turnout, it passes onto the insulated track section beyond. This causes the switch it just passed over to snap to the curved position. It continues on until it reaches the bumper and then returns. Meanwhile the train stopper has started trolley "2" and the lights in the block signal have turned from red to green. Trolley "2" passes over the other turnout and the non-derailing feature snaps the switch to the curved position. Beyond the switch trolley "2" now passes over the remaining section of insulated track and snaps the switch it just passed over back to the straight position. It strikes the bumper and returns. Trolley "2" should return first. When it reaches the switch, it now goes straight through until it reaches the section of track with the insulated outer rails and stops. Trolley "1" is now on its way back and takes the curve into the siding, reaches the insulated track section controlled by the 253 Block Signal, and stops. As its front wheels move onto the insulated track section, the car's axle bridges the non-insulated outer rail to the insulated outer rail. This in turn causes the two outer rails of the adjacent track to become live and trolley "2" starts. This is one complete cycle. The action is continuous.

It will take some adjustment to get the train stopper setting just right. The setting depends on the voltage setting on the transformer, the length of the track beyond the signal (that is how far the trolley controlled by the signal must travel), and the performance characteristics of the trolleys themselves. I recommend using two similar trolleys, either two of the original No. 60s or two more recently manufactured by Lionel Trains, Inc.

The object of making the two trolleys stop and pass one another is to simulate a layover. In prototype small town operation, the passing track was usually in the downtown area where Birneys took their layover until the cars from all routes in the city arrived. Then, at a scheduled time, each started going out to the end of the line and then returned. The track diagram included here is simplified for purposes of illustration. Use your imagination. The passing track might extend through your downtown area. The insulated sections do not have to be exactly adjacent to one another, nor do the tracks themselves. One track might be in one street, while the other is in a parallel street in the next block. By placing the insulated track sections at a street intersection and adding a small painted strip of wood next to the track, your transit riders have a safety island to board and alight. Add additional wiring and on-off toggle switches and the system can be bypassed so one trolley can operate continuously on days when traffic is light. Additional turnouts and a small engine house will make a great car barn and maintenance facility. If you decide to go this route, starting with two-trolley operation is easy. Bring the first car out of the car barn and onto the line. When it reaches the train stopper signal, it will stop for a time and then start proceeding to the end of the line and return. When it reaches the insulated track section controlled by the other car, it will stop and will not start. Now bring the second trolley car out of the car barn and let it proceed to the train stopper. Now the two cars will operate continuously.

As you can see, the electrical connections are very simple. This operation uses all Lionel products, and all of them are currently available. Many operators have avoided using train stoppers because the performance of them with trains is unrealistic, jerky, and too dependent on the length of the train which often changes during the layout's operation. Train stoppers, however, are ideal for trolley cars.

Enjoy! Rapid transit service in your Lionel City or Lionelville will never be better!

SCENERY ON YOUR LAYOUT:
Thinking Small, Thinking Simple, Thinking Cheap
By Jack Robinson

Besides being one of the most entertaining and engaging people I know within the hobby, Jack Robinson is an absolute whiz at miniaturization — the best I've ever seen. Jack is not a train man; rather, he is a talented miniaturist whose dollhouses have become legendary for their exactness of detail, right down to hand-laid miniature shingles and microscopic door hinges and knobs. Jack's quick wit and Southern-gentleman air transfers readily into his miniature world, where everything and anything is a possibility for his exacting craft. In the following article, Jack entertainingly shows you how to turn commonplace objects into scenic wonders on your train layout.

Despite his disclaimers, Jack is an accomplished author. For the Greenberg Publishing Company, he has written Finishing Touches, where he shows how to add realistic detail to miniature house interiors with the assured skill of a master craftsman, which he is. He's working on a second book, Finishing Touches Vol. II — Scaling Down, and slowly but surely he's putting together the main details of the Renwal Toy Company's history. I look forward to rooming with Jack at the summer Pittsburgh Greenberg shows for some first-rate storytelling.

Boy, you'd think that when somebody wants you to help him with a book, you'd get your name in BIG print all over the cover, maybe a big publishing contract, and all the glory that goes with it... Well, as you can see, that's not quite how things turned out. After all the dust settled, all I wrote was one dinky little article. But, after all, as the great labor leader John L. Lewis once said, "He that tooteth not his own horn, the same shall not be tooteth!" And Roland's a good talkin' buddy, so... here goes.

For most of my life I've been in the business of miniature model making, and although they're not really my specialty, I like model trains as well. It seems pretty natural that there is a lot of cross-pollination between the two arts because they share a lot in common. Both crafts want to create the illusion of reality on a small scale.

Now, as I see it, you have a very simple choice with both hobbies. Either you can spend the mortgage money buying all the things you need to create that illusion, or you can use your imagination and create something for that illusion out of everyday household junk. I needn't tell you which of these is the most fun! All you have to do is to observe the world around you... but really LOOK at it! Don't just see an object around the house for what it is. Look at it for what it COULD be!

A lot of the details and ideas you will read about here are basic, simple things which can be applied to your train platform with very little outlay of money, if any. A train layout is more than just trains, track, and motion. When I look at somebody's model pike, I like to take in the scenic details which make up a really nice display. Often, those little extras, which aren't much by themselves, add up to a finishing touch to your layout which will make it a lot more interesting to the onlooker.

For example, if you have a diner, put a couple of trash cans next to it for detail. You can get these commercially, but stop and think. Is there anything around your home, probably in plain sight, which will do the same thing? Sure there is! See that little sewing kit over there? That's right — get those two plastic thimbles. Spray-paint them silver. Now take a fine brush and draw black simulated handles on the top and sides. There are your trash cans! Wasn't that a lot better than just buying them? Smaller ones can be made from painted toothpaste tube caps.

As you can see, all you have to do is to look around your own house, neighborhood, street, and town to get many ideas for little things you can add to your layout, not just to keep costs down, but to stretch your imagination a little. Now, I do exactly that all the time, but after all, miniatures are my business — and hobby. Since I travel quite a bit from show to show, I take in the many signs and sights the highways have to offer, and I try to place these into a miniature perspective. I study the road marking systems from state to state, the billboards, the signs, and anything unusual. For example, out near Strasburg, Pennsylvania there's a little restaurant on Route 41 which must be owned by a guy with a bizarre sense of humor. He's cut an old Volkswagen in half and installed it against his front wall so that it looks like the thing has turned his place into a drive-in. That's a really interesting detail to put into your miniature diner!

Now, don't plan on wearing a pathway to your hobby store for your materials because a lot of what you'll be using may be lurking in the junk drawers and boxes of your own house. I'll grant you that some things may have to be purchased, but the whole idea is to use a little personal creativity, especially if it can be humorous. First, take a good look at your layout as it now exists; study your houses, roads, sidings, and whatever else you

have on your board. After studying what you now have, read through the following few simple ideas I've concocted and try out a few of them. Of course, I won't be able to cover all the possibilities here, but if you have any creativity about you, you can take things from here and create your own improvisations.

ROADWAYS

If you plan to have any type of road for the autos and trucks on your layout, by all means make the roadway out of any appropriate material, but don't forget to put lines on it. Crayon and paint sometimes don't work too well on some road surfaces, but there are materials which will do the job very nicely. Take a little trip to your office supply store. There, you'll find a wide selection of plastic tape in little dispensers and rolls. This tape is used in video transparency presentations and it comes in all kinds of widths and colors. You can even get little black or white arrows. The tape can be applied to your roadways very quickly and removed just as quickly when you make changes to your layout, unlike crayon or paint.

Be sure to plan your road lining details realistically. This means that you should observe the real world roadways and duplicate the kinds of markings you see every day. You should plan double lines, broken lines, striped areas for crosswalks, parking areas for stores, and so forth. Careful use of this tape and some twin-light lamp posts can give you a most realistic parking lot. Don't worry if the markings are not exactly perfect. In the real world, some roadway striping looks as if the crew put it down on Monday morning after a wild weekend!

For the curbs along your roads, if you need them, take some long strips of cardboard three times as wide as the height of the curb off the road. Use a fine knife and score the strips along their length into three equal sections. Don't cut the strips all the way through. Just score them enough so you can fold the strips into a squared-off curb. Now, paint the cardboard a dull light gray, and you'll have good-looking curb surfaces. Storm sewer drains? The upper part can be painted onto the curb in gray with black for the opening and the flat part on the road can be achieved by cutting out part of the road if you've used shingles, painting the hole black and applying dark gray plastic flashing from model kits inside the hole in a cross-hatch pattern.

PIPES

In the real world, piping is all around you. Perhaps big concrete sections of culvert pipe lie alongside a road, waiting for installation. Oil refineries have incredibly complex piping. Any manufacturing business needs pipe of all kinds, and a plumbing shop would certainly have a great deal of pipe around.

The best material for pipe is soda straws. You can spray-paint these straws black for iron piping, gray or silver for galvanized piping, or copper for copper or brass pipes. If you want curves in your straw-pipes, buy a few flexible straws to paint and bend them as you wish. Interconnect them according to your imagination and needs, and use them as loads on your trains and trucks. For larger pipes, wooden dowels cut to fit are excellent once they are painted.

For the complex piping in oil refineries, cut some plastic flashing from model kits and interconnect your oil tanks so that the piping goes every which way, just like the real thing. Small buttons glued to plastic stalks make excellent simulated valves within your piping system. Raid that sewing kit again!

WOOD

Why buy pre-cut dowels and logs when all you really have to do is walk into your back yard to find all the wood you will need? Look at the nearest tree or old limb and notice the terrific amount of twig-lumber you have at your disposal. You can even have different types of wood, depending upon the trees. With this supply of wood readily at hand, you can do all kinds of decorating tricks. Here are just a few:

No doubt you have a few roadside shanties next to your track for materials storage or crew shelter during a railroad job. Many of these shanties would have wood stoves for heat in real life. Well, where's the wood pile? Simple — just cut some twigs to scale, bark and all, and glue them into little pyramids mounted on cardboard. Then put the wood stacks behind the sheds or the gateman houses. For homes, you can bend black wire into log cradles and stack your little wood pieces inside them. Then put the assembled log cradles on the front porches of the houses, where firewood would then be available for the miniature home-owners. Larger logs can be cut for more ambitious wood piles scattered along your layout for scenery. If you cut some twigs into equal lengths and use straight pins and white glue to attach them to each other at 90° and 45° angles, you can have yourself the nicest-looking instant split-rail fences you ever saw. Very large tree limbs (relatively speaking) can become loads for flatcars in a lumber train. That's exactly what Lionel has done recently with its packages of logs. If Lionel can cut branches, why can't you? Get out that jeweler's saw!

WIRE

One neat detail for many uses would be coils of wire stacked and ready for use. Bright copper bell wire has many uses on a layout. If you wrap lengths of bell wire around a wooden dowel, you can make little coils of bright wire which can be stacked in the yard of a factory, placed in the back of a pickup truck, or hung from miniature hooks outside a railroad shed. The same bright copper wire can be used with little wooden stanchions for hand-rails along sidewalks and in other places.

Don't neglect insulated wire, either, especially if it's in green insulation. Most Lionel accessories come with little coils of wire insulated in bright green. With almost no change, these little wire loops can make great simulated garden hoses hanging from the backs of houses. You can also wind this wire carefully around empty thread spools to simulate cable used for underground telephone lines.

ELECTRIC AND TELEPHONE LINES

One of the best ways to add realism and life to your layout is to add electric and telephone lines from pole to pole, pole to building, and building to building. Plastic telephone poles are readily available from Lionel, Plasticville, and many other sources. If you want to make your own, use some wooden dowels for the poles and simulated railroad ties for the crosspieces. Then, get some black or brown fishing line or heavy cotton thread and string it between the insulators on the telephone poles. If you add lines from the poles to your buildings and houses, the effect can be very realistic. Just remember to beware of the presence of these lines when you are reaching across your layout for any purpose. Additionally, make sure that your rolling stock will clear the lines if they stretch across the tracks.

For some whimsical detail, you might consider gluing together a miniature kite out of toothpicks and thin construction paper and "tangling" it in the wires. Perhaps you can even simulate an old pair of sneakers tied together with string and dangling from the wires! This could be done by cutting the feet off an otherwise useless plastic human figure and connecting the pieces with fine thread.

MANHOLES AND TRASH RECEPTACLES

One of the neatest objects for model railroads might be lurking inside your dishwasher, of all places. Unfortunately, this little object usually winds up in the trash can — ironically, in view of what it can become! This is a product known as Jet-Dri; it is used to prevent spotting on dishes and glassware. The material comes in a little white basket with a turquoise cap which hangs from the dishwasher racks. Once the product is used, take this little assembly and look at it. It can be turned into two excellent train platform items!

If you cut off the hanging straps, the basket can be turned into a trash receptacle in two gauges. Use the full-sized basket for G Scale trains such as LGB. For Lionel trains, cut off the top part of the basket down to the first circular divider for the proper scale. You can also use the basket, spray-painted brown, to collect leaves in a back yard. Pencil sharpener shavings make good simulated leaves to fill this basket; strew a few of these shavings around a back yard as well. Make a little paper sign — "Phila. Sts. Dept." — and paste it to the trash receptacle.

The disc in the top of the receptacle can be used as a pattern maker for manhole covers. Place the disc atop a piece of heavy cardboard and trace around the disc, including the holes. Cut out the cardboard with scissors and blacken the holes. Now, place your cardboard disc in the center of your roadway, and you have an instant manhole cover! Note that if you place the disc in the center of the roadway, it should be striped with the road's center lines. However, since many road crews do not place the cover back into the roadway with the stripes exactly parallel with the road, mount the disc so that the stripes are off-center for the most realistic effect. Using the Jet-Dri disc as a pattern, you can make as many of these covers as you choose.

ROAD SIGNS AND ADVERTISEMENTS

If you look through magazines and brochures, you can find many pictures of road signs and advertisements you can use on your layout — speed limits, crossings, curves, and so on. Locate those signs which would suit your layout's size and needs and carefully cut them out. Glue them onto small pieces of cardboard, and then glue this assembly onto poles or small sticks. If you need more than one copy of a particular sign or ad, merely photocopy the signs and color them to suit yourself.

For billboards, it is too easy to use the prepackaged signs which come with ready-made billboard frames. Here is a chance to really exercise some creativity! Instead of using the ready-made signs, cut out pieces of white cardboard and draw your own "gag" products! Can you imagine some of the ad copy? How about "Gassbagg's Garbage Guys...Your Trash Is Our Cash"? Or, there's "Reck & Rewn's Auto Body Shop...We Rebuild The Car You've Killed".

Hopefully, I've been able to give you some insights into how easy it is to add a touch of realism to your layout using creativity instead of money. Look around you, and you can see many inspirations to create some great scenic ideas for your layout. All you need is a little imagination and vision... and everyone has that!

MODULAR LAYOUTS
By William V. Mayer

*Mr. Mayer has contributed several articles to the Greenberg Guides to Lionel Trains. He is the former editor of **The Switcher**, the journal of the Lionel Operating Train Society. In this preface to the **Operating Manual** of the **Tinplate Trackers' Organization**, he explains the many advantages and basic ideas behind shared modular Lionel layouts. We reprint this article with the kind permission of both the above organizations.*

To many operators a first class layout involves distance, distance, and distance. There are some who would go a hundred yards in a straight line if it weren't for the fact that they'd lose sight of the trains completely! The desire for distance and the room available for a permanent layout are always in conflict, and the solution seems to be modular layouts wherein a group of operators gets together and each, independently, prepares a module which, when hooked to the others, forms a layout as large as the members of the modular group decide to make it.

The first problem in any modular layout is standardization. The main items requiring this standardization are the height each module will be from the floor, the placement of tracks at each end of the module so that they will meet with those on adjacent modules, and the electrical connections. Whatever happens in the middle of a module, the ends have to match those of adjacent modules. This is critical. Without standardization on these matters, the entire module concept becomes unworkable.

A second problem with modular layouts is the corner units, assuming, of course, that the module is to be square or rectangular and not point-to-point.

The four corners themselves make a layout, and thereafter any two modules serve to enlarge the layout. But those four corners are critical! It's discouraging when a group of modular railroaders have arranged for a display in a shopping mall or at a meeting for one of the members with a corner module not to show up, for then trains must go forward and back in an incomplete pattern.

The corner problem has been solved in a number of ways. One has been for all members of the group to contribute to the corner modules so that they become common property stored in a single place and brought by one member to the site of assembly. No matter how it is worked out, it is essential that all four corners be at all places where the modular layout is to be run. If you've got four good guys on whom you can always count, don't worry about it. But if a corner is missing at any time, you have trouble!

The use of modules brings modelers very close together, particularly the members with the four corners who are, thereafter, always seen together like the barbershop quartet in The Music Man! Modules allow for a large layout with minimal expenditures of time and effort on the part of each contributor. Except for the standardized ends, each module allows the modeler full freedom to express his or her railroading interest. Bridges, tunnels, trestles, towns, mountains, plains, or any other geographic or railroad preference can be developed. Some modular groups have decided upon a specific theme, and all their modules conform to that. Others end up plugging in a desert module next to one with rivers and lakes. It certainly makes for variety, and those who have watched modular groups operate have become attracted to the hobby themselves.

THE TINPLATE TRACKERS:
Operating an O Gauge Tinplate Modular System
By Albert R. Bailey

*In this introduction to the official **Tinplate Trackers' Manual**, used by permission, Mr. Bailey describes the operating standards and procedures of this exciting, collegial, and truly different way to enjoy Lionel railroading. For the full manual and the particulars of joining the organization, write to Mr. Bailey at 1701 Grandview Avenue, Glendale, California 91201-1207. Why not think of getting your friends together and starting up a local chapter for yourselves? I think this is a great idea. Read on!*

The Tinplate Trackers is a group of people exploring the operation of O Gauge tinplate trains on modules that are basically standardized, yet open to unlimited improvisation. We are not a club or organization in the usual sense. Rather, we are individuals who operate Lionel and other O Gauge tinplate trains and believe that we can have more fun by working with others of like interest in building and setting up large operating systems. Modules can be a very logical way to do this.

THE TINPLATE TRACKERS

The idea for such a modular system that led to the formation of the Tinplate Trackers was proposed by Lew Chilton and Howard Packer to members of the San Fernando Valley Toy Train Club in North Hollywood, California. This is an independent club not affiliated with any of the national groups, although most of its members belong to one or more of these organizations (TCA, TTOS, LCCA, LOTS, TTCS). We like to call the Tinplate Trackers a brotherhood of those with similar interests.

Acting on the Chilton/Packer suggestion, Al Bailey, Myron Moore, and others immediately joined them and started to work developing some standards and constructing some modules. Seven modules were soon built and placed in operation on tables which were available in the Club meeting room.

Since the initial venture, Al Bailey has served to coordinate information for the group and to distribute it to all who might be interested. The small fee charged is intended to offset the printing and mailing expenses.

DEVELOPING STANDARDS

The standards and plans contained in this manual have been altered many times, but they are now developed to a point where they work well and permit much variation in operation. Modules have been built with several construction methods, but with the same overall specifications, by various people at different locations. When brought together, connected with C-clamps and our plug system, they become an immediate operating system.

We realize that there is no perfect system, but we feel that it will be possible to establish standards acceptable to many O Gauge operators everywhere. That's why we prefer to say that these are developing standards, not developed standards, and so we welcome ideas and suggestions. Please feel free to send us yours. The *Tinplate Trackers Newsletter,* published periodically, is a means of disseminating these ideas. We hope you make the most of this opportunity.

FIRST PUBLIC PERFORMANCE

In the fall of 1985, we had our first public showing of the Tinplate Trackers' modules at the big Cal-Stewart train meet sponsored by TCA-TTOS in California. Modules built by several people joined easily and quickly, and trains ran flawlessly for two days. They attracted a lot of attention and served as test tracks for people considering buying locomotives. (Just as often, they were test beds for people to find out after purchase if the engines would run!) They also attracted new converts to tinplate module operation, so the movement is growing and we hope you will become part of it. Welcome aboard!

THE MODULE IDEA

The definitions of module and modular system should be clarified. In our context, we mean a module to be a unit built to standardized specifications so that it can be used with other such units flexibly in a variety of ways. We thus distinguish it from a sectional layout, used by many clubs, which is made up of a set number of units which assemble in only one way. The Tinplate Tracker modules, made in a few basic types, can be assembled in many, many different ways. We're sure you will be able to devise still other ways.

Perhaps the best known and most widespread of the modular groups is NTRAK, which has developed over a period of 14 years or more. **Author's note:** *The NTRAK Organization is a frequent exhibitor at the Greenberg Train, Dollhouse, and Toy Shows on the Eastern Seaboard. I have seen their work, and it is really spectacular!* Under the aegis of Ben Davis and Jim Fitzgerald, this system has spread throughout the United States and to many foreign countries. And we must say that we have adopted and adapted many of their ideas, we hope with their acquiescence, and we certainly give them full credit and many thanks. We have received inspiration, too, from the Los Angeles area HO module groups.

So far, we've considered modules as a way to join with other operators, and this is a great thing to do. But modules can be equally useful at home or in association with a friend. If your home layout, or part of it, is constructed to Tinplate Trackers specifications, you can enjoy it at home, and then on occasion remove one or more modules and take them to a club meeting or convention where they'll become part of a larger system. They can be used for Christmas shows at local businesses, churches, or at train shows or other exhibitions. Take several modules to hospitals to entertain patients, or even to an adult convalescent home or retirement center (they enjoy trains, too!). You can think of more ideas, but basically we advocate modules for your own amusement and to provide more enjoyment from your trains.

SIMPLE STANDARDS

In our basic planning, we decided that modules should be light enough for one person to carry easily, and they should be small enough to fit into almost any passenger car, including compacts and subcompacts. Thus we developed a light 1/4-inch plywood construction with 1" x 4" joists, and a base size of 24" x 48". We adopted a height of 40" from floor to railhead (convenient to operate — especially for those of us over 40 — and the same as NTRAK and several other groups).

And, since these are toy trains, Lionel collectors and operators usually have O Gauge track and 022 Switches on hand or can obtain them conveniently, so we adopted them as standard. Further, we decided on two main tracks, and because trains must sometimes cross from one track to another, we adopted Lionel's spacing of 8-1/2" between the center rails of the main lines, rather than choosing some arbitrary figure that would not mate with so much that Lionel makes. This is the distance required to make a crossover using two 022 Switches (henceforth in this manual called turnouts).

Modules are fastened to each other with C-clamps because they are flexible and allow easy adjustments of height and width and of track. To aid in aligning tracks between modules, we ended the two main tracks 5" from each end of the module. This allows the use of a standard O Gauge 10" straight section for a connecting piece of track, which we call a bridge section. Any inaccuracies in construction or mounting of track can be adjusted easily by using these bridge sections. It will be necessary to cut some track to meet the 48" length of a module, but that's a simple operation anyone can do.

If some of our specifications appear to be arbitrary, please keep in mind a few things: a few basic rules must be followed by everyone, otherwise modules will not be compatible and the whole idea fails; and, in most ways, every builder has a great deal of discretion in how he builds, finishes, and uses his modules.

MODULE STANDARDS IN BRIEF

1. Basic module: 24" x 48". Optional widths 30" and 36"; optional lengths in multiples of 48", although 72" is permissible if two modules are supplied.

2. Height from floor to railhead is 40", with legs adjustable plus or minus one inch.

3. Track: Lionel O Gauge tinplate or equivalent, new or in very good condition.

4. Two main lines, the first with the center rail 3-3/4" from the front of the module and the second with a center rail 8-1/2" off center from the first center rail.

5. Main line tracks end 5" from each end of the module. Each operator to supply two connecting sections (called bridge tracks), one for each main line, of regular O Gauge straight track 10" long.

6. Each module should have a bus wire running its length consisting of four wires no smaller than 16-gauge. Wire should be white for the front main, red for the second main, black for the common, and orange for fixed voltage.

7. Modules electrically connect to each other by having a female socket (Radio Shack 274-205 or TRW-Cinch S304AB) at each end of the rear of the module, with a separate bridge cable having a male plug at each end (Radio Shack 274-204 or TRW-Cinch P304-CCT). An additional four-pin socket should be supplied as a convenient connection for a transformer.

8. Modules structurally connect to each other by C-clamps.

A RELAY SYSTEM WITH AN AUTOMATIC TRAIN CONTROL CIRCUIT
By Richard J. Ziegler

*Richard Ziegler has published the full details of this system in the April 1985 issue of **The Switcher**, the journal of the Lionel Operating Train Society. If you are an electronics advocate and you have been waiting for a nice juicy project to tackle for Lionel trains, your wait is over! Please note this project is for experts only — a thorough working knowledge of electronics is assumed. As this book went to press, we learned of Mr. Ziegler's untimely death at the age of 50. I wish to express my sympathy and that of Greenberg Publishing Company, Inc. We send our regrets to his family and relatives. We will miss his expertise in the world of toy trains.*

Over the years, I have seen many different schemes for operating two trains on the same track. The idea isn't new; many different concepts have surfaced in the model railroading magazines, including many Lionel publications. Sometimes these automatic train control circuits use thermostatically-controlled Lionel signals; others use insulated track sections or weight-activated contactors. If you've tried any of these schemes, you have probably found out that they have some serious limitations. With the thermostats or weight-activated contactors, one slight misadjustment and you have Collision City! Even with the insulated track sections, you give up using these tracks for accessories, and you still have to disable the E-units in the locomotives so that they will only go forward — a decided nuisance if you want to do switching operations. For a long time, I thought I could develop a better way. Eventually, I came up with the circuit you see schematized following this article.

The automatic train control system I have developed for my railroad has several advantages over circuits I have seen in publication. This circuit has at its heart a simple printed circuit board which uses parts readily available from any Radio Shack store. Perhaps its greatest advantage is the use of a resistor which will reduce the voltage in the following block enough to slow down the rear train without having to disable its reversing switch. Unlike an adjustable resistor, this one cuts the voltage to the trailing block in proportion to the voltage in the lead block.

For example, if I am running my forward train at 14 volts and my rear train two blocks behind it at the same voltage, let's assume the rear train is lighter and it begins to overtake the lead train. When the rear train enters the block behind the lead train, it encounters a voltage drop to, say, 11 volts, which slows it down enough to eliminate any chance of collision but still allows it to proceed.

The following drawings, schematics, and parts list will enable you to wire this relay system into your layout. Please note my annotations to certain parts of the circuitry to explain its functions.

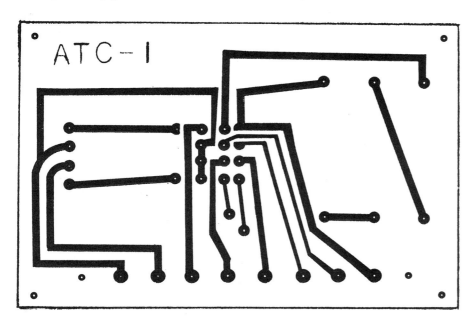

Parts List:

CR1 Full wave bridge
   cat. no. 276-1171

K1 12 VDC plug-in relay
   cat. no. 275-214

R1,2,3 1 OHM 10W resistor
   cat. no. 271-131

TB1 terminal feedthrough-type barrier strip
   cat. no. 274-653

S1 Center off DPDT toggle switch
   cat. no. 275-1533

An actual sized reproduction of the negative for making the printed circuit. (Note: In lieu of creating a printed circuit board, the reader may hard wire this circuit.)

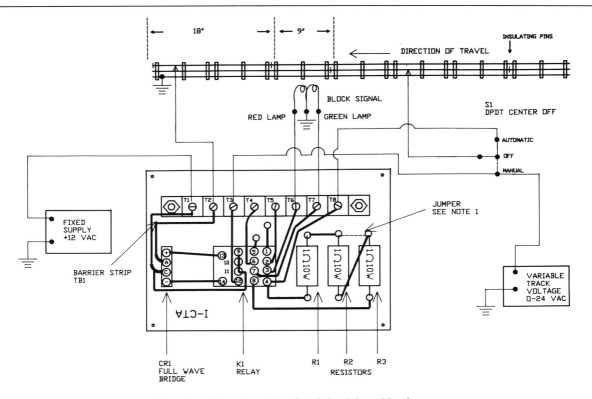

Drawing of circuitry with printed circuit board in place.

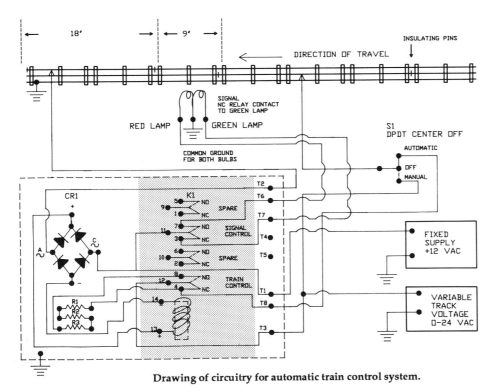

Drawing of circuitry for automatic train control system.

Note 1: Resistors R1-3 are used to permit train to coast to a stop when control block is de-energized. If resistance is too high omit resistor R2 and install jumper as shown.

Note 2: This circuit provides a 12V AC positive lead going into the rectifier. This provides a 12V current to the relay. If more than 12V is supplied to the relay it will be damaged.

Note 3: T1 through T8 are our designations for the terminal posts.

CHAPTER XI

LAYOUT DESIGN AND TRACKSIDE ACTION

By Philip K. Smith and Stan Shantar

(Excerpted from *Greenberg's Enjoying Lionel — Fundimensions Trains*.)

THINKING SMALL: Five 4' x 6' Layouts

One common misconception about tinplate railroading is that if a layout is to be exciting to operate and interesting to watch it must be gigantic. This is not so. The challenge is to build a good-looking, compact, operationally exciting layout. It is a feasible project using Lionel O and O27 track. Given the space available, the time and budget restrictions of many enthusiasts, thinking small is often the only practical approach to building and operating a layout.

Thinking small does not mean that you have to forego the excitement of running two trains simultaneously. Layouts 1 and 2, which follow, both feature two connected independent ovals for this purpose **plus** a pair of spur sidings for switching and loading / unloading operations. Layout 2 will accommodate two medium-sized trains; while Layout 1, designed for one larger and one smaller train, provides more visual interest and operating flexibility. When built with O27 track, either of these layouts will fit on a 4' x 6' board. (The same track plans are suitable for O Gauge track, but approximately ten percent more space will be required.) For those with very limited space who want to run two trains simultaneously, a shortened version of Layout 1 may be built on a 4' x 4' board by omitting the section on the right-hand side which contains the two sidings.

Layout 3 is another 4' x 6' design for O27 track. It demonstrates that more operating features can be incorporated into a limited space if two-train operation is not required. Layout 3 has a number of "classic" features: a large loop for continuous running, a reversing loop in the upper right-hand corner, a mini-yard with two spur sidings in the center, and a corner, a mini-yard with two spur sidings in the center and a passing siding at the bottom. The passing siding allows a locomotive to "run around" a car and push it into one of the spurs.

Larger Lionel equipment will not operate satisfactorily on the O27 track used in Layouts 1, 2, and 3. If you plan to run Berkshires, Fairbanks-Morse diesels, the 773 Hudson, the 746, aluminum passenger cars, or double-trucked depressed-center freight cars and you must limit your model empire to a 4' x 6' board, consider Layouts 4 and 5. These layouts are designed for Lionel O Gauge track which has a wider radius than O27 track. When thinking small with O Gauge track it is necessary to settle for less track, in the same space as you would have used in the

three O27 layouts. However, the two O layouts pictured still offer ample operating diversity: Layout 4 features three spur sidings and an alternate main line, while Layout 5 provides two independent loops for multiple train operation.

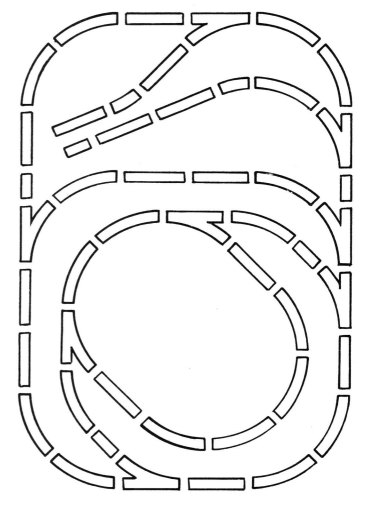

Layout 1: **14 straight sections, 19 curved sections, 5 half-straight sections, 2 half-curved sections, 2 pair switches, 2 left-hand switches. Drawing by D. Price.**

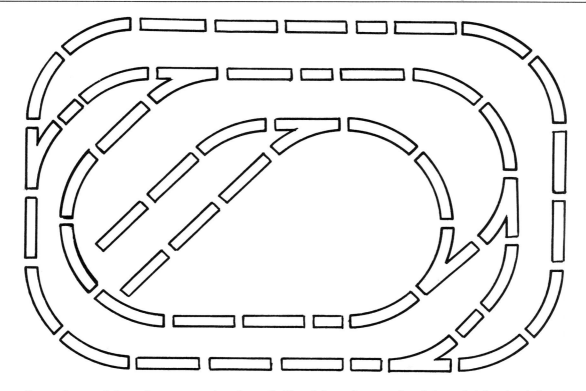

Layout 2: 9 straight sections, 19 curved sections, 6 half-straight sections, 2 pair switches, 2 left-hand switches.
Drawing by D. Price.

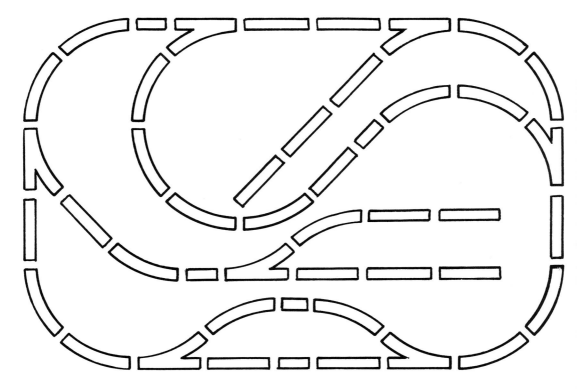

Layout 3: 16 straight sections, 18 curved sections, 5 half-straight sections, 1 pair switches, 5 left-hand switches.
Drawing by D. Price.

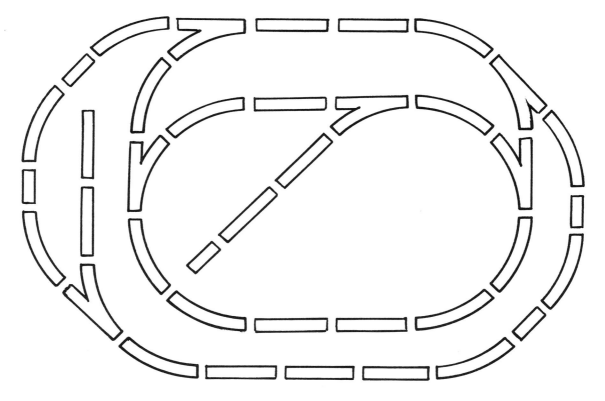

Layout 4: 14 straight sections, 15 curved sections, 5 half-straight sections, 2 pair switches, 1 left-hand switch.
Drawing by D. Price.

Layout 5: 12 straight sections, 15 curved sections, 5 half-straight sections, 3 pair switches.
Drawing by D. Price.

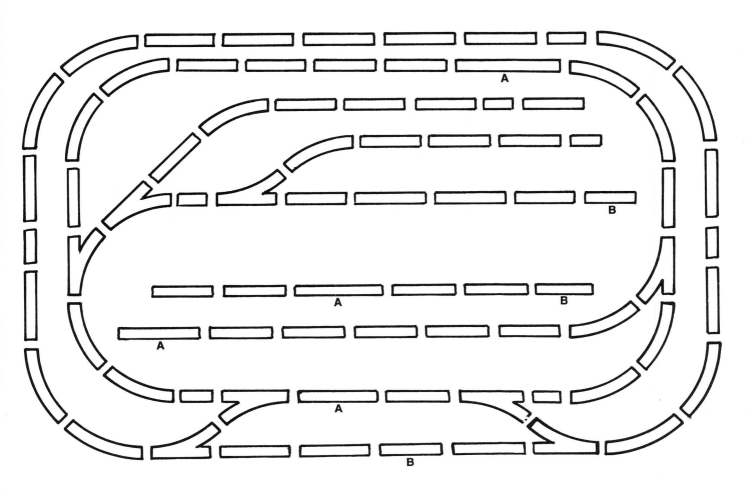

Outer loop is O Gauge track. Inner loop is O27 track. Inside track must be raised to the height of O Gauge track by the use of 3/8" wooden ties. All turnouts are No. 1121 Lionel O27 Gauge. Layout may also be built with all O27 track. To allow the O Gauge track pins to fit into the O27 switches, very carefully use an awl to widen the opening. A = Extra long Marx O27 track (if Lionel track is used it will have to be cut to fit). B = Cut sections of O and O27 track. Drawing by D. Price.

1. 1121 Turnouts (prewar metal covers)
2. 8603 Chesapeake & Ohio Hudson with 2046W-style Tender
3. 9581 Chessie Steam Special Baggage Car
4. 9582 Chessie Steam Special Combine
5. 9586 Chessie Steam Special Diner
6. 19808 New York Central Icing Station Car
7. 3424 Wabash Operating Brakeman Car
8. 8772 Gulf, Mobile, and Ohio GP-20
9. Telltale fringes for Operating Brakeman and Giraffe Cars
10. 153 Block Signal
11. Marx Operating Banjo Crossing Signal
12. Control box for Operating Gantry Crane
13. 362 Barrel Loading Platform
14. 2323 Operating Freight Station
15. 45N Operating Gateman

16. Marx non-operating Water Tower
17. 2283 die-cast lighted Bumpers
18. 3562-50 ATSF Operating Barrel Car
29. 9336 CP Rail Gondola with barrels and scrap metal
20. 12700 Erie-Lackawanna Operating Magnetic Gantry Crane
21. 9385 Alaska Gondola with canister loads
22. 3454 PRR Operating Merchandise Car
23. 155 Ringing Highway Signal
24. 77N Operating Crossing Gate
25. Marx street lamps
26. Colber street lamps
27. Life-like O Scale telephone booth
28. 18404 San Francisco Trolley
29. Latrobe street lamps
30. Tonka cherry-picker truck

Drawing by Maureen Crum

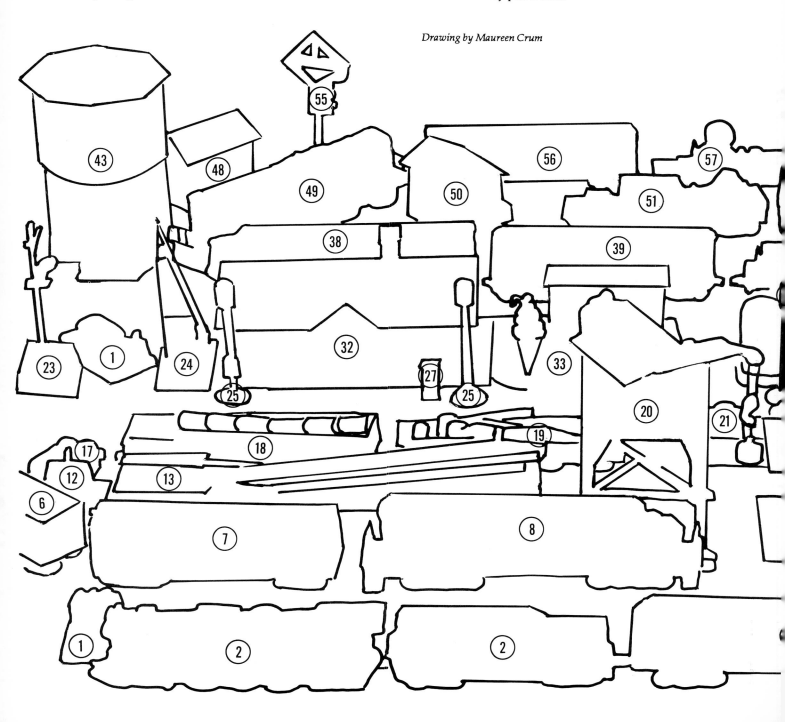

31. Marx lighted ringing signal
32. 2783 Freight Station kit
33. 12719 Animated Refreshment Stand
34. 397 Coal Loader
35. 3462P Milk Platform
36. 3356P Horse Corral
37. LTC Track Lockon (illuminated)
38. 8465 Rio Grande F-3A (dummy)
39. 9221 Operating Poultry Dispatch Car
40. 3469 Operating Coal Dump Car
41. 3462 Automatic Refrigerated Milk Car
42. 3356 Santa Fe Operating Horse Car
42. 30 Operating Water Tower
44. K121 K-Line Bubbling Oil Tower (Marx remake)
45. 12723 Microwave Relay Tower

46. Marx single-light Searchlight Tower
47. Bachmann Plasticville Switch Tower
48. 2127 Diesel Horn Shed
49. 8867 Minneapolis & St. Louis GP-9 (dummy)
50. 2125 Steam Whistle Shack
51. 9307 Animated Gondola
52. 9308 Aquarium Car
53. 9866 Pennsylvania Work Crew Combine (custom painted)
54. 151 Operating Semaphore
55. 69N Ringing Highway Signal
56. 5724 Pennsylvania Bunk Car
57. 9345 Reading Searchlight Car
58. 6560 Crane Car
59. 19807 Pennsylvania Smoking Caboose
60. 12720 Rotary Beacon

FURTHER READING:
AN ANNOTATED BIBLIOGRAPHY

The list of books given below is a rather widely varied lot. Some of them deal specifically with Lionel; others have more to do with railroad lore or other areas of model railroading which may be of interest to the Lionel reader. Following the list of books is a list of current video productions of some interest. You will then find the addresses of the major train collecting clubs in the nation, in case you may wish to contact them for membership information.

Ball, Don Jr. *America's Colorful Railroads.* New York: Bonanza Books, 1978. 210 pp., epilogue, photos.

This book is perhaps the best-known photographic text on real railroads, both in the age of steam and in the age of the diesel. The late Mr. Ball was well known for his excellent photography, and this book captures some of his best. It's a real education about the glory days of the railroads in every region of the country, and you may get some scenic ideas from these photos. The text is nostalgic and entertaining, too.

Botkin, Benjamin A. and Harlow, Alvin F., eds. *A Treasury of Railroad Folklore.* New York: Bonanza Books, 1953; 530 pp., railroadiana appendix, index, illustrations.

This book really has it all! If you have any interest in the history of railroading in America, you'll find something about it here, from tall tales, legends, and songs to technical discussions. Better than that, the work captures the intangible spirit of old-time railroading and gives the reader a real appreciation that this country was built on the railroads. Highly recommended!

Greenberg, Bruce C., gen. ed. *Greenberg's Guide to Lionel Postwar Parts.* Sykesville, MD: Greenberg Publishing Company, Inc.; 1989. 32 pp.

If you're a collector and operator of Lionel postwar (1945-1969), you'll really value this book. Here you will find a long list of parts dealers who can get you that missing front truck for your 224 Locomotive or even a replacement helicopter for your 3519 Helicopter Launching Car. This book can save you many annoying hours of searching!

Greenberg, Bruce C., gen. ed. *Greenberg's Guides to Lionel Trains.* Prewar (1901-1942), 2 vols., ed. Christian Rohlfing; Postwar (1945-1969), 2 vols., ed. Roland E. LaVoie (Vols. 1-2); Lionel (1970-1988), written and ed. Roland E. LaVoie. Sykesville,

MD: Greenberg Publishing Company, Inc.; 1987- 89. All volumes have photos, tables, charts, and quick-locating indices.

Granted, in recommending these books I'm speaking from a somewhat biased point of view, since I'm involved with them. However, from that involvement I know this: Lionel guides simply do not come any more comprehensive and thorough! No matter what volume you choose, you'll find terrific color photography, superb toy train scholarship by the best collectors in captivity, and very complete listings of every known variation of every piece of Lionel equipment along with current values in the marketplace. No wonder it takes nearly a thousand pages to document these trains! Plans are afoot for another volume just on Lionel's accessories. There are several other price guides and "pocket"-type guides for those interested in prices alone, but for documentation and real understanding of Lionel trains, there's nothing even coming close to these books. All are highly recommended.

Greenberg, Bruce C., gen. ed. *Greenberg's Lionel Catalogues, Vols. 1-4.* Sykesville, MD: Greenberg Publishing Company, Inc.; 1985-88. Vol. 1: 1902-1922. Vol. 2: 1923-1932. Vol. 3: 1933-1942. Vol. 4: 1945-1955.

The middle two volumes of this series have already been printed, and the others are planned for some time in 1989. From the very beginning of Lionel's reign over the toy train world, the consumer catalogues have been the "dream books" for generation after generation of children and adults. Collectors pay handsome prices for originals of these catalogues, but now you can have the whole Lionel catalogue record in beautifully printed full-color volumes. They're quite expensive, but their limited-production status assures these books of being collector items in their own right.

Greenberg, Bruce C., gen. ed. *Lionel Parts List and Exploded Diagrams, 1970-1987.* Sykesville, MD: Greenberg Publishing Company, Inc.; 1987. 552 pp., diagrams, charts, periodic supplements.

This large compilation of parts was achieved with the full cooperation of Lionel Trains, Inc. It has parts lists by number of every Lionel product in the years of the modern era, and if you're wondering what parts carry over from the postwar era, or if you need a part for a modern era item, this is the book for you. It comes in a large loose-leaf binder for the insertion of periodic supplements. It is indispensable for repair work as well as general interest.

Greenberg, Bruce C., gen. ed. *Greenberg's Repair and Operating Manual for Lionel Trains*, ed. Susan Pauker. Sykesville, MD: Greenberg Publishing Company, Inc.; 1985. 736 pp., illustrations, track plans.

The advertisements state that this book will pay for itself in terms of helping you do your own repairs, and those ads are absolutely correct. Here are many of the original instruction sheets and service manual literature pieces which will assist you in securing parts and repairing your own rolling stock and accessories. Heaven only knows how many transformers I've rewired and locomotives I've repaired with the assistance of this book. There are some other pretty good repair guides available, but this one is the most logically arranged and comprehensive. Strongly recommended!

Greenberg, Linda, ed. *Greenberg's Operating Instructions With Layout Plans*. Columbia, MD: Greenberg Publishing Company, Inc.; 1978. 452 pp., track plans, illustrations.

This book has been out of print for some time now, but occasionally copies show up on the used train book market. Although for the most part it has been supplanted by newer compilations, this book is still an excellent collection of Lionel's terrific instruction sheets, those little papers packed into every one of the millions of Lionel pieces from the postwar era. If you can't find this book, you can get the same information from several other sources, but this book is still a fine reference work.

Hodgson, Lee K. *The History of Toy Train Engineering*. Sykesville, MD: Greenberg Publishing Company, Inc.; 1989. 200 + pp., diagrams.

This ought to be an interesting book with a great deal of competitive history behind it. Mr. Hodgson has searched through the U. S. Patent Offices for the patents of the various train manufacturers since the turn of the century. There's some fascinating information here. How many people know that the idea for insulated rail sections, which seems like a great discovery every time it is used, was actually patented in 1911? Learn about the Great Whistle War between Lionel and American Flyer in the late 1940s. This one's not to be missed!

Hollander, Ron. *All Aboard! The Story of Joshua Lionel Cowen & His Lionel Train Company*. New York: Workman Publishing Company, Inc.; 1981. 253 pp., photos, charts, index.

This is the definitive biography of Joshua Lionel Cowen, the founder of Lionel Trains and the guiding spirit behind the firm's success. In a very entertaining, affectionate style, Hollander has shown the place of these trains in America's history, and his portrait of Cowen and his associates is unforgettable. The book is richly illustrated with well-chosen photos and colorful little "side bar" essays. A sample of Hollander's excellent writing style: "There was no way to control the speed of the trains. Like Cowen himself, Lionel trains only ran full speed ahead." If you want to understand the appeal of Lionel trains, this book is an absolute necessity for your library. Very highly recommended reading!

Lang, Cliff, ed. *Greenberg's Layout Plans for Lionel Trains*. Sykesville, MD: Greenberg Publishing Company, Inc.; 1987. 32 pp., 110 track plans of various sizes.

This book is a good beginning for the selection of a track plan for your layout. Each of the track plans is explained for its advantages, and each has a materials list of necessary track and dimensions. Many of these track plans have been adapted from those originally appearing in Lionel's own publications, which have been out of print for many years. Somewhere in here, there's a track plan for you!

Moedinger, William M. *The Road to Paradise: The Story of the Rebirth of the Strasburg Rail Road*. Lancaster, PA: Strasburg Rail Road Shops, Inc., 1983. 40 pp., photos, maps.

This is basically a souvenir book available by writing to the Strasburg Rail Road or through a visit to the well-run and managed tourist railroad right in the heart of Pennsylvania train lover's country. I recommend it here for its inspiration to everyone fighting the odds; this is a remarkable story about a group of truly dedicated railfans who refused to yield to "progress" and insisted upon preserving history. This would be a great railway to model point-to-point, too! Look at the excellent photography for some scenic tips about countryside settings. This place has always been one of my favorite "getaway" spots!

Osterhoff, Robert J. *Greenberg's Guide to Lionel Paper and Collectibles*. Sykesville, MD: Greenberg Publishing Company, Inc.; 1989. 150 pp., photos, index.

This book is an extensive compilation of listings for Lionel's many catalogues, instruction sheets, service bulletins, and so forth over the firm's long history. The catalogue listings, for example, show every known major catalogue and dealer bulletin right from the beginning to the present day. There are also comprehensive lists of Lionel's instruction sheets — a major undertaking and accomplishment. Perhaps the best part of the book is the listing of Lionel's dealer displays and service station tool sets. The Lionel Corporation treated its toys much as a major auto manufacturer treats its cars, with all the supportive literature that implies. This book records it all. Highly recommended!

Robinson, Jack. *Finishing Touches*. Sykesville, MD: Greenberg Publishing Company, Inc.; 1987. 64 pp., photos, schematics, diagrams.

Now, why would I possibly recommend to you a book concerning dollhouse construction in a toy train book? Just take a look at the craftsman's tips Jack Robinson has put into this book, and you'll see the connection right away! There are many, many scenic construction ideas from this fellow's highly creative mind which can be put to use on your train layout. Read this book and you'll be able to make the best scratch-built houses you ever saw! Highly recommended!

Schleicher, Robert H. *The Lionel Train Book*, ed. John W. Brady. Mount Clemens, MI: Lionel Trains, Inc.; 1986. 131 pp., glossary, diagrams, photos.

Lionel has issued many train-building books over the years, from the great articles in its magazinee *Model Builder* to the famous Bantam paperback book series of the 1950s. Of all those books, this one is the best. As a basic book for the Lionel enthusiast, it is very comprehensive, even though the overall treatment is in breadth rather than depth. I differ with this book in a few ways, but it is a fine how-to-do-it book which belongs in your library. The Fritz von Tagen photography is excellent. Highly recommended!

Simpson, T. Hood. *Guide to Catalogued Sets of Lionel Trains, 1917-1969*. Dover, DE: THS Enterprises; 1980-82. 153 pp., tables, appendices, charts.

If you're trying to put an original Lionel set together at a train shop, this book is indispensable. Basically, it's a compilation of all of Lionel's catalogued sets arranged in handy tabular form. Suppose, for example, you want to put together that special Lionel train set you had when you were a child. If you can find the engine, you can reconstruct the set with the aid of this book. It will save you many hours of leafing through catalogues, when you can find them! This is an excellent reference book. Highly recommended!

Smith, I. D., ed. *Greenberg's Lionel Service Manual, Vols. 1-4*. Sykesville, MD: Greenberg Publishing Co.; 1987. 1,800 pp. total, indices, diagrams, charts.

If the Greenberg Repair and Operating Manual isn't comprehensive enough for you, here's a set of books for the true specialist. The Lionel Corporation issued huge amounts of literature to its officially approved Service Stations to assist in repairs and parts. No other toy company documented its production like this, and here is the complete compilation of all that literature, including every known parts listing for every piece of Lionel equipment of the postwar era! This exhaustive (and no doubt exhausting) task took years for Mr. Smith to compile; he's been a Lionel repairman for many years and has been a terrific help on all the Greenberg books. Now you can trace the development of Lionel's engineering efforts, sometimes culling valuable clues to variations in many pieces. This is an expensive set of books, but I strongly recommend them.

Villaret, Eugene. *Realistic Revenue Operations*. Sykesville, MD: Greenberg Publishing Company, Inc.; 1987. 36 pp., illustrations, glossary.

If you want to run your railroad like a real one, this book is for you. Mr. Villaret has detailed a card-order system to duplicate real train order sheets; by using this system, you can work with other layout operators in all your timetable and freight operations. He shows how to prepare waybills and orders, and you can even computerize your layout's operations by using the principles in this book. If you're a real stickler for absolute realism, this book can be very helpful indeed!

Weaver, Carl. *Greenberg's Layout Building Handbook for Operators of Marklin HO Trains*. Sykesville, MD.: Greenberg Publishing Company, Inc.; 1987. 77 pp., glossary, photos, schematics, diagrams.

Why do I recommend a book on HO operations — Marklin at that? Isn't HO the sworn enemy of Lionel? Take a look at Mr. Weaver's chapters on assembling tools, platform construction, and wiring and you'll see why this book can be very helpful to the Lionel layout builder as well. Besides, the Marklin firm is the oldest toy train company in the world, and their products are of extremely high quality. Look at Mr. Weaver's station houses and layouts, and if that scenery can't give you ideas, you don't observe very well! The book is very crisply written with an excellent glossary; I particularly like Mr. Weaver's discussion of maintaining friendly family relationships while you build your toy train hobby — an often-overlooked topic. This is a fine, fine book!

VIDEO PRODUCTIONS

All of the following are available in VHS or Beta formats, and all are available by direct order from the Greenberg Publishing Company, Inc., 7566 Main Street, Sykesville, MD 21784. Write for a current brochure.

American Flyer Boys' Club. TTOS Film Library, Volume III. This video details the promotional efforts on film of Lionel's chief competitor during the golden years of the toy train, American Flyer. It features tours of the Gilbert factory in New Haven and the Gilbert Hall of Science in New York as well as out-takes of American Flyer's early television commercials.

The Fairbanks-Morse Trainmaster. Don Shaw. This video documents the many varieties of the big double-motored diesels produced by Lionel in the postwar years. Perhaps more importantly, it shows how to tell the real Lionels from the many reproductions on the market. Also includes a five-minute cartoon, "Play Safe."

Lionel In Action. TTOS Film Library, Volume I. This video includes three separate films, "Railroad Story" (1951), "Iron Ponies" (1952), and "The Wonderful World of Trains" (1960). They show Lionel's best trains in action, Joshua Lionel Cowen and the staff executives, and some factory assembly sequences.

Lionel — The Movie. TM Productions, Inc. This video shows nearly all of Lionel's great postwar trains in action as well as "Iron Ponies," a 1949 Lionel promotional film.

Toy Trains In Action. TTOS Film Library, Volume II. This video is my personal favorite. It features many Lionel and American Flyer TV ads, a rare silent Dorfan promotional film, and, above all, a hysterically funny Joe McDoakes short comedy from the 1940s about a man obsessed with his trains. Don't miss this one!

AUDIO CASSETTE

Hear Ye! Model Railroad Sound Effects. TTOS Library. This little cassette has 26 recordings of the many sounds of old toy trains which you may remember from your childhood: the Noma and American Flyer Talking Stations, Lionel's little records, Marx, and Colber sounds. Great fun on this one!

TRAIN ASSOCIATIONS AND CLUBS

For membership and other information, write to the following organizations:

THE LIONEL COLLECTORS CLUB OF AMERICA (LCCA): 6355 Westland Drive, Westland, MI 48185.

THE LIONEL OPERATING TRAIN SOCIETY (LOTS): 135 76th Street, Boulder, CO 80303.

THE LIONEL RAILROADER CLUB: Managed by Lionel Trains, Inc. Send a $3.00 check or money order for membership and the newsletter, The Inside Track, to the club in care of Post Office Box 748, Mount Clemens, MI 48046.

In Canada: THE LIONEL COLLECTORS ASSOCIATION OF CANADA (LCAC): Box 976, Oshawa, Ontario, Canada L1H7N2.

THE TINPLATE TRACKERS SOCIETY: Write to Albert Bailey, 1701 Grandview Avenue, Glendale, CA 91201-1207 for the excellent Manual and information.

THE TRAIN COLLECTORS ASSOCIATION (TCA): P. O. Box 248, Strasburg, PA 17579.

THE TOY TRAIN OPERATING SOCIETY (TTOS): 25 West Walnut Street, Pasadena, CA 91103.

GLOSSARY

REAL AND MODEL RAILROADING TERMS

AC (Alternating Current): This term is used for the most common household electrical current; it changes polarity between positive and negative, or alternates, sixty times, or cycles, per second. Most Lionel motors are made to run on this current, though they also can run on direct current.

Airbrush: A small paint-spraying device which produces a very fine paint mist for detailed model painting.

Alligator clips: These are small sprung clips with toothed jaws which can be attached to ends of wires to make temporary electrical connections for test purposes. The long, narrow clips resemble the jaws of an alligator (one wonders why they aren't called crocodile clips).

Amperes: Usually abbreviated as Amps, this is a unit of measurement determining the strength of electrical flow within a circuit. The greater the amperage, the more forceful is the current passing through the circuit.

Ash pan: On steam locomotives, a large basin below the firebox used to catch cinders from the burning of coal until they can be dumped at an ash pit. Lionel's larger steam engines simulate this with a metal plate just below the cab. Also, a pipe smoker's ash tray.

Bad order track: On real railroads, a siding where rolling stock needing repairs can be stored until they can be serviced.

Baggage smasher: A less-than-affectionate term used on a real railroad to describe a baggage handler at a passenger station. One of American Flyer's best accessories was a small station with an automated figure carrying this name.

Bakelite: A trade name for a compression-molded plastic powder which, because of its resistance to heat, is used in appliances and stoves. Lionel has used compression-molded plastic for transformer casings and rolling stock.

Ballast scorcher: On real railroads, the term for a fast express train. In model railroading, a term of scorn used to describe a person who insists on running trains too fast for track conditions, thereby causing derailments all the time.

Ballast tamper: A track installation machine used to tamp down the rock ballast used on real railroads to hold the ties in position on the roadbed. Lionel has made a model of this machine, which replaced laborers who tamped this rock down by hand.

Bell wire: The name given to light-duty solid insulated wire often used in telephone applications or for household doorbells. It is usually 18- or 20-gauge in thickness and ideal for model railroad uses.

Benchwork: A generic term used to describe the structure supporting a train layout.

Bent: One section of a model train trestle set. On real railroads, the curved section of the trestle.

Big hook: A railroading nickname for a crane car used to lift cars and locomotives back onto the track after a wreck or derailment.

Blocks: The term used for sections of track in model railroading which are insulated electrically from other sections of track. The most common application of block circuitry is in the system known as cab control.

Bus bar: An electrical terminal strip with a large number of screw or clip connectors which can be interconnected into a common point of connection for ease of wiring ground and hot leads for accessories, etc.

C clamps: Small to very large clamps with thumbscrew devices used in carpentry to hold pieces of wood together temporarily. These can be very handy in layout building applications.

Cab control: A system for switching control of a series of blocks on a model railroad so that two or more throttles are capable of controlling those blocks, depending upon which engine is to use the blocks of track at any given time. By this system, the Lionel railroader can perform intricate switching maneuvers without fear of collisions.

Can motor: A small electric motor which is permanently sealed inside a cylinder, resembling a tin can. These motors are usually made to run on DC current, but Lionel has used them with rectifying circuits for AC applications quite successfully in recent years.

Catenary: A system of overhead wires suspended from girders to provide power for electrically-driven locomotives. Some model railroads feature elaborate hand-soldered catenary for an extremely realistic look.

Circuit breaker: An electrical trip switch which shuts off the flow of current to a circuit when there is a short circuit. It is usually tripped by excessive heat. This prevents damage to the transformer and wiring, which would otherwise overheat and melt. Most Lionel transformers are equipped with these devices.

Classification yard: A large group of tracks and turnouts used to break up and make up trains prior to shipment. The more complex of these yards in real railroading are computer-controlled.

Clear board: A railroading term used to describe an unobstructed right of way for a train with all green signals ahead.

Closed-top layout: The most common form of toy train layout, in which a solid sheet of wood is mounted to a frame and legs to be the foundation for the layout.

Common ground: The use of one ground wire, or ground rail, from the track, to complete the circuit for operating many accessories. This one lead substitutes for many wires leading back to the transformer.

Commutator: The rotating part of a locomotive motor which contacts stationary carbon brushes and completes the circuit. There are flat types in most modern Lionel locomotive motors, but some of the older types had drum-type commutators.

Compression molding: A manufacturing process where a plastic compound in the form of powder is subjected to extreme heat and pressure inside a die to produce a thick, rugged, heat-resistant plastic. One of the main trade names for such plastics is Bakelite.

Consist: A railroading term used to describe the units of rolling stock within a particular train. A "mixed consist," for example, describes a train with both freight and passenger cars.

Contactor: A special track clip which operates by means of the train's weight or by the completion of an electrical circuit to operate a track side accessory.

Cornfield meet: A colorful railroading term used to describe a violent head-on collision between two trains. Definitely not desirable on your layout!

Culvert: A large, short pipe for storm sewers, usually made of concrete. Lionel's examples are metal and are found on the culvert loader and unloader.

Cut: A method of railroad construction where a huge trench is cut through a hillside to keep track on a level grade. "Cut and cover" describes this process when the cut is covered by a roof of some kind.

DC (Direct Current): The type of electrical current where current flows in one direction only and the positive pole is always positive and the negative pole always negative. Most of Lionel's motors can operate on DC as well as AC. Some are meant for DC-only operation. Lionel's postwar whistles were specifically made to operate on a shot of DC current sent along the rails to a relay by a rectifying device within the transformer.

Deadhead: A colorful railroading term used to describe any train or locomotive which makes a run without income-producing freight or passenger service, as when a locomotive has to be transferred to another terminal. Also, any fan of the group, "The Grateful Dead."

Dead Man's Control: A throttle on a real locomotive which had to be continuously operated by the engineer. If he released the throttle for any reason (including the extreme one

suggested by the title), the engine would stop. American Flyer duplicated this feature on some of its transformers.

Die-casting process: A method of manufacturing models where powdered metal is subjected to great heat to convert it to a strong solid metal casting within a die, or form. This process permits very fine detail within the casting.

Diodes: Electrical devices which work like valves to activate relays or to rectify AC into DC. Some are gated diodes; they will permit electrical flow in only one direction. Others open only at specific voltages.

Drawbar: The large hook-like device which attaches a steam engine to its tender. To "pull out the drawbar" can mean an attempt to haul a train much too heavy for the particular locomotive to handle.

E-unit: Lionel's name for its solenoid-operated mechanical sequence reversing switch used to make its locomotives go forward, reverse, or stay in neutral. There are two-position models with only forward and reverse, and three-position models with a neutral position added.

Eccentric crank: A large forged casting attached to the main drive wheels of a steam engine which allows a rod to rotate in an elliptical path and thus open and close the slide valves of the cylinders. In railroading, definitely not a term referring to a grouchy elderly person!

Emery paper: A black or brown sandpaper-like substance in many grades of abrasiveness used in model railroading to clean track, sand wood, and many other uses. This is usually available in any hardware or auto supply store.

Frog: An intersection of two railway tracks to permit the wheels and flanges moving on one track to cross to another. This intersection is named for its resemblance to a frog's spread legs.

Grade: The degree of elevation of the track's surface over a given distance, usually expressed in percentage. "Making the grade" is still used as a term for achieving success.

Gremlin: Any electrical or mechanical problem on a layout which seems incapable of being diagnosed or solved. Every layout has them!

Homasote: A trademark name for an insulation board which is often used by model railroaders over the base plywood sheet on a layout to cushion against noise.

Hot lead or line: The center-rail of an electrical circuit. In most Lionel transformers, the A or B posts are meant for the hot leads, which are usually connected to the track's center rail by means of a lockon.

Hump track: In a large classification yard, an inclined track leading to the various sidings. A train to be broken up and classified is backed over this track, and each car is uncoupled and rolled by gravity to its proper track in the yard. Some hump tracks have scales for weighing cars of freight. On modern railroads, these tracks are computer controlled.

Hydrocal: A trademark name for a powdery substance which can be mixed with water to form a quick-drying, durable paste for use in mountain and scenery building on a model railroad.

Injection molding: A process by which liquified plastic compounds, especially Styrene, are squirted into a mold and cooled so that they take on the shape of the mold. Most modern Lionel car bodies are made in this way.

Joist: A term of construction practices for the long strips of wood which form the internal supports for a frame. On a layout, these are the cross strips which connect the long boards of the frame internally.

Junker: (1) A tinplate locomotive or car which has become so battered that it is useful only for parts; (2) A tinplate collector and/or operator who likes to rummage around in boxes of battered junk at train shows for salvageable track, switches, and parts at bargain prices.

Jumper wire: A wire soldered or clamped between two points when the original connection has lost its electrical efficiency. In model railroading, this is most frequently done on the center rails of permanently ballasted track to bypass a corroded center rail pin. Can also refer to any temporary connection used to bypass another electrical circuit.

Kitbashing: A colorful term used to denote the making of a model railroad structure from parts of two or more ready-to-assemble kits.

Klutz: A general term of scorn used to describe any person who is extremely clumsy, accident-prone, and awkward around a train layout.

Ladder track: The track which leads to a large number of spur sidings in a switch yard.

Lichen: A moss-like plant which, when dried, treated with glycerine, and dyed, is very effective as a scenic decoration to simulate brush and undergrowth on a layout. Very handy for hiding electrical connections and wiring.

Lockon: A device used to connect wiring to tracks on a model railroad, making it easier to hook up a circuit than by direct soldering of the wire to the tracks. Usually these devices contain two or more wire terminals attached to a spring steel clip which snaps onto the tracks.

Magnetraction: Lionel's patented name for magnets attached to the frames or axles of locomotives to allow them to grip the track and thus attain more pulling power and greater speeds on curves with the use of slightly more voltage.

Module: A section of a train layout which is designed to hook up with other similar sections built to special standards to form a complete train layout. These are not usually designed to operate independently. Refer to the *Tinplate Trackers* essay in Chapter X for examples.

Nichrome: A very fine heat-conduction wire used in Lionel's earlier smoking locomotive units. When the wire heats, it melts a pellet or vaporizes a liquid, producing smoke.

Nippers: A small pair of pliers with sharp pointed jaws which can snip off the ends of wires. Also refers to young children when they become pests in a given situation.

O Gauge: A size of model railroading where the models are 1/48 the size of the prototypes, or a scale of 1/4 inch to the foot. This track is 1-1/4 inches between the outside rails. A circle of regular O Gauge track has a diameter of 31 inches at the outer rails.

O27 Gauge: This track has the same distance between its outside rails as O Gauge, but its circle is just 27 inches in diameter. In addition, O27 Gauge track is less high off the board and much lighter in weight than is O Gauge, making it incompatible with O Gauge track except under special circumstances.

Ohms: A unit of electrical measurement which describes the resistance of a circuit to the flow of electricity passing through it.

Open-top layout: A type of layout design which uses a wooden frame with joists allowing the roadbed to rise and fall beneath the top level of the frame by means of cross members and long, narrow strips of wood called stringers. In this layout, there is no solid sheet of plywood laid across the framework.

Oxidation: A process whereby oxygen in air combines with other elements to form another compound. Rust is one common form of oxidation. Oxidation inhibits the electrical flow on track and should be removed by abrasives or solvents.

Pantograph: A sprung diamond-shaped device with a large sliding shoe at the top for the collection of electrical power from an overhead wire; used in electric locomotives and duplicated by Lionel in several models.

Papier-mache: An old-fashioned but effective way of building scenery by using water, flour, or wheat paste and newspaper strips. The newspaper strips are soaked in the flour and water mixture and allowed to dry before decorating after they are spread across a framework, usually screening supported by wooden strips.

Pawl: A lever or rod equipped with a catch for mechanically releasing another object. The most common use of a pawl in Lionel trains is in the reversing switches of locomotives.

Peddler: The railroad name for a freight train which makes many stops along a route to deliver and pick up freight cars.

Phasing: In model railroading, the connection of two or more transformers in such a way that the movement of the alternating current in all the transformers from positive to negative is identical.

Pike: Another term for any train layout.

Pilot: The term used to describe the wheel set on the front of a locomotive, or the proper term for what was once called a "cowcatcher" on a steam locomotive.

Pony truck: The trailing truck behind the drive wheels on a steam locomotive.

Prototype: A general term used by model railroaders to refer to the real item on a railroad. If a model is "true to the prototype," it is in exact proportion and details.

Rectifying: A process by which alternating current is changed, or rectified, into direct current by the use of diodes or other electrical devices. In the new Lionel can-type motors, the track's alternating current is rectified by a solid-state circuit into direct current which then runs the motors.

Rivet counter: A term of scorn used by model railroaders to describe anyone who is excessively concerned with exact realism or minute, insignificant details.

Roadbed: The surface upon which track is laid, whether on a real or a model railroad. This surface is usually raised from ground level by rocks and wooden or concrete ties, upon which the tracks are laid and ballasted.

Rollers: Small cylindrical devices attached to a bracket to collect electric current from the center rail in Lionel layouts to power lighted or functioning freight or passenger cars and locomotives.

Rolling stock: Any model railroad car which runs upon the rails and is not self-propelled but meant to be pulled by a locomotive.

Roundhouse: A circular or curved building meant to house a railroad's locomotives; it usually faces a turntable which switches a locomotive onto and off of one of the roundhouse's tracks for servicing.

Scale: The relationship in size between the prototype and the model. Model train scales range from the very small (Z Gauge) to the large (G Scale).

Scratch-building: The process of constructing scenery, buildings, rolling stock, or locomotives from raw materials by hand instead of from a ready-to-assemble kit.

Shoofly: The railroading term which describes a temporary stretch of track laid around a construction site or a wreck to allow normal traffic to bypass it. Usually hastily constructed, this track demands a slowdown of any train which uses it.

Short circuit: The improper interference with an electrical circuit, usually caused by metal-to-metal contact, allowing the current to take a short-cut across the interference. This creates heavy current flow and heat which can damage wiring or circuitry unless current is cut off manually or by a circuit breaker.

Siding: A section of track, usually a dead-end spur, which leads off a main line by means of a turnout. There are spur sidings for freight deliveries and passing sidings to allow one train to overtake and pass another on a single-track line.

Skirting: The strips of wood attached to the side of a flat surface, such as a train layout top, for cosmetic and structural reasons.

Sleepers: Three different definitions: (1) The nickname of a passenger car with overnight berths for travelers; (2) The ties used beneath track rails in European prototype track work; and (3) An exceptional item for train collection which is scarce but perhaps unappreciated and therefore not very expensive at the time of purchase, although it may become so later when it is "discovered" by the train collecting fraternity at large.

Slip switch: A crossover, usually 45° or less, between two tracks which has a turnout in it. A double slip switch has two switches in the crossing.

Slow-order territory: A stretch of track which demands relatively slow train speeds because of sharp curves, construction, or congestion.

Solderless connectors: Any of several types of connecting devices which link wires together without the use of heated solder. Examples are plastic or ceramic cones and solderless terminals of a wide variety which are crimped onto the ends of wires.

Solenoid: An electrical device consisting of an electromagnet with a metal rod inside its core. When current is introduced into the electromagnet, the rod moves, and so does anything attached to its end. Lionel uses these devices, which are very reliable, in many applications.

Spade lugs: Metal wire fasteners crimped onto the end of a wire to aid connection to screw terminals.

Spur: A short track leading off a main line, usually a siding with a bumper at its end for train or rolling stock storage.

Styrene: A plastic compound in pellet or liquid form which is heated and injected into a mold to produce a finely-detailed and shaped plastic model.

Switch yard: A group of tracks and sidings off the main line used to store freight cars for unloading and loading, among other purposes. In large yards, the track work can be extremely complex.

Tender: A special car carried immediately behind a steam locomotive to store the water and the coal or oil needed for its operation; sometimes referred to as a coal car.

Third rail: A rail mounted aside the running rails on a real railroad and between the running rails on Lionel track. It supplies electrical power in both instances.

Throttle: A mechanical lever or knob on a transformer in model railroading which varies the electrical current in the track and thus regulates the speed of the locomotives.

Tinplate: Stamped-steel surfaces which have been coated with a layer of tin to prevent rust and corrosion. Most toy train track is tinplated, and this term has by extension been used to refer to all toy trains and their operators ("Tinplaters").

Track clips: Devices used to attach two ties of adjoining track sections together in a toy train layout. These are used to fasten track in temporary layouts; otherwise, the weight of the train might cause the tracks to separate.

Transfer table: A laterally moving geared set of rails used to move a locomotive or cars from one track to another. These replaced turntables and were used for diesel and electric engines which could be run in either direction without turning, unlike steam locomotives.

Trestle: Any structure designed to carry train tracks above ground level; these often span rivers or valleys. In model railroads, tinplate trains are carried above table top level by trestle sets, which can be graduated or elevated. The height of Lionel's largest bents (trestle girders) is 4-3/4 inches.

Trucks: On both the real railroads and toy train layouts, the wheels, axles, and their assemblies on railroad rolling stock.

Turnout: The proper name for what is usually called a switch; a track section with movable pivot rails which can transfer a train from one track to another.

Turntable: A large circular device which rotates within a pit to turn around locomotives for operation on a different track. These were mostly used for steam engines and discontinued after dieselization.

Uncoupling track: A special section of track in tinplate railroading which separates cars within a train electrically. Lionel made several types to match its trackage; some of them had magnets in their centers, and some others had special rails to activate the couplers on the cars. Since the special rails also operated automatic cars, Lionel made some uncoupling tracks with both magnets and special rails.

Vibrator motor: An electromagnet which, when energized, vibrates a pocket of air to set up a vibration making figures or belts move. Lionel has used vibrator motors in many operating cars and accessories.

Volt: A unit of electrical measurement which determines the level of pressure behind an electrical current. The more the voltage, the more powerful the current.

Water bottle: A tank car filled with fresh water and placed directly behind a steam locomotive tender as an extra source of water for its boiler, should water sources be scarce on a given stretch of track.

Watt: A unit of electrical energy expended on powering a device. This term is used to illustrate the top power capacity of an instrument such as a transformer or light bulb.

Whyte classification system: A numbering system once used to describe types of steam engines by their wheel arrangement. The system uses three numbers: one for the number of wheels on the pilot, one for the number of drive wheels, and one for the number of wheels on the trailing truck. Most of the steamer types have nicknames as well. For example, a steam locomotive with a Whyte classification of 4-6-4 is called a Hudson. Some European classification systems count the number of axles instead of wheels. The Hudson would be a 1-C-1 configuration in Germany and 1-3-1 in France.

Windings: The parts of a toy train transformer consisting of long sections of copper wiring wound tightly around an iron core. The electrical current flows from one end of the long wire to the other down the iron core, and through a process called induction, the high-voltage household current is transferred from one set of windings to another set which produces the low voltage used for the trains.

Wye: A special section of track to reverse a locomotive without the use of a turntable. This track configuration is in the shape of the letter Y — hence its name — with the top of the letter connected by a section of track.

ABOUT THE AUTHOR

Roland E. LaVoie, 45, is a Philadelphia native whose youth was spent in Collingswood, New Jersey, just a few blocks away from the residence of Bruce Greenberg and the old Pennsylvania-Reading Seashore Lines tracks. A graduate of Bishop Eustace Prep School in Pennsauken, N.J. and Philadelphia's LaSalle University, Mr. LaVoie began his teaching career in 1967 at his old high school. This is his 22nd year as a teacher, the last 17 of which have been as a Reading and English teacher at Cherry Hill High School East in Cherry Hill, N.J. He is also the former director of the nationally-recognized Cherry Hill Study Skills Program.

Mr. LaVoie began his involvement with Lionel trains in 1976 after having enjoyed American Flyer as a boy. He currently demonstrates his 5' x 8' Lionel layout at the Greenberg Train, Dollhouse and Toy Shows in the Philadelphia, Baltimore, and Pittsburgh areas. His writing includes the editing of the Lionel Prewar and Postwar Guides and the authorship of the *Greenberg's Guide to Lionel Trains 1970 - 1988*. He is a member of the Train Collectors Association and the Lionel Operating Train Society. In addition to his train activities, Mr. LaVoie is also an avid reader of non-fiction and a classic movies enthusiast. He resides in Cherry Hill with his wife Jimmie and his 16 year-old son Tom.